# EMPOWERING CATECHETICAL LEADERS

EDITED BY
THOMAS H. GROOME, ED.D.
AND MICHAEL J. CORSO, PH.D.

NATIONAL CATHOLIC EDUCATIONAL ASSOCIATION

National Catholic Educational Association
1077 30th Street, NW, Suite 100
Washington, DC 20007-3852

ISBN 1-55833-219-7
REL-24-1208

# TABLE OF CONTENTS

# PART THREE
# THE REALITIES OF CATECHESIS

# Acknowledgment

The Mission 2000 Plan of the National Catholic Educational Association stated that one of its objectives is "to promote and inspire excellence in leadership development and renewal." To help realize this leadership objective in the field of religious education, the executive committee of the Chief Administrators of Catholic Education (CACE/NCEA) established a committee to **develop formational materials for parish directors of religious education**. It was this decision that led to the writing of *Empowering Catechetical Leaders* (ECL).

As with any important document, ECL is the fruit of many labors. Initially, it was envisioned as a similar project to the three-volume work entitled: *Formation and Development of Catholic Education* (United States Catholic Conference in conjunction with the NCEA). The development committee for ECL included the following: Dr. Joseph P. Sinwell (chair), diocesan director of religious education, Providence, RI; Virginia Infantino, diocesan director for evangelization and catechesis, San Diego, CA; D'Esta Verdicchio, diocesan director of religious education, Oklahoma City, OK; Rev. Richard Walsh, secretary for education, Joliet, IL; Frank Savage, executive director, CACE; and parish directors of religious education from the National Association of Parish Catechetical Directors (NCPD): former executive committee presidents Jan Kayser, St. Thomas Parish, Crystal Lake, IL and Eileen Loughran, St. John Fisher Parish, Rancho Palo Verdes, CA. Dr. Barbara Campbell, associate executive director, NCEA department of religious education, served as staff.

This committee worked diligently to develop a detailed outline for the project. Eventually in the fall of 1996 the department of religious education assumed responsibility for completion of the project. Dr. Barbara Campbell contacted Dr. Thomas H. Groome and Dr. Michael Corso and asked them to serve as general and managing editors. Almost immediately they invited others to assist them in writing for ECL: Wilkie Au, Fran Ferder, Michael P. Horan, Carl J. Pfeifer and Janaan Manternach, and Diana Dudoit Raiche, Jane E. Regan, and Mary Angela Shaughnessy.

With the planning and development of any quality text, the energies of many people are necessary. Besides the committee and the outstanding authorship team, ECL is indebted to William H. Sadlier, Inc., which gave wonderful encouragement and support to this effort through the personal involvement of Frank Sadlier Dinger, Chairman of the Board, William Sadlier Dinger, President, Dr. Gerard F. Baumbach, Executive Vice President and Publisher, and Dr. Eleanor Ann Brownell, Vice President. In addition Sadlier made a significant financial gift in an effort to keep the cost of this text at a reasonable level for catechetical leaders. In short, ECL was truly a community effort.

In closing we are confident that *Empowering Catechetical Leaders* will serve as an excellent resource for veteran parish catechetical leaders as well as in developing future leaders. The **General Directory for Catechesis** emphasizes how "any form of pastoral activity is placed at risk if it does not rely on truly competent and trained personnel" (GDC, #234). May this text enrich, challenge, and affirm all who use it and make them ever mindful of their special and important task of sharing the Good News of Jesus Christ!

Joseph P. Sinwell, D. Min.          Robert I. Colbert, Executive Director
President, NCDRE-CACE              Department of Religious Education

# Preface

First, let us thank you and thank God for your ministry as a catechetical leader. Surely the Church carries on no more important work than sharing its faith and nurturing people to live as disciples of Jesus in the midst of the world. And you are in the frontline of this crucial ministry—vital to the Church carrying on its central mission of evangelization and catechesis. You have an august responsibility. Thank you for taking it so seriously.

Be assured, too, that the authors of these essays realize full-well how challenging a task is yours, the importance of it, and how demanding to do it effectively. All who write to you here, at one time or another, have held "job descriptions" similar to yours in a parish or school setting. It is our commitment to help meet the challenge of faith-filled and life-giving catechesis that prompts us to offer this ready-to-use resource— both inspiring and practical—*Empowering Catechetical Leaders*.

Stand back a bit to view the scholarly resources required by this ministry. For good religious education/catechesis one needs to draw upon the best of scripture study and informed theology that reflects the faith of our Church, upon educational theory and practice and the relevant social sciences, and then upon the theoretical and practical resources that are particular to this ecclesial function. While every pastoral minister should continue to read to enrich one's own faith and enhance effectiveness, no busy leader can keep up with such a vast breadth of literature and array of resources.

So, writing as a team with expertise and experience in those various resources of catechetical ministry, we make readily available here the best of scholarship relevant to the work of catechetical leaders. We have done so always with a view to pastoral practice and to promoting effective catechesis in our parishes, schools, and homes. Whether you are a neophyte in this ministry or a seasoned veteran, we hope you will find here a text that is both inspiring and useful, both theoretically sound and practically helpful.

The themes of these essays vary from the grand vision of educating for the Reign of God to the practicalities of how to constitute a parish committee for catechesis. Such is the breadth of horizon and down-to-earth issue that every catechetical leader must address regularly.

We have gathered the nine principal essays into three parts: *The Foundations of Catechesis*; *The People of Catechesis*; and *The Realities of Catechesis*. Each part, however, is equally important to the work of catechetical leaders; all nine essays are an essential piece to the mosaic of catechesis. We conclude with a brief review of the *General Directory for Catechesis*; it will serve as a guide for your own reading of this important document. We are confident that you will find in these ten essays an informed and insightful treatment of all the major aspects of your ministry as a leading catechist to your faith community.

We hope this collection of essays can serve as a ready reference—a desk top book that you keep close at hand and turn to often. Take opportunities to spend reflective time with *Empowering Catechetical Leaders*, to mull over its questions and proposals. It will be most effective to gather with a few other leaders for shared conversation around each essay; this will also nurture a community of support for each other in your ministry. We have inserted questions for reflection throughout each essay—not just at the end—to facilitate such "sharing faith" together.

We wish you God's best blessings on your wonderful ministry as a catechetical leader, and on your family and faith community. We assure you of our prayers and ask you to remember us likewise.

Sincerely,

Thomas H. Groome

# THE
# FOUNDATIONS
# OF CATECHESIS

## PART ONE

# 1
# The Purposes of
# Christian Catechesis
## Thomas H. Groome

It is so obvious a question as to sound ridiculous: "Why should the Christian community hand on its faith?" Surely we can take the answer for granted. Did not Jesus give a farewell mandate to the disciples assembled on a mountain in Galilee, "Go, make disciples of all nations . . . baptizing them . . . teaching them . . ." (Matt 28:19-20). And long before Jesus, had not Moses warned God's people "never to forget" their divine story of salvation and covenant, and commanded them to teach it faithfully "to your children and to your children's children" (Deut 4:9). Consequently, and since the earliest days, the community of Jesus' disciples— the Church— has considered evangelizing people to live God's Good News of salvation in Jesus Christ as essential to its mission in the world. So, why ask "why" about catechesis, let alone write an essay in response?

That the Church is to catechize is beyond doubt, but in practice it would seem that catechists are often confused about why we are to do so—in the sense of the purposes we should have in mind. The new *General Directory for Catechesis* (*GDC*) claims that confusion about purposes is a major cause of "defects and errors" in catechetical ministry, insisting that good pastoral practice is possible "only if the nature and end of catechesis . . . are correctly understood" (#9).

Probably no foundational issue has more impact on how we go about catechesis and what we teach than our sense of why we do it—what we hope to achieve in people's lives, for the Church, for society, and for the whole world. And surely we must choose ways of proceeding that are likely, by God's grace, to serve our purposes.

Of course, our defining purposes are not ours to choose, as if we can decide them arbitrarily for ourselves. As catechists, we are ministers of the Church; our commission is to share with faithfulness the faith of our Christian community. The Holy Spirit calls and empowers us to be instruments of God's grace for the "learning outcomes" intended by Jesus; all our work participates in Christ's mission to the world. The *GDC* notes that "the principle sources of catechesis" are "the word of God contained in Sacred Tradition and in Sacred Scripture" as both are given "an authentic interpretation" by the teaching office of the Church—"the Magisterium which teaches with authority" (#95 and 96).

This tripod of Scripture, Tradition, and the Church's Magisterium—constituting and mediating "the Faith handed down"—reflects within it a strong sense of purpose for catechesis; this essay will review and summarize this purpose. And yet, in the reality of every catechetical event or program, the catechist—be that teacher or parent— is the primary agent of such purposes. In other words, catechists must make their own the purposes suggested by Christian faith itself, integrating them into our catechetical approach, becoming their agents in ways authentic to our own gifts and personhood.

## At Least Three Levels of Purpose

We can think of Christian catechesis and catechists as having at least three layers of purpose, reaching in depth from immediate, to intermediate, to ultimate. Perhaps an old medieval tale may help us recognize the contours.

A passing pilgrim came upon a work site outside the city of Paris. The traveler was intrigued by the massive boulders that workers were hauling and stopped one to ask, "Why are you working so hard?" The worker responded laconically, "A large building requires large stones—I must get them to the building site." The traveler stopped with another worker, and asked, "Why are you working so hard?" This one replied with equal simplicity, "To support my family." The visitor asked the purpose of a third worker. This one paused, wiped his sweaty brow, smiled, and said with a glint in his eye, "I am helping to build Notre Dame Cathedral."

In a sense, catechists could echo all three workers encountered by the medieval traveler. We have an ultimate vision, a great horizon of possibility that motivates and permeates all that we do—our Notre Dame Cathedral. Then, we have more intermediate hopes for what we can bring about now or later in people's lives, how they may live in response to Christian catechesis. I will sometimes refer to these as our formative purposes in that they pertain to the formation we intend for people in Christian identity and character. And then, like all educators, we have immediate hopes about what learners may learn and come to know for themselves. Let us call these our knowing purposes; for example, that people may know the Ten Commandments—a great stone needed to build the Cathedral of Christian faith.

Of course, all three layers of purpose overlap and support each other. Our sense of ultimate purpose should influence what we attempt, by God's grace, to form in people's lives, and then what we desire people to know and how we want them to know it. Likewise, what and how we teach people to know their faith should form their Christian identity and promote their ultimate end.

In my own work as a catechist, I confess that there are days when my noble-sounding purposes are vividly before me—always in September—but then, other days—often in February—when they seem quite faint. Yet I know that the best days are when all three layers are alive in my heart and reflected in my work. And though my purposes are shaped by the great tradition of Christian faith that I teach, and are guided by my Catholic community, they function as authentically my own and with the unique spin that I, like every catechist and parent, must give them. Before reading my proposals, however, pause here to name and reflect on your own sense of the purposes of Christian catechesis. And let this first pause be a "blue sky" moment—about ultimate purposes.

## Questions for Reflection

- Sit for a while and contemplate your sense of ultimate purposes— what do you finally want for the people with whom you catechize? For the whole Church? For our society? For the world?
- How did you come by such purposes? Reflect on some of the story behind them. Recognize some of the concrete ways that they affect your work as a Catechetical Leader.
- Do you have a symbol or phrase that summarizes all your ultimate hopes?

## For The Reign of God

Turning to the Bible and Christian tradition, we find one overarching symbol of God's ultimate purpose for humankind and creation: the Reign of God. This is God's great vision that every aspect of creation may fulfill what God desires for it—only out of love; the intent of God's reign reaches from each human heart to the entire cosmos.

Catechists over the centuries have recognized that their work has such great ultimate purpose, and often referred to it as the "kingdom of Heaven"— the phrase preferred in Matthew's Gospel. (Matthew, being a good Jew, preferred to use a synonym instead of the Holy Name.) This encouraged catechists to think of their final purpose as pertaining only to the next life— to save souls for Heaven. Undoubtedly, we must always affirm such ultimate purpose; surely catechesis must always be about "saving people's souls." It is inspiring and sobering for catechists to recognize that our ministry can have eternal consequences in people's lives.

The development that has occurred of late, however, is a broadened interpretation of what the Scriptures mean by the reign of God. More than an other-worldly place for souls later, God's reign is to begin now for all humankind and every aspect of creation. The holistic nature of God's reign is reflected in how Jesus taught us to pray: first, "Thy kingdom come" and then to add immediately, "Thy will be done on earth as it is in heaven." God is to reign now, in this life and world, with people doing in every aspect of their lives what God desires.

The Hebrew Scriptures portray God's desires for humankind as love and compassion, peace and justice, mercy and forgiveness, freedom from all forms of oppression or exclusion, and freedom for living in "right relationship" with God, self, others, and creation. Their summary word for what God wills for people and creation is the beautiful term *shalom*. The *shalom* of God's reign is to be realized on every level of human existence—personal, interpersonal, and socio-political—and throughout creation; there is no aspect or arena of life in which God's desire of fullness of life for all is not to be realized.

The Hebrew Scriptures also emphasize that God takes humankind into covenant on behalf of God's reign; we are to be partners in actualizing what God wills for us. Logically, then, God's vision—*shalom*—becomes the law by which we are to live. God desires us to have justice, so we must live justly; God desires that we experience compassion, so we must live compassionately, and so on for every aspect of *shalom*. God's will, then, is not an arbitrary law, but only what is in our best interest "for life."

The *GDC* refers to Jesus with the lovely title of "catechist of the Kingdom of God" (#163)—how fitting! It notes that he "proclaimed the Kingdom of God as the urgent and definitive intervention of God in history, and defined this proclamation "the Gospel," that is the Good News (#34). And it is Good News precisely because God's reign demands "the integral development of the human person and of all peoples" (*GDC* #18).

Scripture scholars now agree that Jesus understood the coming of God's reign as the central purpose of his life and ministry. He subsumed the values it represented in his Hebrew tradition, but emphasized and deepened the law of love as the "greatest commandment" (Matt 22:36) of God's rule. For Jesus, this supreme mandate is not so much three different loves—of God, other, and self—but more like one love with three expressions, each sustaining the others. And he pushed neighbor to the ultimate point of inclusion— even enemies. As the *GDC* notes, God "offers the gift of integral salvation" (#102), a phrase it uses frequently to capture the holistic nature of God's reign in Jesus.

We can get a felt-sense of what the symbol reign of God means by looking into our own hearts for our deepest and most authentic desires. As we long for love, freedom, compassion, justice, peace, hope, integrity, inclusion, security, well-being, true happiness, and so on, we can know that God desires the same for us, and God reigns as such values are realized. And though Jesus often preached the reign of God as for people's hearts, he also made clear that its values are to prevail in the world as well. So, commitment to God's reign requires people to help realize *shalom* values for all people and throughout God's creation.

In St. John's Gospel, Jesus stated his own sense of purpose as having come in order for people "to have life, and have it abundantly" (John 10:10). The *GDC* says that Jesus' "Good News of the Kingdom of God . . . includes a message of liberation" (#103), calling it a "radical liberation" (#104) that clearly has both personal and social consequences. For example, it requires catechists to "arouse in catechumens and those receiving catechesis 'a preferential option for the poor'" (#104), and to "stir Christian hearts to the cause of justice" (#17). Clearly God's reign is a holistic affair!

It may help to capture the comprehensiveness of God's reign by thinking of it more as both/and than either/or. So, it is both a spiritual symbol calling people to holiness of life and a social one demanding that Christians work for justice in the world. It is to be the disposition of our own hearts and we are to work for its realization in the public arena. It indeed symbolizes our hope of everlasting life "in the eternal kingdom of our Lord and savior Jesus Christ" (2 Pet 1:11), but its values must be lived now—it is always for here as well as hereafter. Our baptismal commitment to the reign of God should permeate our prayers and politics, our spirituality and sociality, how we relate to God and to others, influencing how we live in our homes and communities, what we contribute to the mission of our church and to the common good of society. In sum, there is no nook or cranny of life, no time or place, where God is not to reign.

The vocation of every Christian is to live life passionately and completely for the reign of God in Jesus. The purpose of the Church in the world is to function as a sacrament of God's reign, or, as the *GDC* states repeatedly, to be "the universal sacrament of salvation for the life of the world." (E.g., see #83.) This calls the community of faith to be a visible, credible, and effective agent of God's grace that helps to bring about what God desires for all. Given that God's reign is the purpose of the Church, we can well state the ultimate purpose of catechesis as to help bring about, by God's grace, "the kingdom of God and of Jesus" (Eph 5:5).

So, the ultimate purpose of catechesis ever remains eternal and spiritual but is now expanded to include all time, the whole person, all people; in the words of the Third Eucharistic prayer, "to advance the peace and salvation of all the world." Though it may sound pretentious to state it, and certainly we should never presume to do it by our efforts alone—without God's help—yet if someone inquires about the ultimate purpose of Christian catechesis, we could make bold to reply, "to save the world."

To be conscious of the reign of God as the ultimate purpose of catechesis could have far-reaching effect on how we go about it. Not only would we teach about God's rule but would allow such ultimate purpose to permeate everything we do as catechists—our process and context as well as our content. Every aspect of our catechesis would be fashioned to serve the reign of God and the "integral salvation" that it symbolizes. Let us take an example to make the point.

So often, catechists and parents have presented the Ten Commandments as curtailments upon human freedom or as arbitrary "hoops to jump through" in order to save our souls. I remember well getting the impression as a child that we could have a lot more fun if we did not have these old rules to keep—basically a nuisance. The choices, however, were patently clear: break them and go to hell; keep them and get to heaven.

Now, it will always be true that we can indeed "lose our souls" and "go to hell" if we consistently live outside of God's law. And, like salvation, the danger of perdition is not postponed until the next life—it can certainly begin in this one. We can choose to destroy ourselves now by consistently violating the Ten Commandments.

But much more than a negative prohibition, God's commandments are positive guidelines toward authentic freedom; to live them is to become fully alive as human beings. And to live one's life in violation of these divine guidelines is a formula for misery and unhappiness—for a hell of one's own making—wrecking destruction on ourselves, others, and creation.

In a rap session with a youth ministry group, a young person offered the opinion that "life would be a ball if we didn't have the ten commandments." For fun, but also to make a point, I said, "O.K.—let's play pretend—we will imagine that they are gone; yeah gone—and now it's totally up to us to make our own rules. God gives us a couple of blank pages (the old story had two stones) and says, "O.K., make up your own commandments—include nothing more than you absolutely need."

They entered into the exercise, and soon we were debating what would be the barest minimum by way of moral laws in order to live humanly, with some sense of security and to find happiness. As vibrant young people, they began with sexuality, determined to have as little law as possible.

At first, it sounded as if they would allow a great life-long orgy, but as we probed, they began to agree that such would be license rather than freedom, that it would destroy the prospect of true love—impossible without trust, commitment, faithfulness—that such liberality could quickly become slavery. And thus they worked their way through all the great moral issues of life; if one can steal then everyone can steal and nothing we have would be safe; if one can lie then everyone can lie, and we are constantly deceived. False gods always enslave, and life without rest would be bondage. By the end of our session, my young friends had "reinvented" most of the Ten Commandments, agreeing that life would be a misery without them.

When we look closely, we find that Holy Scripture itself alerts us to interpret and present the Commandments with such an emphasis—as signposts to freedom. Both versions of the Decalogue in the Hebrew Scriptures—Deuteronomy 5:6-21, and Exodus 20:1-17—are prefaced with the exact same statement, "I am the Lord your God, who brought you out of the land of Egypt, out of the house of slavery." The old rabbinical commentaries proposed that this opening verse is the clue to what follows. It is saying that our God is a God of freedom, One who intervenes in human history to liberate people from slavery. It is as if God is saying to the Israelites—and through them to humankind—"I have set you free! Now, if you wish to remain free . . . put me first in your life because other gods will enslave you," and so on with the other nine commandments.

This one example of "the spin" that a reign of God perspective would put on teaching the Ten Commandments can be extended to every aspect of the faith tradition, alerting catechists that they must always teach with content and process that is life-giving and liberating—that builds up the reign of God. We Christians claim that the Gospel of Jesus is Good News; we will be more likely to teach it as such if we remember that our ultimate purpose—and Jesus'—is the realization of God's reign.

## Questions for Reflection
- What are your own sentiments about making the reign of God the ultimate purpose of Christian catechesis?
- What difference might commitment to the reign of God make in your work as a Catechetical Leader?
- The reign of God clearly calls Christians to live their faith in the world. What do you consider to be the core characteristics of a life of Christian faith?

## A Life of Christian Faith
To stop and reflect for even a moment, catechists recognize that the formative purpose of catechesis is a life of Christian faith. And the catechist's

intent is indeed formation; to shape people's very "being"—as noun and verb—who they are and how they live. The *GDC* proposes "a comprehensive and systematic formation in the faith," and "an apprenticeship of the entire Christian life" (#67). And precisely because the intent is "formation in the Christian life, [catechesis] comprises but surpasses mere instruction" (#68—strong language indeed!). But what is this Christian life to which we aspire ourselves and intend, with the help of God's grace, to form other people?

I will propose a general response and then elaborate on it. To be a Christian is to live as a disciple of Jesus Christ, in the midst of a community of disciples—the Church—and for God's reign in the world.

## To Live as a Disciple of Jesus Christ

The core of Christian identity is to be a disciple of Jesus. It is interesting to note that the term *mathetes*—typically translated as disciple—in the social world of the Gospel actually meant "an apprentice." Perhaps apprentice is a more appealing term in that disciple can sound a bit daunting— almost too much to take on. Apprentice clearly implies that one will always be learning from Jesus, and in the meantime allows tolerance for shortcomings; no one expects perfection from apprentices. Whichever term one uses—and the *GDC* interchanges "apprenticeship in the Christian life" with "Christian discipleship"—the baptismal vocation of every Christian is to live a life of faith following "the way" of Jesus.

Christian faith demands that one live as Jesus lived for the reign of God, to make his passions and commitments one's own. At the beginning of his public ministry, when Jesus first reached out to call disciples, his invitation was "come follow me" (Mark 1:17). At the end of his life, as he spent a final evening with disciples—and St. John's Gospel gives a moving account of the farewell discourse—we hear Jesus drawing together the core of what it means to be apprenticed to him.

He began with the extraordinary act of washing disciples' feet and then said simply, "I have set you an example, that you also should do as I have done for you" (John 13:15). Then he went on to say, "I give you a new commandment, that you love one another. Just as I have loved you, so you should love one another" (John 13:34).

Jesus could never have preached the Great Commandment—love of God, neighbor, and self—as something "new", he had learned its centrality from his own Hebrew tradition and knew well its source in the Sacred Scriptures of his people. But that apprentices should love as Jesus himself loved — this is a "new" and extraordinary commandment. Let us interpret it in its context of St. John's Gospel.

As the Last Discourse unfolds, Jesus elaborates his "new" commandment. First, he roots it in the premise that "As the Father has loved me, so I have loved you" (John 15:9). So, the love between himself and the Father is the same love with which Jesus loves disciples, in other words, with divine love. Then he repeats again, "This is my commandment, that you love one another as I have loved you" (John 15:12). Wow! What an extraordinary invitation for apprentices—to love as God loves. No wonder that Jesus specifically included enemies. At the very core of the formative task of catechesis, then, is to nurture people to be lovers like their God—as modeled by Jesus.

## In a Community of Disciples for God's Reign in The World

Christian faith is deeply communal; a "private Christian" is an oxymoron. A central theme of the Hebrew Scriptures is that to live as a person of God one must belong to a people of God. God enters into covenant with a people, calling them to live together as the People of God. Indeed, each member is held responsible to the covenant and invited to personal relationship with God, but this identity in faith must be lived out in a community of faith.

Inviting people into community was central to the ministry of Jesus. He called disciples into a bond around him— welcoming even sinners and outcasts, appointed leaders to be of service to the rest, promised the Holy Spirit to guide them, commissioned this community to share in his ministry, to celebrate his memorial meal, to go make disciples of all nations, and promised to be with them until the end of time.

At the first Pentecost, Mary and "a group of about one hundred and twenty persons" (Acts 1:15) were gathered in Jerusalem when they experienced being "filled with the Holy Spirit" (Acts 2:4). Immediately they began their commission to evangelize. That very day, through the sacrament of baptism, "about three thousand persons were added" (Acts 2:41) to the small community of Jesus' disciples. The Holy Spirit had officially launched the Church.

All mainstream Christian churches hold that to be Christian requires belonging to a community of faith. They also understand the nature of the Church as a new community of God's people in Jesus Christ, and its mission to be a sacrament of God's reign in the world. But the communal nature of Christian faith is a particular emphasis of Catholic Christianity.

At the Reformation, many great Protestant Reformers like Luther and Calvin were so critical of the institutional Church that they downplayed its importance, giving greater emphasis to a Christian's personal relationship with God. At the Council of Trent (1545-63), however, Catholicism recognized anew the importance of one's personal relationship with God but reiterated the Church's crucial function as an instrument of God's grace, insisting that active membership in a Christian community is essential to Christian faith.

That the Church is to be a community of faith in which all members actively participate was one of the great themes of the Second Vatican Council (1962-65). Its great metaphors for the Church—new People of God and Body of Christ—are both radically communal. And Vatican II made clear that the Church as community never exists for its own sake but to be an instrument of God's reign in the world. This teaching is expanded in various places by the *Catechism of the Catholic Church* (CCC); for example, "The Church in the world is the sacrament of salvation, the sign and instrument of the communion of God" with humankind (#780). And, as noted, the *GDC* frequently refers to the Church as "the universal sacrament of salvation."

The communal nature of Christian faith means that catechesis has the purpose of nurturing people in ecclesial identity—as people of the Church. It must nurture a sense of belonging to the Church, fostering people's gifts to contribute to the community, convincing and preparing them to take on what Vatican II called "full, conscious, and active participation" (*Constitution on the Liturgy # 14*) in the whole mission and ministry of the Church in the world. As the *GDC* states boldly and often reiterates, "Catechesis prepares the Christian to live in community and to participate actively in the life and mission of the Church" (#86).

Gone are the days when Christians can think of the Church as a thing apart from themselves, as if it is a service agency where they can "pull in," receive service, and "pull out" again into the world. Now, the word "Church" for every Christian must have the connotation that "we are all in this together." Each baptized person is responsible, according to gifts and circumstance, to participate in the mission of the Christian community, enabling it to be a sacrament of God's reign in the world. To nurture not only a sense of identity within the Church—of belonging to it—but also of agency—of being responsible for it—is a challenging purpose of catechesis.

Taking these general aspects of Christian faith— discipleship and community—we can unpack what they mean for everyday life, making more explicit the formative purposes of Christian catechesis. Again, a summary statement: Christian faith is to be lived and living, whole and wholesome, personal and communal. What might these dynamics mean for the purposes of catechists?

## Lived and Living Christian Faith

By lived faith I mean faith that gets done, that is realized by Christian persons and communities in every context of life and level of society. Lived faith is sustained by and relies upon knowledge of one's faith and being convinced of its divine truth, but goes beyond knowing or confessing to a spiritual relationship with God and to living for the reign of God in every time and place.

Surely a lived faith is what Jesus had in mind when he warned apprentices that people who confess "Lord, Lord" will not inevitably enter into God's kingdom, but "the one who does the will of my Father in heaven" (Matt 7:21). And John's Gospel has Jesus make a statement that seems to place priority on Christian praxis. In fact, Jesus reverses our typical Western assumption that knowledge comes first, then relationship, and finally the lived response. Placing lived faith first in the sequence, Jesus states, "If you live according to my teaching, you are truly my disciples. Then you will know the truth, and the truth shall set you free" John 8:31; *JB*).

To make lived Christian faith our defining purpose will shape what and how we teach as catechists. Regarding what to teach, it alerts that as we give people access to this great rich tradition of belief, worship, and ethic that is Catholic Christianity, we should emphasize what will entice and nurture them to live it, to take it on as their lifestyle. The *GDC* states, "The aim of catechetical activity consists in precisely this: to encourage a living, explicit and fruitful profession of faith" (#66).

That people may come to live their faith should be the first priority of catechetical curricula, and this is not always the case. For example, some groups in the Church become so concerned about religious literacy that they seem to make it the end in itself. We must indeed teach people a sound knowledge of their faith, but, as the *GDC* often reiterates, knowledge alone is not enough; our primary intent is that people choose to live it.

Likewise, this lived-faith intent should shape how we catechize. For instance, we must explicitly invite people— as part of the curriculum—to make choices that are Christian, encouraging them to practice their faith. Enticing such decision-making can be done in umpteen ways; for example, telling stories of people who have lived as disciples of Jesus, or giving direct experience of people who live or apprentice themselves to Jesus now. It would also seem imperative that the catechetical process turn people to their own lives in the world, inviting reflection on experience and to see for themselves how they can live their faith in the everyday. The *GDC* advises the catechist that "one must start with praxis to be able to arrive at praxis" (*GDC* #245).

By a living faith I mean one that is ever vibrant and vital, growing and maturing, that is life-giving for self and others, for Church and world. Christian tradition has a rich image of the life of faith as a journey, with the

Christian community being a pilgrim People of God. A journey into the realization of God's reign cannot be a rambling in circles, a "re-run" of what has been in the past—for either person or community. To journey is to break ever new ground, to remember and learn from where one has come, to imagine and forge ahead into new horizons. The Church as a pilgrim people should offer old familiar ways and new paths to trod, a secure home and the impetus to journey on, deep roots and reaching wings.

A living faith is one that provides comfort and consolation in the midst of life's struggles, but challenge and confrontation as well, always inviting onward. Faith that is alive remembers and reclaims the past, engages and celebrates the present, imagines and creates the future. Jesus surely had a vital faith in mind when he counseled that every scribe learned in the reign of God—a good description of a catechist—is like the head of a household who can take from the storeroom both the new and the old (see Matt 13:52).

A living faith requires catechists to represent Christian tradition as a lively and life-giving affair. And let us be honest—we have been known to present our faith in a "deadly" way. People should be led to experience this great Christian tradition as a flowing river that refreshes and spawns new life rather than stagnant water. Catechists must represent it in ways that foster curiosity instead of boredom, that give the impression of a constant challenge and discovery rather than "the same old stuff."

Catechesis for vibrant Christian faith should encourage openness instead of closed-mindedness, giving people a sense of reverence for what is ultimate Mystery rather than the attitude that Christians "know it all." It is surely poor catechesis when we sound as if we have easy answers to the great mysteries of life. Our stance should be to prepare people for the surprises that the Holy Spirit ever has in store for us—personally and as a faith community—to be ready to respond to how and wherever the Spirit moves.

The *GDC* reflects the development in the Church's consciousness since Vatican II that catechesis is not just for children; that the journey of faith is life-long and needs the support of good catechesis from beginning to end. It champions "continuous education in the faith" or "permanent catechesis" (#51). It says that "ongoing education in the faith" is needed in order to maintain "the process of continuing conversion" (#69), "which lasts for the whole of life" (#56). Later it states that "Catechesis not only brings to maturity the faith of those being catechized but also brings the community itself to maturity" (#221).

I am convinced that the seeds of faith as a life-long journey must be sown from the very first moments of catechesis—at the parents knee. In other words, whether or not faith development is likely to continue throughout people's lives depends, in large part, on their initial catechesis. In a sense, adult faith education must begin in kindergarten! This calls for a catechetical style that conveys, in one way or another, "we have an old and always new Story of faith, and we can grow in understanding and living it our whole life through."

## Whole and Wholesome Christian Faith

By a whole faith I mean one that permeates every aspect of human "being," that engages every feature and capacity of people. Jesus' own preaching of the Great Commandment reflects such a comprehensive understanding of Christian discipleship. He brought together from his Hebrew tradition the commandments to love God with all one's being (Deut 6:5) and to love the neighbor as oneself (Lev 19:18), making explicit that these three loves are "like" each other (see Matt 22:39). Christians are to love God, self, and others— the primary law of discipleship—with their whole mind, heart, and strength, with all their soul. A holistic affair!

Throughout Christian history this wholeness of faith was reflected in the Church's insistence that being Christian entails right belief (*orthodoxa*), right ethic (*orthopraxis*), and right worship (*ortholeitourgia*). Cyril of Jerusalem (d. 386) was likely the first to portray the totality of Christian faith as right belief, morality, and worship. Since then, and down to the present day, all the great catechisms have followed the schematic outline (varying only in sequence) of creed, code, and cult—doctrines of belief, code of ethics, and sacraments of worship. The *Baltimore Catechism* captured well the wholeness of Christian faith with the question "Why did God make you?" and the response "to know . . . to love . . . and to serve . . ."

The *GDC* is a new champion of Christian faith as a whole way of life. It speaks of "the profound unity of the Christian life" which entails—in old traditional terms—*lex credendi, lex vivendi*, and *lex orandi*—"law" of belief, of living, and of prayer (#122). It says repeatedly that "the faith demands to be known, celebrated, lived and translated into prayer" (#84, 144, etc.)—reflecting the sequence of the *Catechism of the Catholic Church*. In another section it refers to "the contents of catechesis" (note the plural) as "cognitive, experiential, and behavioral" (#35). Clearly, though there are different aspects to a life of Christian faith, they make up a whole mosaic, engaging people's heads, hearts, and hands.

For catechists to make holistic Christian faith their purpose has far-reaching implications for what and how they catechize. For example, it would seem that catechesis must include sound instruction in the doctrines and dogmas of the Tradition, but must reach far beyond "mere information" (*GDC* #29). Needed too is direct experience of and active participation in liturgy and worship.  Likewise, catechesis must entail a curriculum of moral formation, including instruction in the moral code of Christian faith, formation in its virtues, and opportunity to practice its ethic of life.  The intent cannot be simply that people learn about worship but that they become worshippers of God, not simply that they learn about justice but become just, and so on.  Catechesis in a holistic faith demands a holistic curriculum.

Catechists should also teach Christian faith as a wholesome affair.  Such a positive emphasis has often been neglected to the diminishment of our message and ministry.  It is imperative—out of faithfulness to the tradition and concern for people's "integral salvation" (see *GDC* #102)—that we present Christianity as a way of being human and religious that is essentially life affirming, life embracing, and life celebrating.

Throughout its history, the Church has experienced many efforts to deny the wholesomeness of Christian faith.  In the early centuries there were movements like Docetism, Gnosticism, and the Manichaeans; in the Middle Ages there were groups like the Albigensians, and more recently the Jansenists.  What all of them had in common was a dismal attitude toward life, insisting that everything human—and especially the body—is essentially evil, that Christian faith should be life-denying rather than life-affirming.  Though there is evidence that some of their attitudes "rubbed off," the greater truth is that the Holy Spirit guided the Church to condemn all such negative movements as heresy.  Christianity is essentially a wholesome faith.

Catechists should ever present Christian faith as the possibility of living into fullness of life, confident, as St. Irenaeus said so long ago, that "the glory of God is the human person fully alive."  On the other hand, and let's face it, our catechesis has often presented Christian faith as a negative curtailment upon people—as "bad news" instead of "good."  The philosopher Friedrich Nietzsche (d. 1900) once commented that for him to believe in God, Christians would need to "sing better songs and look happier than they do."  Nietzsche needed Christianity to be a positive and life-giving affair but, sadly, could not find sufficient evidence.

The symbol of God's reign should remind catechists to present Christian faith as a wholesome way of *shalom*, of living into fullness of life.  At the Last Supper, Jesus prayed that his disciples might be filled with joy, with his own joy being completed in them (see John 16:22-24 and 17:13).  Since the beginning, Christian apprentices have been convinced that the life and preaching, death and resurrection of Jesus is great Good News—the very word Gospel means as much.  Let us represent and catechize it as such.

## Personal and Communal Christian Faith

As personal, Christian faith makes a deep claim upon the individual person and likewise engages her or him as an agent of faith—a "doer" rather than simply a "done for" or a "done to." A Christian understanding of the human condition maintains that every person is made in the image and likeness of God, is saved/liberated by Jesus Christ, has abiding human rights that must be respected, and has profound responsibilities which, by God's grace, she or he is capable of fulfilling. Within God's family, and explicitly for Christians within the Body of Christ, each one of us is irreplaceable and must function as a full participant—no one else can substitute for us or alleviate our accountability. As St. Paul explained to the Corinthians, just as "the eye cannot say to the hand, 'I have no need of you,' nor again the head to the feet" (1 Cor 12:21), likewise, each member in the Body of Christ is vitally important and has a distinctive role to play.

God's word through the Prophet Isaiah is addressed to every human being, "I call you by your name" (Is 45:4). In God's eyes, each of us is a unique person—one of a kind. I have the general vocation of every Christian—to live as an apprentice to Jesus—but I also have my own particular vocation and am held responsible for how I do or do not live my faith as a person. In the life of faith I must be a team player, not merely a spectator.

From the perspective of Christian anthropology, the term "person" is more apt than "individual." Person comes from the Greek *prosopon* which means "turned toward another," whereas "individual" literally means to be "divided from." The Christian must always be turned toward others, toward relationship; rugged individualism or isolationism is antithetical to the call of Christian faith. And yet, the person never becomes a cog in a wheel, nor a dependent without rights and responsibilities. In our origin, in our living, and in our destiny, each of us stands before God and toward each other as a person. From this perspective we can say that Christianity is a deeply personal faith, with each one having "the sublime vocation" of "communion with Jesus Christ" (*GDC* #116).

For catechesis, the personal aspect of Christian faith highlights the need to nurture each person's spirituality, to enable her or him to grow in holiness of life. The great Catholic theologian Bernard Lonergan (d. 1984) never tired of saying that full conversion in Christian faith is to fall in love with God, and rather than being one cataclysmic moment, Lonergan, too, saw conversion as a life-long affair. Catechists are instruments of God's grace who enable people to grow ever more deeply in knowing and loving God.

Personal faith also requires catechesis that enables each Christian to make the tradition his or her own. It must help people to see for themselves the truth of Christianity and how to live it in their lives. Our Christian faith is indeed a family heirloom, an inheritance to which we are entitled from our foremothers and forefathers in faith. But we cannot simply inherit it in a passive way. If it is to be a living and vibrant faith, a whole and wholesome faith, then we must embrace it by choice and persuasion. The *GDC* states boldly, "In the catechetical process, the recipient must be an active subject, conscious and co-responsible, and not merely a silent and passive recipient" (#167). Perhaps this is another way of saying that catechesis should never be by indoctrination but by personal appropriation.

The communal nature of Christian faith was highlighted at the beginning of this section; baptism calls people into a Christian faith community that is to be an effective agent of God's reign in the world. What I accent in this section is that every aspect of the life of a Christian community must participate in its evangelizing and catechetical mission, that the shared life of the Church is its primary curriculum.

Again, this is a common sentiment throughout the *GDC*. For example, "the Christian community is in herself living catechesis. Thus she proclaims, celebrates, works, and remains always a vital, indispensable and primary locus of catechesis" (#141). And within the Christian community, "catechesis . . [is] the particular responsibility of every member . . ." (#220). The whole Christian community—every aspect of its life and each member—is to be catechist.

Perhaps the communal nature of catechesis—required by the communal nature of Christian faith—can be elucidated by brief reflections on each of the Church's core ministries and their potential for faith formation. Of course, as the *GDC* repeats often, catechesis is essentially "a ministry of the word." But the proposal here is that we think of all the Church's ministries as having catechetical potential and of needing to be done with "catechetical consciousness." The fact is that classrooms and programs are not enough to form Christians—important though they are; it takes communities—parish and family.

And we must explicitly include "family" as a crucial community of Christian faith, especially by way of catechesis (for detailed elaboration see "Parish and Family as Catechist" by Dr. Michael Corso in this series). As the *GDC* notes, "In a certain sense, nothing replaces family catechesis, especially for its positive and receptive environment, for the example of adults, and for its first explicit experience and practice of the faith" (#178). By way of the ministries of the Church, we must also embrace the notion renewed by Vatican II that the Christian family is "the domestic church" (*Constitution on the Church*, #11). If this be true, then every family needs to reflect within its own life the essential ministerial functions of any Christian community.

It is also imperative that we broaden our notion of family beyond the "nuclear" image to include extended and blended families, indeed any bonded network that serves as one's primary community of personal sustenance. What then is the catechetical potential of all the ministries of a Christian community—parish or family?

There are many ways to elaborate the functions of the Church's mission in the world—what parish and family are to do in carrying on the ministry of Jesus. Since the earliest days of the Church, however, six Greek terms have had pride of place in summarizing Christian ministry: *koinonia* (to be a life-giving community); *marturia* (to bear witness to faith); *kerygma* (to evangelize and preach the Good News); *didache* (to teach Christian faith); *leitourgia* (to worship as a community); and *diakonia* (to serve human needs). I will summarize them in a fourfold schema (pairing *koinonia* and *marturia*, *kerygma* and *didache*) as the functions of Witness, Worship, Welfare, and Word. I place Word last since catechesis is the focus of this entire essay and my hope in this section is to raise catechetical consciousness around the other three.

- The Church is to be a community of witness. It is to live the Good News that it preaches, to be readily recognizable as a community of Christian faith, hope, and love, as one that lives the way of Jesus and functions as an instrument of God's work of salvation in the world.

- Parishes and families must look to their witness for how well they catechize. Does this parish or family live by values that are truly Christian, is the ethos suffused with faith, hope, and love, does its structures and roles reflect commitment to the reign of God? Are people likely to "catch the bug" of Christian discipleship simply by living in the midst of this parish or family?

- The Church is to be a community of worship. It is to carry on the "public work" (original meaning of *leitourgia*) of assembling as a people to worship God together, praising and thanking God, offering repentance and petition, and anticipating God's promise of eternal life.

Parishes and families should be communities of life-giving worship. Surely nothing that a parish does is more formative of Christian faith than its liturgy. We have come to realize that good liturgy nurtures people in faith, whereas poor liturgy can be hazardous to people's faith. And every family must celebrate its sacred rituals in order to nurture each other in faith.

I once asked a devout Jewish friend how she came by her strong Jewish identity; she immediately responded, "Oh, from the rituals in my home." Surely every Christian family can create or rediscover—old Catholic cultures had plenty of them—sacred rituals for the home that will nurture members in faith.

- The Church is to be a community of human welfare. It is to participate in God's work of salvation by caring for human need—spiritual and physical, personal and social. By its faith, every Christian community—parish and family— must engage in works of peace and justice, of mercy and compassion, to be ever reforming itself and society toward the realization of God's reign.

Parishes and families should be communities of care for human welfare. To be catechetically effective, the parish must have outreach to the poor and marginalized, be involved directly in the works of mercy, and participate in the social struggle for justice and peace. Likewise, the Christian family as catechist must be a place of compassion and justice within its own shared life, with similar commitment and outreach to the world.

- The Church is to be a community of God's word. It is to evangelize, preach, and teach the word of God that is mediated through the Hebrew Scriptures, through the New Testament, and through the Tradition of the Church over time.

Formal programs of intentional catechesis are indeed the very core of the Church's evangelizing and catechizing ministry—its ministry of the word. But God's word should also be encountered throughout the whole life of a Christian community. Parishes and families will each do this in their own way, but there is no doubt that family and parish can give access to the word of God in Scripture and Tradition. I know a family who every week sits down together for what they call "a family scripture moment." They re-read the Sunday Gospel and then share together what each heard from the text. What a powerful ministry of God's word within that family and done as a "sharing faith" dynamic—so effective for catechesis.

Let me reiterate the catechetical point I am making with the above review of Church ministries. Indeed, every Christian community is to carry on these four functions by mandate of its faith. But I am highlighting that doing them faithfully and well is needed for the community to be effective as catechist—in order to catechize people in Christian faith. For example, a family or parish must fulfill the ministry of *diakonia*—service to human welfare—and do so because its faith requires as much. But by such ministry it is also more likely to form people in lived and living, whole and wholesome Christian faith. Whereas a parish or family that does not do the works of mercy and justice most likely fails in its function as catechist.

In sum, everything about a Christian community—parish or family and let me also add Catholic school—can and should be harnessed for catechesis. Doing so intentionally requires parents and community leaders to ask of every aspect of communal life "what is this teaching by way of Christian faith?"—supporting what catechizes well and changing what does not. Every aspect of the life and ministry of a Christian community must be reviewed often with a "catechetical consciousness."

## Questions for Reflection

- What in this description of Christian faith rings true to you? What would you add to it?
- Reflecting on the context of your faith communities—parish, school, or family—what are some practical implications of such a description of Christian faith for your work as Catechetical Leader? What decisions are emerging for you?
- Looking to our last section, when you think about catechizing people to "know" their faith, what would be your best hopes? How do you want people to "know" Scripture and Tradition? At what level of their "being"?

## Catechesis for Wisdom in Christian Faith

Like the first worker at the medieval building site outside of Paris—with the purpose of getting the needed stones to the building site—every catechist, like every educator, teaches so that people may come to "know" certain things. More specifically, the catechist's purpose is that people may come to know Christian faith. But what does it mean to know Christian faith? What do such knowing and knowledge entail?

It is possible to know "about" something, to hold it apart from oneself and not allow it to affect one's identity. One may have accurate information but without making any difference to one's commitments or values. Knowing "about" something keeps it at a distance, maintaining a kind of objectivity; it never goes to the heart.

Knowing "about" is usually by weight of authority; one takes what is known as reliable because of the credibility of the one teaching it. Conviction does not arise from one's own agency; it does not come from the person as "subject" of the knowing but more as a passive recipient of knowledge, accepting the authority that proposes it.

In Christian faith and catechesis there is certainly a place for knowing "about" the faith tradition—what is sometimes called "religious literacy." And the truth of what is taught is ever assured by the authority of the "fonts of revelation"—the Bible and Christian Tradition as interpreted and taught by the Magisterium of the Church. But the purpose of Christian faith as a whole way of life means that catechists cannot settle for bringing people to know "about" it, nor to simply accept it in a non-reflective way on the grounds of authoritative sources. A lived and living, whole and wholesome, personal and communal Christian faith surely requires a deeper kind of knowing—that engages the very souls of people. Likewise, commitment to the reign of God seems more likely if one knows Christian faith by personal conviction.

Another way of stating this point is that catechists must intend a knowing that honors and engages the presence of God's Holy Spirit in each person's life. And it is imperative to remember that nurturing people as apprentices to Jesus is realized only by the grace of the Holy Spirit. It is the Spirit—not our efforts but nevertheless working through our efforts—that "gives the growth" in Christian living.

The *GDC* makes clear that catechesis is "before all else and forever the work of the Holy Spirit" (#138) and insists that "the charism given (to each person) by the Spirit constitutes the soul of every method" (#156). God's Holy Spirit, moving in each person's life, gives them the capacity to "know" their faith for themselves—at a deeply personal level. Catechists must intend that people come to know their faith at the depth of their very souls. This will be a "knowing" that informs, forms, and transforms people in Christian faith. Reaching beyond what the *GDC* calls "mere information," catechesis should enable participants to comprehend and embrace Christian teachings with conviction, to allow such convictions to shape their identity and holiness of life, and their commitments to forging God's reign in the world.

It may be illuminating for catechists to reflect on one of Jesus' own statements about "knowing." "And this is eternal life, that they may know you, the only true God, and Jesus Christ whom you have sent" (John 17:3). What kind of "knowing" did Jesus have in mind? Clearly, he was using "know" as understood in his Jewish tradition. There "knowing" in its fullness is deeply personal and relational; it engages one's total being, affecting who one becomes and how one relates to others.

The verb for knowing in Hebrew is *yada*. It is an activity of the whole person—including the mind but the emotions and will as well. Instead of feigning objectivity, it is profoundly subjective in that it engages the person as subject of the knowing—as its agent. Much more than knowing "about," *yada* means to experience and live what is true.

An indication of the deeply personal, experiential, and relational sense the Hebrews had of knowing is the fact that the verb *yada* also means lovemaking, and the past participle of *yada* is used of a good friend. The Book of Genesis states that Adam "had knowledge" of Eve (Gen 4:1). The New Testament has a similar meaning. Though the verb *ginoskein* is more prone to a Greek emphasis on objective knowing, the personal connotation is retained. For example, Mary protests at the Annunciation, "How can this be since I know not man" (Luke 1:34; Douay Rheims).

Thus, to "know" God—and for Christians, to "know" God in Jesus Christ—is to enter into a loving relationship with God in which the knowledge permeates one's whole "being." One knows Christian faith by living it, and such knowledge is to be lived with love. What would be a compelling way to describe such an "intended learning outcome"?

My proposal is that the "knowing" and "knowledge" intended by catechists is well described by the biblical notion of wisdom. Wisdom includes knowledge in the Western sense, but reaches far beyond it to affect the knower's whole being— permeating thoughts, desires, and choices. A wise person is someone who lives what one knows. Wisdom and becoming wise in Christian faith may best describe the immediate purpose— the stones needed for the cathedral of God's reign—of Christian catechesis.

## Wisdom in the Bible

The most frequent term used for wisdom in the Hebrew Scriptures is *hokmah*, translated in the Septuagint (ancient Greek version of the Hebrew Scriptures) as *Sophia*. It seems to evolve over the span of biblical tradition from a practical craft (Exod 31:6) to the Craftsperson whom God employs in the work of creation—a personification of God. In the Wisdom literature itself, Wisdom is the giver of life (Prov 4:13), the one who saves the people (Wis 9:18); it is She who creates and renews the earth (Ps 104:30). (Note well that Wisdom as the personification of God is a feminine figure). But always biblical wisdom has a practical and life-oriented meaning of doing what is right in one's everyday life and for the right reasons—in faithfulness to the covenant with God. For people of God, wisdom is to do God's will— to keep the covenant—and especially by doing the works of justice, compassion, and peace (Prov 2).

One becomes wise from reflection on life experience (Job 12:12), but wisdom is also learned from tradition (Prov 19:20) and from other wise people (Isa 19:11). The seat of wisdom is the *leb*, a term that means the very core of a person (Eccl 10:3). The *leb* is the intellectual source of thought and reflection (Isa 6:10), the center of affections (Ps 4:7), and the seat of volition and conscience (1 Sam 24:5). In other words, situated in the *leb*, biblical wisdom engages people's heads, hearts, and hands.

Contemporary scripture scholars propose that an overarching view of Jesus in the New Testament is as the *Sophia* of God; Paul specifically names Jesus "the wisdom of God" (1 Cor 1:24). To be wise in Christian faith is to be an apprentice to Jesus, and vice versa. Christian wisdom is making one's own the totality of Christian faith, allowing it to permeate and shape one's entire "being."

Throughout other religious and philosophical traditions, too, wisdom has the connotation of living wisely and choosing rightly, of caring for self and others, of doing what is good and true, being loving and compassionate, just and peaceful. Wisdom always entails living with integrity—integrating what one knows with how one lives. "Wisdom in Christian faith"—what a fitting and challenging purpose for catechesis. What are its implications for our pedagogy?

Bernard Lonergan offered a most helpful description of the dynamics that take place when a person comes to "know" something at the depths of oneself as a subject. Though Lonergan favored the term "cognition," his description of its dynamics resonate with the biblical notion of wisdom.

The first act, says Lonergan, is "attending to the data" to be known. In more colloquial terms, this means learning the information—be that from life, or from some tradition of wisdom or science of knowledge. Then, one must strive to understand it in the sense of comprehending it for oneself, seeing what it means, being able to express it in one's own words. The third moment is judgment about what we understand—whether it be true or false, and whether our understanding is accurate. And lastly, we need to decide about it—allowing what we know to affect how we live and who we become. Reflecting on these four activities—attending, understanding, judging, deciding—apropos the dynamics of catechesis, will illustrate what it means to educate for wisdom in Christian faith.

**To Inform Well:** Every Christian is entitled to have access to the breadth and depth of the rich storehouse of Christian faith, "to the entire treasure of the Christian message" (*GDC* #112). The *GDC* also notes that this must be done "gradually" and with "adaptation . . to the capacity of those being catechized." The point is that though level of interest, need, and capacity will vary, everyone has a baptismal right to "the whole Story" of Christian faith.

This includes: its scriptures, traditions, and liturgies; its creeds, dogmas, doctrines, and theologies; its sacraments and symbols, myths, gestures, and religious language; its virtues and values, ethic and laws; its spiritualities, expected life-styles, and models of holiness; its songs, music, dance, and drama; its art, artifacts, and architecture; how it sanctifies time, celebrates festivals, and recognizes holy places; its community structures and forms of governance, and so on.

Though there may have been some loss of emphasis on the "content of the Faith" in the early 70s, there is now a strong catechetical consensus that all Christians should be thoroughly informed in their Faith Tradition, and that such knowledge is essential for living it and sharing it with others. "By deepening knowledge of the faith, catechesis nourishes not only the life of faith but equips it to explain itself to the world" (#85).

**To Foster Personal Understanding:** Catechesis should encourage people to think about their faith, to understand it, and to personally recognize what it means for their lives. This means encouraging them to use all their gifts of mind—reason, memory, and imagination—to fullest capacity, to contemplate, to probe and analyze, to really think for themselves.

Encouraging such personal understanding reflects the ancient confidence of Catholicism that faith and reason are partners, that encouraging people to understand their faith is likely to foster living it. The *GDC* says that personal probing and "searching" enhances faith and promotes "a firm option" (#56). Surely this affirms for the catechist the importance of raising provoking questions and of welcoming the questions that students raise. Later the *GDC* adds that helping people to develop "the rational foundations of the faith . . . in conformity with the demands of reason and the Gospel . . . helps to overcome certain forms of fundamentalism as well as subjective and arbitrary interpretations" (#175). In other words, getting people to think for themselves about their faith is not only permissible but necessary in catechesis.

**To Encourage Sound Judgment:** In order to reach toward wisdom, it would seem imperative that people make up their own minds about what they know, that they weigh its truth, goodness, or value. In Christian catechesis this implies encouraging participants to appropriate and integrate Christian faith as their very own. They must be encouraged to take it to heart—literally—to allow it to seep into the very depths of their being, into their souls. It must move beyond something "known" in people's heads to shape who they are and how they live.

**To Invite Decision:** Catechesis for wisdom in Christian faith will invite people to discipleship—to decide to live it. Catechists are to constantly raise up and challenge people to choose the Vision that arises from the Christian Story—symbolized by the reign of God. Giving access to the Christian Story is always done with this intent and hope—that people may choose to live it. But rather than leaving the call to discipleship implicit, the dynamics of catechesis should explicitly invite people to decision—being sensitive to age and readiness—for Christian faith.

It is significant that Jesus constantly invited people to choose, to make a decision whether or not to live as disciples—a decision that has present and eternal consequences. It is indeed important that people know and understand their faith, and come to make it their own, but ultimately it is to be lived. We cannot stop short of the invitation to so choose—if our learning intent is wisdom in Christian faith.

## A Pedagogy for Our Purposes

Catechetical process will be the primary focus of another essay in this series by Janaan Manternach and Carl Pfeifer—two of the finest catechists of our day. But here we can briefly suggest a general pedagogy that seems fitting to the purposes of catechesis as outlined in this essay. My proposal reflects two sources of "wisdom in Christian faith" and then a style for correlating them.

First—to reiterate a point made earlier—catechesis for the reign of God and a life of Christian faith advises that people's own lives be directly engaged in the catechetical process—as an aspect of the curriculum. Such a holistic faith must be grounded in and return to people's own praxis.

That people should learn from experience, by doing, from praxis—or however this pedagogy is described—has been a central proposal of the major educational theorists of the 20th century—Dewey, Montessori, and Freire, who, in turn, echo such architects of modern education as Comenius, Mary Ward, Rousseau, Pestalozzi, and Herbart. However, in the curriculum of Christian catechesis, we have a distinctive rationale for turning to people's lives, and it can be stated simply: a) God constantly reaches out through people's own lives, through the ordinary and everyday, inviting response to God's love; and b) to educate for faith as a way of life, educators simply must engage people's own lives. Without drawing upon people's experience, what we teach may go to their heads but is far less likely to reach their hearts and hands. As the *GDC* advises, "Every dimension of the faith, like the faith itself as a whole, must be rooted in human experience and not remain a mere adjunct to the human person" (#87).

The second but "principle sources of catechesis"—as the *GDC* notes—are "the word of God contained in Sacred Tradition and in Sacred Scripture" as both are given "authentic interpretation" by the teaching office of the Church—"the Magisterium which teaches with authority" (#95 and 96). I have also referred to this source as "the Faith handed down" and as the "whole Story" of Christian faith and the Vision of God's reign, inviting lived response.

So, catechesis should give people access to "the entire treasure of the Christian message" (*GDC* #112), and likewise engage participants' own lives, drawing upon their experiences, reaching into their very souls. That catechesis must correlate these two sources—life and Faith—then, seems self-evident, suggesting that the core dynamic of catechesis is enabling people to bring their lives to the Faith and the Faith to their lives. The *GDC* encourages such integration of life and faith.

It makes clear that the pedagogy of catechesis is charged with "correlating faith and life" (#207), and should constantly establish "the relationship between the Christian message and human experience" (#116). It explains further that "catechesis is . . . realized in the encounter of the word of God with the experience of the person" (#150). It says that "Interpreting and illuminating experience with the data of faith is a constant task of catechetical pedagogy," that it must enact "the correlation and interaction between profound human experiences and the revealed message" (#153). So fitting to the purposes of catechesis, a dynamic of "from life to Faith and from Faith to life" is clearly recommended by the "catechetical mind" of the Church.

## Questions for Reflection
- What are your own responses to the notion of catechesis for wisdom in Christian faith?
- From your conversation with this entire essay, to what decisions are you invited as a Catechetical Leader.

## Bibliography

Boys, Mary. *Educating in Faith: Maps and Visions.* Kansas City: Sheed and Ward edition, 1992.

Dooley, Catherine and Mary Collins, Eds. *The Echo Within: Emerging Issues in Religious Education.* Allen, TX: Thomas More, 1997.

Groome, Thomas. *Educating for Life: A Spiritual Vision for Every Teacher and Parent.* Allen, TX: Thomas More Press, 1998

Harris, Maria and Gabriel Moran. *Reshaping Religious Education: Conversations on Contemporary Practice.* Louisville, KY: Westminster John Knox Press, 1998

O'Hare, Padraic. *The Enduring Covenant: The Education of Christians and the Enduring Covenant.* Valley Forge, PA: Trinity Press International, 1997.

# 2
# Principles of Catechesis from Ecclesial Documents
## Jane E. Regan

As catechetical leaders our days are shaped by the weekly and monthly and annual rhythms of the structures and opportunities we provide for the faith formation of those within our parishes and schools. Many times the focal point of our work is keenly attuned to the daily requirements of our programs and the particular needs and dynamics of our pastoral setting. The requests of catechists and parents, the questions or concerns of learners—adults and children—can be all-encompassing in their demands on our time and energy. It is easy then to lose track of the broader context within which we engage in catechetical ministry.

A key presumption for this essay is that the backdrop for the work of catechesis extends beyond a particular parish or Church and is, in fact, shaped by the vision and direction of the Church in the United States and ultimately the Church universal. While on a day-to-day basis that influence may not be explicit, as we reflect on the fundamental direction of and hope for catechesis into the future, this broader framework is essential. This essay is designed to provide a perspective on that wider context by exploring the principles of catechesis articulated in some of the Church's major catechetical documents.

In considering the documents and the principles that shape them, it is helpful and even necessary that we begin by reflecting on the central principles that form our own present approach to the catechetical enterprise and their relationship to what we believe to be the focus for our diocesan Church as well as the universal Church. You might begin this by giving thought to these questions either alone or in conversation with others.

## Questions for Reflection
- In a series of words or short phrases—five or six, perhaps—list the primary descriptors of catechesis as you understand it. What words or phrases describe the core dimensions of catechesis for you?

Why are these important to you? It would be helpful here to reflect on both the present reality as well as your future hopes and vision.

- As you reflect on your experience within your diocese, what phrases or words best describe your sense of the direction and vision of catechesis? What words or phrases describe the priorities which shape the diocesan catechetical work? In what ways are these complementary to your own understanding of catechesis? In what ways are they challenging to you?
- How would you describe the sense of catechesis that is at the core of the vision held by those leading the universal Church? What experiences shape your perception of that vision? In what ways does this vision complement and/or challenge your own sense of the core dimensions of catechesis? With our own understanding of the core principles of catechesis before us, we turn now to a consideration of some of the Church's major catechetical documents.

## Reading Ecclesial Documents

Before entering into an analysis of the details of these key documents, a prior conversation concerning the process for reading ecclesial documents in general and documents addressing catechesis in particular is necessary. Here a number of questions can be explored: What are the factors which shape and direct the writing and promulgation of these documents? What are the relationships among the documents that are under consideration here? What role do these documents serve within the catechetical enterprise? In providing a sense of direction for how we enter into the process of reading ecclesial documents, let me propose three overarching guidelines.

First: Each document must be read and understood in light of the formative context which shaped its writing, promulgation and reception. There are a number of dimensions which shape ecclesial documents, including those on catechesis. An understanding of the historical setting in which a document is written provides an important starting point: *To Teach as Jesus Did*, *(TTJD)* for example, which was published in 1972 is very much a document of its time. While the structure of community, message and service which is prominent in this document is helpful, other elements of *TTJD* are less applicable in today's Church. Recognizing the historical realities which influenced the document's composition allows the reader to acknowledge the limitations of a given text while appreciating its potential contribution to the present and future.

Attending to the historical context also allows the reader to recognize developments in the understanding of catechesis and the articulation of the key issues related to it. The place of adult catechesis, the relationship between catechesis and liturgy, the role of the experience of the learner and the significance of culture—our perception of all of these have undergone significant changes in the years following Vatican Council II. This is reflected in the documents.

The issue of our developing understanding of catechesis is particularly interesting at this time with the promulgation of a new *General Directory for Catechesis (GDC)* which replaces the *General Catechetical Directory (GCD-71)* issued over twenty-five years ago. As a major ecclesial document, the *GDC* provides an articulation of the central dimensions of the catechetical endeavor and in some ways speaks of the hopes for catechesis into the new millennium. Its publication invites reflection on the developments of catechesis over the past quarter century and the areas in need of yet further attention.

Having a clear sense of the source of the document and the basis under which it was promulgated provides another helpful lens in support of a valid reading of the text. *Catechesis in Our Times (CT)* promulgated in 1979 is an apostolic exhortation under the authorship of Pope John Paul II; it had its origin in the gathering of bishops for the Synod on Catechesis in 1977. The locus of authority for the text is different from, for example, *The Challenge of Adolescent Catechesis: Maturing in Faith (CAC)* which was produced by the National Federation of Catholic Youth Ministry in the mid-80s. While the focus of attention for these two documents may be similar, their authority and "weight" within the various conversations concerning the nature of catechesis—local, national, universal—are different.

In general terms, as American Catholics look at the catechetical documents that have been promulgated since the close of Vatican Council II we can speak of three primary sources. One set of documents originates from the National Conference of Catholic Bishops (NCCB) here in the United States or from offices, committees and conferences that are related to it. At their best, these documents provide a window for viewing the present dynamics of catechesis here in the United States and an angle for imagining the future. Their specifically U.S. coloring, while limiting their applicability to other settings, makes clear that an essential element of catechesis is to correlate between the Christian message and the experience of the learner rooted in a specific culture.

Another set of documents originates from offices, committees, and congregations within the Vatican structure. While the focus of these documents varies, their audience is the universal Church and usually more specifically those who have responsibility for catechesis at the national and local levels: the bishops, priests and catechetical leaders. In many cases, the sweep of these documents is fairly broad and their role is to provide guidance for the application and adaptation of catechetical principles to the national Churches. As will be examined in a bit more detail below, this is clearly seen in the relationship between the *General Catechetical Directory*, prepared by the Sacred Congregation for the Clergy and promulgated in 1971, and *Sharing the Light of Faith: The National Catechetical Directory for Catholics of the United States (NCD)*, prepared under the direction of the NCCB and published in 1978. The intended use for the *Catechism of the Catholic Church (CCC)* is also universal—it is to serve "as a point of reference for the catechisms or compendia that are composed in the various countries" (*CCC* #11).

The final group of documents are those that have their foundations in the deliberations of representative bishops from throughout the world gathered in Synod. Three recent Synods pertain particularly to catechesis and their documents have been included in this list. Such documents are known as "Apostolic Exhortations" and though arising from the deliberations of the Bishops' Synod, are issued under the authorship of the Pope. They are designed to establish a vision and tone for addressing issues of pastoral concern which shape the life of the Church. Rooted in the consultation with bishops from around the world, these documents are intended to provide a universal perspective and to have local application.

Using these three categories of documents, the listing of post-conciliar catechetical documents is given below. One could debate at length what documents should or should not be included in this list. The ones listed here are those that give explicit attention to describing the nature and purpose of catechesis. Also included are those documents which specifically intend to be used as a resource for catechesis, *Basic Teaching for Catholic Religious Education (BT)* and the *Catechism of the Catholic Church*, for example.

| Year | Roman Documents | Synod Documents | United States |
|------|-----------------|-----------------|---------------|
| 1971 | *General Catechetical Directory (GCD-71)* | | |
| 1972 | | | *To Teach as Jesus Did (TTJD)* |
| 1973 | | | *Basic Teaching for Catholic Religious Education (BT)* |
| 1975 | | *On Evangelization in the Modern World (Evangelii Nuntiandi) (EN)* | |
| 1978 | | | *Sharing the Light of Faith (NCD)* |

| | | | |
|---|---|---|---|
| 1979 | | *On Catechesis in Our Time (Catechesi Tradendae) (CT)* | |
| 1981 | | *The Christian Family in the Modern World (Familiaris consortio) (FC)* | |
| 1986 | | | *The Challenge of Adolescent Catechesis (CAC)* <br> *Serving Life and Faith: Adult Religious Education and the American Catholic Community (SLF)* |
| 1988 | *Rite of Christian Initiation of Adults (RCIA)* | | |
| 1988 | *The Religious Dimension of Education in a Catholic School (RDE)* | | |
| 1990 | *Adult Catechesis in the Christian Community (ACCC)* | | *Guidelines for Doctrinally Sound Catechetical Material (GDSCM)* |
| 1992 | | | *Go and Make Disciples: A National Plan and Strategy for Catholic Evangelization in the United States (GMD)* |
| 1993 | *Guide for Catechists (GC)* | | |
| 1994 | *The Catechism of the Catholic Church (CCC)* | | |
| 1997 | *General Directory for Catechesis (GDC)* | | |

Because the sources of the documents differ, the perspective and audience of the various documents also vary, another reality that shapes the ecclesial texts. Returning to the documents compared earlier: *CT* is addressed to the universal Church; it attempts to articulate the challenges and realities of catechesis as the Church comes to expressions in all parts of the world. It asks questions and raises concerns which may not be fully applicable to every local Church. *CAC*, on the other hand, is an expression of the leadership of the Church in the United States. Given the diversity of the US Church, its applicability is not uniform, but the document is intended for a much more limited audience that share some common linguistic, epistemological and cultural experiences.

An awareness of these dimensions which serve as the context for the document—the times in which it was written, the ecclesial source from which it was promulgated and the audience to which it is addressed-is essential to an adequate and valid reading of these texts.

Moving from the context of the document, the second guideline for effectively reading Church texts on catechesis attends to the actual text: The articulated focus and goals of the document itself serve as an essential tool in guiding the reader's approach to the text. Within its own historical context, reflective of its source and audience, each document has its own specific focus which serves as an essential starting point in the process of interpretation. At some level, this is self-evident: a given text needs to be understood and evaluated in light of what it says it is trying to accomplish. But too often, ecclesial documents or excerpts from these texts are seen as full articulations of the present state of catechesis and of the mind of the Church regarding the catechetical enterprise, disregarding the ways in which the text itself sets limits on its intended scope and application. An awareness of the specific goals of a document allows the reader to ask the right questions in approaching the text and to draw from its content helpful insights for the formation of catechesis into the future.

A few examples: *CT* makes clear that, reflecting the focus of the synod of 1977, it is attending particularly to catechesis "meant for children and young people" (*CT* #2); that puts into context somewhat the minimal attention within the document to the experience and needs of adults. *Adult Catechesis in the Christian Community (ACCC)* on the other hand specifically addresses the issue of the catechesis of adults. Its lack of attention to children and youth is a function of its focus rather than a slight to these important groups. A text like *Basic Teaching for Catholic Religious Education (BT)* makes clear in its introduction that it is not attempting to provide a complete articulation of the catechetical ministry; it simply serves as an expression of the key themes and teachings that are to be present in catechesis (*BT*, Introduction).

It is in reflecting on a text like *BT* that the third guideline comes into focus: the documents are best read in relationship to one another. The writers of *BT* make clear the necessity of seeing the relationship among documents.

> This document is not to be confused with either the *General Catechetical Directory* or the planned *National Catechetical Directory* (to which this document will be helpful input). This document should however be read in the light of the *General Catechetical Directory*, by which its admittedly limited scope can readily be understood. (*BT*, Introduction).

In some ways, *BT* can be recognized as an expanded excerpt from *GCD-71* and as an outline for the preparation of the *NCD*'s Chapter 5, "Principal Elements of the Christian Message." But, more importantly, a text like *Basic Teaching for Catholic Religious Education* can never be effectively read in isolation. The contribution of *BT* to the general catechetical enterprise can best be recognized only when it is placed in relationship to other documents which provide a balance between *BT*'s focus on content and the need for similar attention to the setting and process of catechesis.

From another perspective, the importance of recognizing relationships among the documents is also evident in an examination of the *General Catechetical Directory* and *Sharing the Light of Faith: National Catechetical Directory for Catholics of the United States. GCD-71*, published in 1971, was written following the directive of the Vatican II document, *Decree on the Bishops' Pastoral Office in the Church (CD)*. Affirming the role of the bishop in fostering effective and vital catechesis, *CD* calls for the publication of a directory which would provide guidelines for establishing the content and approach to catechesis and for the composition of catechetical materials (*CD* #44). Throughout the universal Church, this call for a directory marked a significant shift in the understanding of the central concern of catechesis, a shift that had been in process for several decades leading up to the Council. Without denying the importance of defining the content of this instruction, the move toward a directory affirmed that effective catechesis and its power to make faith "living, explicit and active" (*CD* #14) is rooted in the broader challenge of bringing the message into active dialogue with the experience of the learners and the culture within which the Church strives to live the Gospel. For this reason the writers of *GCD-71* made explicit in the foreword that it was to be used as the foundation for the "production of catechetical directories and catechisms." The task of "applying the principles and declarations contained in this *Directory* to concrete situations properly belongs to the various episcopates, and they do this by means of national and regional directories . . . " (*GCD-71*, Foreword). Thus the creation of the *National Catechetical Directory*.

Placing the *NCD* within the wider framework of *GCD-71* leads to some important conclusions regarding the role of the *NCD* and to some insights regarding the task of catechesis. The *NCD* reflects the attempt to bring to particular expression the wider Church's vision of the nature and purpose and approach to catechesis. By beginning with the realities and challenges of American culture, the *NCD* reiterates the perspective of *GCD-71* (and other documents) that catechesis takes place within a particular culture and a specific time and place. The presumption of *GCD-71* that national directories are essential to the effective realization of the goal of catechesis affirms the core insight that catechesis is ultimately a local activity. Catechesis at its essence is to be directed and evaluated by the local Church.

At the same time, this relationship between *GCD-71* and the *NCD* reminds us that even the most "local" catechesis has an important point of reference in the universal Church. The work of catechesis is oriented not primarily for membership in a specific parish community but in the universal Church with eyes directed outward toward the Reign of God. As Thomas Groome points out in his article on "The Purposes of Catechesis," the Reign of God is the overarching symbol of God's ultimate purpose for humankind and creation. Keeping that relationship between national and universal documents in focus allows us as catechetical leaders to attend to our own parish and diocesan concerns while maintaining that essential tie with the broader goal of catechesis that moves us beyond the specifics of our day.

Reading any ecclesial document requires care and attention. At some level, the valid reading of any text, including ecclesial documents, requires us to enter into the "world of the text," that is, the context and presumptions which allow the text to make sense, to be reasonable.

A good novel sets out for the reader a particular world which is given expression through a certain historical context, a defined set of motives and motivations, and a specific group of characters whose actions and attitudes both reflect and shape the world of the novel. Within the world set out by the novelist, the plot and movement of the story unfold in a way that makes sense, is reasonable, is even believable. The reader enters into that world and is rightly disappointed when the novelist finesses the ending in a way that is not true to the world which he or she had created or portrays the characters acting in ways that breach the contexts and presumptions of the world of the novel.

However, the created world of the novel does not stand in isolation. As reader I enter into the story bringing expectations and assumptions about how the world works and how people think and act based on my own experiences. The world set out by the novelist is appealing to me or not, engaging for me or not depending in part on my ability to bring my context, my presumptions—my "world of the reader"—into dialogue with the world of the book. As reader my "world" both provides the possibility of my reading the novel at all and sets the limits of how I understand the novel and enter into the world set out there. So the reading of any text, a novel or an ecclesial document, engages the reader in dialogue between the world of the text and the world of the reader.

Each of the three principles for reading ecclesial documents which we have been exploring here—naming the context which shaped the composition, promulgation and reception of the document, giving consideration to the goal and focus of the document itself, and recognizing the relationship of the document with similar texts—each of these contributes to an effective and reliable reading of the text. Each give us access to the world of the text. As we approach the documents, we bring our own world as readers, our pre-understandings concerning the nature of catechesis and the place of Church documents in shaping and directing our perception and expressions of catechesis. These pre-understandings are susceptible to challenge, confirmation, questioning, strengthening, enhancing and negating as we genuinely engage in dialogue with these texts.

So it might be helpful to pause again and reflect alone or with others on your own pre-understandings of ecclesial documents.

## Questions for Reflection
- Name one or two insights into the reading of ecclesial documents that you gained from the essay thus far.
- What in the above presentation do you disagree with or find problematic?
- Return to the questions set out in the beginning of this essay to explore the way in which your responses to those questions have been influenced by catechetical documents. How have they influenced your own understanding of catechesis? In what ways have Church documents given you insights into the diocesan or national sense of catechesis?

## Naming the Issues

As we have already seen, there is a wide range of sources, goals, and points of view shaping the ecclesial documents under consideration. In many ways, they form an eclectic collection of writings; and the complexity of describing the "mind of the Church" on catechesis is particularly clear as older documents are compared with more recent ones or Roman documents are compared with national ones. This diversity thwarts any attempt to express the richness and variety of these documents in simple summary statements about the nature of catechesis and its expression in the Church today.

On the other hand, there are a number of key themes, central to the way in which we understand and engage in the catechetical enterprise, which echo fairly consistently throughout the documents. It is as though we were asking each of the documents a set of questions that they are all prepared to answer. While some attend more to one question over another, or emphasize this dimension of the question rather than that, each document answers from a particular perspective reflecting the faith of the Church—

and all contribute to an overall understanding of contemporary catechesis.

Four sets of questions can be used to explore the understanding of catechesis as set out in the Church's documents. Reflecting on your response to these questions is a helpful way to begin to enter into dialogue with the text.

- First, what is the nature of catechesis? A perhaps obvious and exceedingly broad question, it is important to begin by articulating the place of catechesis within the overall life of the Church. How does catechesis relate to other dimensions of ecclesial praxis? Is it possible to speak of distinguishing characteristics of catechesis and what might they be?

- Second, what are the resources of catechesis? How does catechesis take place? If we grant, as the documents do, that catechesis extends beyond instruction, what are the realities of parish or school life that give shape to the catechetical enterprise?

- Third, who is the learner and how do we understand the participants in catechesis? Many immediately think of children when the question of the learner is raised. Can the documents' view of learners provide us with a broader, more "across the life-span" approach? Part of this also includes asking about the relationships among the multiple and diverse groups that are invited to participate in catechesis.

- Finally, where are we going and how will we know when we get there? In other words, what are the purposes of catechesis? In some ways returning to the first question on the nature of catechesis, here the issue revolves around our hopes for the catechetical work, the purpose of it all.

While there are other issues to be kept in mind when interpreting these documents, these serve as significant markers for navigating and exploring the depth of the documents and for bringing to light some of the key concerns and tensions present in contemporary catechetical conversations.

We turn now to the documents themselves and consider the contribution they make to our sense of catechesis in light of the four questions cited above. Since the *General Directory for Catechesis*, (*GDC*) promulgated in 1997 by the Congregation for the Clergy, the Roman congregation responsible for catechesis, is the most recent and universal of the documents considered, it serves as the beginning point of our discussion; the other documents are brought in to expand or nuance or complete the *GDC*'s perspective.

## The Nature of Catechesis

Defining the nature of catechesis necessitates our stepping back a bit and seeing catechetical activity within the comprehensive framework of the life of the Church.  A number of documents make clear this broader and broadening dimension by situating catechesis within the activity of evangelization.  So this discussion of the nature of catechesis begins with a consideration of evangelization and then explores the distinctive nature of the catechetical enterprise and its relationship to other elements of ecclesial praxis.

Evangelization is the complex and multi-faceted process by which the Church proclaims in actions and words the depth and significance of the revelation of God in Jesus Christ. Its concrete expression is diverse:  acts of charity and justice, explicit proclamation of the gospel, celebration of sacraments, community living, invitation to conversion, and many others. It is the Church's response expressed ever new to the imperative of Christ to proclaim the Gospel and make disciples (Matt 28:19-20).

## Evangelization is an Ecclesial Action in Three Ways.

First, evangelization is at the heart of the Church's mission and identity; it represents its primary mission and reason for being.  In the final analysis, evangelization is not something the Church does but something it is; the Church exists in order to evangelize (see *EN* #14).

Secondly, evangelization is the task of the whole Church. Roles and specific tasks are distributed among the membership, but it is the whole life of the Church that stands as witness to the Good News of the Gospel.  It is the transformed lives of the members that evoke from others a desire to know the foundation of the believer's hope (1 Pet 3:15). The Church's capacity to evangelize rests not primarily on the effectiveness of a group of designated evangelizers but on the authenticity of the lives of believers and of the communal life of the Church.  And finally, evangelization is an ecclesial action in that the whole Church is not only called to be evangelizer but is also always itself in need of evangelization.  The Church "is evangelized by a constant conversion and renewal, in order to evangelize the world with credibility" (*EN* #15).

Evangelization includes all those ways in which the Church engages in "bringing the Good News into all the strata of humanity, and through its influence transforming humanity from within and making it new" (*EN* #18). While the first proclamation of the Gospel and the call to conversion that is inherent to it is at the core of evangelization, it cannot be simply equated with making possible the faith commitment of an individual. The movement toward the transformation of the individual and the process of freeing him or her from all that oppresses (*EN* #s 30-31) is at the heart of evangelization. However, it extends beyond the impact it has on individuals. In evangelizing, the Church seeks to convert "both the personal and collective conscience of people, the activities in which they engage, and the lives and concrete milieus which are theirs" (*EN* #18). In its essence, "evangelization would not be complete if it did not take account of the unceasing interplay of the Gospel and of [humanity's] concrete life, both personal and social" (*EN* #29). Inner conversion and social transformation may be seen as two dimensions of evangelization, but they cannot be separated.

How does this description of evangelization provide insight into our notion of catechesis? Set in the context of the Church's evangelizing mission, "catechesis receives from evangelization a missionary dynamic which deeply enriches it and defines its own identity" (*GDC* #59). Described as "one of those moments - a very remarkable one - in the whole process of evangelization" (*CT* #18), catechesis shares in many of the characteristics of evangelization: it, too, is an ecclesial activity which presumes the complementarity between interior adherence and exterior transformation within both the personal and social contexts.

As the *General Directory for Catechesis* often points out, catechesis, like its umbrella category of evangelization, is an ecclesial activity: engaging in the work of catechesis, the Church expresses and enlivens its identity and advances its primary mission. It flows from and returns to the life of the Church as expressed in local parishes and communities of faith. As an ecclesial activity, catechesis cannot simply be understood as something that the Church does or as one of many items on the parish's to do list. Catechesis is of the essence of the rhythm that defines Church as Church; engaging in catechetical activity is itself formative of the identity and direction of the parish.

One perspective on this: we understand a family to fulfill many tasks—providing safety and security, a place to live and adequate food are primary, certainly. But we also expect a family in some way to give to all members, though particularly the children, a sense of identity, a way of seeing the world, an understanding of how "we," i.e., members of this family, do things and think about things. Sometimes that is quite intentionally done as when a parent explains to a child why certain family traditions are important, or teaches a son or daughter how to make a favorite dessert, or tells the important stories that formed the family, stories of birth or adoption, baptism and marriage.

Quite often, however, the process of forming the identity of the family members and shaping the way they understand themselves and the world around them is done in the simple flow of life: children learn that reading is important because their mother or father reads to them and because they see their parents reading in their leisure time. Children learn the habits of the family—the actions and perspectives that give shape and identity to this particular family—simply by being part of the family. The informal formative aspects of the family go hand-in-hand with the more intentional ones. In this sense, we can say that the process of bringing members into the family and shaping them within the vision of a particular family is a function of the family itself. It is not something the family does; it is the core activity that makes a family a family. And all members have responsibility for this; while parents clearly have specific roles, everyone in the family is shaped and formed by the process of identity formation.

There is a similar dynamic at the heart of understanding catechesis as an ecclesial activity. Viewing catechesis as a process of socialization in this way goes beyond thinking about programs and requires that we think of the whole life of the parish as formative. We will look at this idea more closely when we consider the resources of catechesis. Here, however, it is important to hold in mind that when we speak of the nature of catechesis, situated within the Church's primary mission of evangelization, we speak of the multiple ways in which the parish shapes and reshapes itself and its members into a Christian community. The intricate relationship between catechesis and the community is expressed in the *GDC*: "The Christian community is the origin, locus and goal of catechesis" (#254). To speak of catechesis as an ecclesial activity is to recognize that "it is from the whole life of the Church that catechesis draws its legitimacy and energy" (*GDC* #168).

Sharing in the vision of evangelization, catechesis recognizes the essential link between the proclamation of the Gospel and human realities. "Like evangelization, catechesis is incomplete if it does not take into account the constant interplay between gospel teaching and human experience—individual and social, personal and institutional, sacred and secular" (*NCD* #35). Catechesis is concerned with "initiating people into the fullness of Christian life" (*CT* #18), with putting "the human person in communion with Jesus Christ" (*GDC* #116). At the same time, the broader community and social implications are not ignored. Like evangelization, catechesis shares in the work of Jesus Christ which centers on the proclamation and fulfillment of the reign of God. Individual growth in Christian faith, personal and ecclesial conversion, and social transformation are intricately related.

As a moment of evangelization, catechesis shares in common with evangelization some core characteristics: it is an ecclesial action, it is concerned with the initiation of the individual within the context of a community, and it recognizes as its final point of reference the fulfillment of the reign of God. But what are the distinctive elements of catechesis? Where does catechesis pick up and other moments of evangelization fade off? While clear lines of demarcation are difficult and probably unhelpful, an attempt to name the characteristics that are at the heart of catechesis is important.

> All in all, it can be taken here that catechesis is an education of children, young people and adults in the faith which includes especially the teaching of Christian doctrine imparted, generally speaking, in an organic and systematic way, with a view to initiating the hearers into the fullness of the Christian life. (*CT* #18)

We can draw three points from this description. First, catechesis presumes an initial proclamation of the core message (*kerygma*) and an initial response of faith. (*NCD* #34) It is a matter "of giving growth, at the level of knowledge and in life, to the seed of faith sown by the Holy Spirit with the initial proclamation . . ." (*CT* #20). Catechesis is designed to build on and support that first faith with the "teaching of Christian doctrine." Secondly, catechesis is more than simply the transmission of propositions about the faith. It clearly includes that aspect, but the reality of continuing to enter into the "fullness of Christian life" requires more than knowledge about the faith. As the *GDC* explains, "Catechesis, distinct from the primary proclamation of the gospel, promotes and matures initial conversion, educates the convert in the faith and incorporates him into the Christian community" (#61). In other words, the priority of catechesis is formation in Christian faith (see *GDC* #66). This requires experiences of the faith and of the community of faith. In light of this description of catechesis and its goal of Christian formation, the process of "teaching Christian doctrine" expands far beyond what the *GDC* refers to as "mere instruction" (#29) It is to be "an apprenticeship in the entire Christian life" (#30).

A third point from this description: catechesis is an on-going process in the life of the Church and in the lives of believers. Entry into "the fullness of the Christian life" is a life-long process which is sustained by an "organic and systematic" teaching of Christian doctrine. Catechesis goes beyond the initial proclamation and invites hearers to engage deeply the meaning of the Gospel message for their lives. That process of taking in the significance of Christian teaching for one's life and one's responsibilities in the world is a continual one, sustained by systematic catechesis. This is one of the core reasons that the call of adult catechesis echoes across the catechetical documents published over the past twenty-five years. To accomplish its goal, to contribute to personal conversion, to support the work of social transformation, catechesis must be sustained, on-going and oriented to adults. The link between catechesis and evangelization takes on a new shade here: adult catechesis is essential in that it enables and empowers adults to participate in the Church's key mission—evangelization.

## Questions for Reflection

- What images come to mind in response to the term "evangelization?" Does this form a helpful framework for your understanding of catechesis? Why or why not?
- Many of the documents describe catechesis as an "ecclesial action." What does that mean to you? In what ways might that concept be expressed in the concrete realities of parish or school catechetical programs?
- The description of catechesis taken from "Apostolic Exhortation on Catechesis" (see p. 71) is echoed in the *Catechism of the Catholic Church* as well as in the *General Directory for Catechesis*. In what ways is that description helpful to your own understanding of catechesis? What would you want to add or how would you nuance it to reflect your experience or faith community?

## The Resources of Catechesis

As the prior discussion of the nature of catechesis indicates, the ecclesial documents presuppose that catechetical activity extends beyond instruction, if we understand instruction in a narrow classroom sense. As an ecclesial activity that forms people in Christian identity, catechesis is situated at the heart of the life of the faith community and it is from that community that catechesis draws its energy and resources.

One of the earliest documents to point to the relationship among catechesis and the multiple dimensions of Church life is *Sharing the Light of Faith: National Catechetical Directory (NCD)* published in 1978. It speaks of the source of catechesis as "God's word, fully revealed in Jesus Christ and at work in the lives of people exercising their faith under the guidance of the Magisterium, which alone teaches authentically" (*NCD* #41). It then goes on to say that this one source is manifest in four signs: biblical ("the varied and wonderful ways, recorded in scripture, by which God reveals Himself" [#43]); liturgical ("the celebration of the liturgy, the sacramental rites and the Church Year" [#44]); ecclesial ("grouped under two headings: doctrine or creedal formulations and the witness of Christian living" [#45]); and natural ("examining at the most profound level the meaning and value of everything created, including the products of human effort, in order to show how all creation sheds light on the mystery of God's saving power and is in turn illuminated by it" [#46]).  This emphasis on the multi-faceted expression of the one word of God revealed in Jesus Christ opens out for us the depth and richness of the resources that catechesis uses to continually draw people "into the fullness of the Christian life."

In the twenty years since the promulgation of the *NCD*, one of the ways in which these dimensions have come together most clearly and effectively is in the implementation of the Order for the Christian Initiation of Adults (*RCIA*). It is not surprising then, in attempting to set out a way of thinking about the varied reality of catechesis today, the *GDC* points to the *RCIA* as the "inspiration for catechesis in the Church" (#90).  The significance of the initiatory catechesis for our understanding of the full catechetical enterprise is a central theme within the *GDC*.  So to explore the resources which are drawn upon for the work of catechesis, it is helpful to examine the central components of a catechumenal catechesis.  Set out in paragraph 75 of the *RCIA*, they are:  suitable catechesis, the community as context for journey of faith, liturgy, and call to service and Christian witness.  In concert, these four elements of Church life serve as the foundational resources for effective catechesis.

The description of "suitable catechesis" is similar to the call in *CT* as well as in *GDC* for catechesis that is organic and systematic.  Described as "gradual and complete in its coverage, accommodated to the liturgical year, and solidly supported by celebrations of the word," the goal of this catechesis is to lead the catechumens "not only to an appropriate acquaintance with dogmas and precepts but also to a profound sense of the mystery of salvation in which they desire to participate"(*RCIA* #75).  This idea is echoed in the *GDC* when it states that the "definitive aim of catechesis is to put people not only in touch, but also in communion and intimacy, with Jesus Christ" (#80).

As we look at the first resource or dimension of catechesis—the element of instruction—we recognize, as we did in the discussion on the nature of catechesis, that the intent or goal is not simply the acquisition of knowledge about God or about Church teaching.  The purpose is continued growth in faith and an appropriation of the experience of who God is and who God is for us; it is the experience which sustains and supports the specific teachings.  In order to accomplish this, the instructional dimension of catechesis needs to be situated within the dynamic energy of the other elements—community, liturgy and service.

The primary context for catechesis is the parish—"the most important locus in which the Christian community is formed and expressed" (*GDC* #257).  While the structure of the parish is undergoing significant change in many parts of the United States, it is nonetheless, the primary point of reference for Christians, even those who are not involved with Church life. The parish serves as the usual place that faith continues to grow and to be expressed.

But beyond simply being the setting in which catechesis takes place, the parish community serves as the primary catechist; it is the shared life of the parish that is the agent of catechesis. This was echoed earlier in considering the nature of catechesis as an ecclesial action, but it bears repeating here: formation takes place in all the formal and informal ways in which the community gathers or fails to gather. The parish as community as well as the members of the parish are being formed within the very rhythm of parish life. While as catechetical leaders we attend to and have specific responsibility for the more intentional expressions of formation, it is essential that we recognize the formation that takes place in how the community makes decisions, welcomes others and expends its resources—in its whole life as a faith community.

There is a story told of a congregation in Chicago that was faced with a dilemma in the days following the bombing of Pearl Harbor by the Japanese: A community of Japanese-American Christians had been evicted from the place where they gathered each week, and they came to this large, suburban congregation with the request that they be able to use a small room in their complex for weekly worship. The congregation was divided in their opinion, but given the anti-Japanese conviction which dominated, the majority seemed to be against welcoming the Japanese into their space. When the leadership of the congregation met to make their decision, one of the Sunday school teachers asked if she could speak. She said, "This is an important decision you're making here tonight. The Sunday school teachers met last night to pray about this situation and to pray for you in your decision making. And I was sent by them to tell you this: if you do not allow this Japanese-American community to share our space, then none of us will teach Sunday School again. We cannot teach our children and young people and adults about the love of God if we as a community cannot express that love to others." The Sunday school teacher left and the decision was made: the Japanese-American community was welcomed in. In this sense the community is the primary catechist.

At the same time, the full community is also the "learner" in the catechetical enterprise. Catechesis attends not only to the individual believer in his or her journey of faith, but to the whole community. The whole community is being shaped and formed into a welcoming and evangelizing community; the whole community is called to enter into and participate in the "fullness of the Christian life."

What would catechesis look like if we wished to enhance the parish community's role both as catechist and as full participant? The *GDC* sets out a few proposals for describing such a blossoming faith community. The document affirms that priority be given to adult catechesis, that those who are alienated or indifferent toward religion need to get specific attention, and that the fostering of small faith communities is an important means for nurturing mature faith (#258). While these may sound like simple proposals, implementing them will have the effect of transforming the faith community in its essential role as a resource for catechesis.

A third resource essential to catechumenal catechesis and central to the broader catechetical endeavor is the liturgical life of the Church. Liturgy here is used in its broadest sense as all those times that the community gathers for prayer and worship, gathers to celebrate and participate in the saving work of God in Jesus Christ. (*Catechism of the Catholic Church* # 1069-1070). Holding pride of place is, of course, the Eucharistic liturgy: it is here that the paschal mystery of Christ—the saving reality of Jesus' life, death and resurrection—is celebrated and made present. It is within the celebration of the Eucharist that those gathered are invited to connect the realities of their lives with the paschal mystery (see Vatican II, *Constitution on the Sacred Liturgy* #2). The Eucharist, therefore, is at the heart of our identity as Catholic Christians; it is at the heart of providing the community with the opportunity to enter ever more deeply into the fullness of Christian life.

Enhancing the liturgy's formative energy is the role of liturgical catechesis. Much more than simply preparation for the celebration of a particular sacrament, liturgical catechesis "aims to initiate people into the mystery of Christ by proceeding from the visible to the invisible, from the sign to the thing signified, from the 'sacraments' to the 'mysteries'" (*CCC* #1975). By introducing the core symbols of the liturgy and by providing opportunity for participants to reflect back upon their engagement with those symbols, liturgical catechesis enhances the community's ability to participate more fully in the liturgical celebration. If, as we said earlier, the liturgy provides the opportunity for us to connect the experience of our lives with the saving reality of Christ's paschal mystery, then liturgical catechesis serves as the opportunity to articulate that connection and draw out its implications for how we live as Christians in the world.

As we speak about liturgy as a resource for catechesis, we recognize the complex relationship between these two central elements of parish life. "Both are rooted in the Church's faith, and both strengthen faith and summon Christians to conversion, although they do so in different ways" (*NCD* #113). There is a dynamic circular relationship such that effective catechesis leads to fuller participation in the liturgy which, in turn, enhances catechesis. This is not simply a closed circle of ever more effective catechesis and liturgy, but one that is in service to the community and the community's ability to engage in service and Christian witness—the fourth resource for catechesis.

The *RCIA* makes clear that Christian witness and service are essential to initiation into the Christian life (*RCIA* #75). From the first signs of commitment to the Christian community, marked by entry into the catechumenate, participants are introduced to the evangelical nature of the Church. Implicit in this is the recognition that participation in service, in action for justice, is not simply the consequence of formation but is itself formative. Engagement in activities of service opens up in a new way the implications of the Church's teachings and the challenge of evangelization. This is true for individuals as well as for communities: The congregation that welcomed the Japanese-American community into their church was forever changed by that. Having once recognized their responsibility to the other, the community could never again turn its back on those marginalized by society or wider culture. This congregation in Chicago was in the vanguard of the civil rights movement in the 1960's, has supported the dignity of all persons whenever that is threatened and continues to take an active role in overcoming the systemic causes of poverty and discrimination. While effective catechesis complements and provides insight into actions of service and justice, it is the actions themselves that form and transform individuals and communities of faith.

These four dimensions—systematic catechesis, community life, liturgy, and Christian witness and service—give indication of the central dynamics of catechesis. Two points worth noting: First, catechesis is more than simply speaking about these four elements—not only are we called to develop community, but participation in the life of the community is itself formative; not only do we teach about the sacraments, but participation in the liturgical life of the Church contributes to our identity and our capacity to enter more fully into the Christian life. And, secondly, in reflecting on these four resources it becomes clear that catechesis involves the dynamic interaction of instruction, community, liturgy and service. Programs of instruction need to be clearly linked in some way with the liturgical life of the parish, particularly the Sunday liturgy; actions of service and justice are seen as an integral aspect of the formative life of the parish, rather than the separate responsibility of a few.

The implications of this discussion for our understanding of catechesis are challenging. It is clear that catechesis and the process of formation extend beyond the once-a-week session with children and youth or even the more extended time in the parish or regional school. Reflecting on the interaction of these resources of catechesis invites us as catechetical leaders to see our task as wider than the specific programs for which we may be responsible. As catechetical leaders our task involves enhancing and at some level contributing to the coordination of all the ways in which the individual and the community is formed and transformed in light of the Gospel.

## Questions for Reflection

- A number of documents draw on the *RCIA* as an model for understanding the nature and task of catechesis. Reflecting on your own experience with the *RCIA* and/or your understanding of the process inherent to it, what two or three insights can you draw to illumine your understanding of catechesis?
- We have highlighted here the essential interconnection among instruction, community, liturgy, and service. In what ways are those interconnections already present in the structure and dynamics of catechesis in your parish or school? How might you facilitate their further interaction?
- What elements in your setting can be used to enhance the connection among these four resources? What elements challenge such connection?

## The Learners

The next question can appropriately be asked of each of the catechetical documents under consideration: who is the learner? While at some level the answer is self-evident—the learners include adults, young people and children, as the *GDC* proposes, from infancy to old age—the point of emphasis and the understanding of the relationship among them continues to evolve.

With the exception of documents pertaining specifically to the content of catechesis *Basic Teaching for Catholic Religious Education* or *Guidelines for Doctrinally Sound Catechetical Materials*, for example) every catechetical document published over the past thirty years has referred to the importance of adult catechesis. Those documents particularly concerned with the catechesis of children and youth, speak of the importance of forming the adults who are engaged in such work. For example, see *Challenge of Adolescent Catechesis*, Part V and *The Religious Dimension of Education in a Catholic School*, Part Four, no. 5. In both cases the formation of the adults is recognized as being in service not only to the particular children or youth with whom they are working but to the wider mission of the Church. Documents that are more general in nature speak not only of the importance of adult formation but of its centrality to the catechetical mission and its necessity to the vibrant life of the Church.

Over the past thirty years the primary ecclesial documents on catechesis have become increasingly insistent on the indispensability of regular, systematic, on-going catechesis of the adult community. While the earlier documents regularly included reference to the importance of adults, the amount of attention given within a particular document to the issue of adult catechesis has increased significantly over the years. Comparing the earlier *General Catechetical Directory* (*GCD-71*) with the more recent *General Directory for Catechesis* (*GDC*) illustrates this. The recent *GDC* quotes *GCD-71* in support of the importance of adult catechesis:

> Catechesis for adults, since it deals with persons who are capable of an adherence that is fully responsible, must be considered the chief form of catechesis. All the other forms, which are indeed always necessary, are in some way oriented to it. (*GDC* #59)

So both the 1971 and the 1997 documents make the case for the centrality of adult catechesis and its role in serving as point of orientation for all other catechesis. The evolution of the place of adult catechesis comes clear, however, in comparing the way in which the discussion of adult catechesis develops within the two documents. While arguing for the orienting role of adult catechesis, in delineating the characteristics of catechesis at each age, *GCD-71* begins with children and youth, developing these sections in significant detail and concludes with a brief section on the catechesis of adults. (See Part Five: "Catechesis According to Age Level.") In the comparable section of the *GDC*, the discussion begins with adults, arguing in the introduction that the various stages in the faith journey need to be integrated and "hence it is pedagogically useful to make reference to adult catechesis and, in that light, orient catechesis for other times of life" (#171). (Part Four, Chapter Two: "Catechesis According to Age.") More significant is that as one reads the *GDC*, it becomes clear that the writers of the document considered the primary referent for learners to be adults. This is rooted, at some level, in the formative vision of the *RCIA* which is one guiding focus of this document. The catechumenal catechesis of non-baptized adults "should serve to inspire other forms of catechesis" (*GDC* #68).

To examine the rationale for saying that the formation of adults is the core expression of catechesis, we return again to the relationship between catechesis and evangelization. As we have already seen, catechesis builds on the first faith established with the earliest proclamation of the Gospel in actions and words. Evangelization and catechesis are "essential and mutually complementary: go and welcome, proclaim and educate, call and incorporate" (*GDC* #61). But while attention must be given to initiatory catechesis—the immediate response to the faith evoked through evangelization—the task of catechesis requires that we continue beyond that in order to mature the faith of the believer and the believing community.

This formative level of catechesis takes many forms (see *GDC* #s 69-72, *ACCC* #s 61-65), but all are in service to enabling the participants to enter more fully into the Christian life and to embrace their role in the mission of the Church. Here is where the relationship between catechesis and evangelization takes on a new depth: initiatory catechesis builds on the work of evangelization. But evangelization is made possible through the actions and words of the mature believer as he or she lives and works and engages with the world.

*Adult Catechesis in the Christian Community* makes the point this way: at the heart of the Church's mission is the building up of the reign of God by allowing the message of the Gospel to permeate all of human existence. This is accomplished through the day to day witness of the Christian whose faith has depth and maturity. In light of this, *ACCC* concludes:

> Hence, it is not only legitimate, but necessary, to acknowledge that a fully Christian community can exist only when a systematic catechesis of all its members takes place and when an effective and well developed catechesis of adults is regarded as the central task in the catechetical enterprise. (#25)

Here again, we return to the ecclesial nature of catechetical work. It is ecclesial in that it enlivens and expresses the Church's identity and promotes the Church's fundamental mission. While there is a communal dimension to this mission, it is accomplished in the lived experience of adult Christians "who are capable of a full response to God's word" (*NCD* #32).

We should be clear that the group included under the large heading "adult" is not monolithic. Members of this group, who range from young people in their twenties to elders who are home bound, bring a diverse set of needs and experiences, questions and perspectives to the catechetical enterprise. The designation "adult" extends from those who are in the midst of the initiation process, the catechumens, to those whose wisdom and maturity of faith call and welcome others to the Christian community. Looking to the catechesis of adults as our central task makes clear that the work of catechesis is not easily addressed by a set program but must evolve from the life of the faith community and the dynamic interplay of the various elements of parish life (see *ACCC* #29).

We must be clear about our emphasis on adult catechesis. This in no way diminishes the importance of or need for the catechesis of children and youth. Rather, it serves to provide a meaningful context and sense of direction for this work.

Adult catechesis cannot be conducted to the exclusion or slighting of catechesis for other age groups. When coordinated with them, it becomes the catechesis of Christian maturity and the goal of other kinds of catechesis. (*ACCC* #29)

While much of the catechesis with children and youth is initiatory in its nature, there is the recognition that that is not an end in itself. Adult catechesis potentially provides a horizon against which the catechesis of children and youth is understood. As the *GDC* notes, all catechesis of children and youth should build harmoniously toward adult faith and catechesis (#71).

## Questions for Reflection

- In what ways is the catechesis of adults a core element of your pastoral setting? How would you describe the main goals of the direction of adult catechesis in your setting?
- How would your understanding of your task as catechetical leader change if the parish leadership embraced the vision that "well-developed catechesis of adults is regarded as the central task in the catechetical enterprise" (*ACCC* #25)? What would you name as some of the core benefits of engaging such a vision? What would be the challenges?
- At the conclusion of this section, it was argued that giving emphasis to adult catechesis benefits the work done with children and youth. In what ways do you think that is true? What would be your concerns in this regard?

## The Goal of Catechesis

One final question is in order before we conclude this discussion of the "mind of the Church" concerning catechesis. To some degree it is a circling back to the first question which examined the nature of catechesis. Here we ask about the fundamental focus or goal of all catechesis. This question invites us to push against the goal of "mature faith" or "initiating into the fullness of the Christian life," central elements of the definitions of catechesis that we have been exploring here, and ask about the broader goal within which catechesis has meaning. Here we ask: Why is fostering mature faith important? What is the point of helping people enter every more deeply into the fullness of Christian life? In exploring these questions we are reminded by the documents of the significance of catechesis within the Church's mission.

As we have seen already, the documents characterize catechesis as a complex reality which includes the interplay of effective instruction, a formative community, engagement with the liturgical life of the Church, and participation in the mission of the Church through service and Christian witness. It receives its mandate and energy from evangelization within which it is a significant moment. To gain insight into the fundamental focus and goal of catechesis requires that we examine the focus and goal of evangelization and then make application to catechesis.

In engaging in evangelization, the Church is merely following the example of Jesus Christ, the first evangelizer.

> As an evangelizer, Christ first of all proclaims a kingdom, the Kingdom of God; and this is so important that, by comparison, everything else becomes "the rest," which is "given in addition." Only the Kingdom therefore is absolute, and it makes everything else relative. (*EN* #8)

And so, the short answer to the question of the focus or goal of evangelization is the proclamation of the kingdom or reign of God, "the urgent and definitive intervention of God in history" (*GDC* #34). While it is impossible to fully explicate the reality of the reign of God, it is clear that it includes announcing divine love and the gift of salvation (see Pope John Paul II, *Redemptoris Missio* #14); it is to declare a message of liberation (*EN* #9); it is to echo the call to justice which marked the life and preaching of Jesus and the responsibility all believers share in bringing that justice to fruition (*GDC* #102).

At the heart of the work of evangelization, the focus or goal of evangelization, is the proclamation of the reign of God. Catechesis is in service to this same goal. The *GDC* fittingly calls Jesus "catechist of the Kingdom of God" (#163).

In expanding on this concept—that catechesis is in service to the proclamation of the reign of God—the *GDC* highlights some basic aspects that catechesis is to underscore: God as loving Father; the integral gift of salvation; God's call to justice and our responsibility; the call to conversion; the role of the Church in service to the kingdom; and the fulfillment of all human hope within the reign of God (*GDC* #102). It is clear that this is not a syllabus of content, but the descriptors of an orientation of life. Catechesis is not to teach us about the reign of God, but to participate in its fulfillment. The reign of God "is absolute, and it makes everything else relative" (*EN* #8).

This final focus on the reign of God provides a vital lens to our work as catechetical leaders. It puts in perspective everything we do—all is relative to the reign of God. But "relative" does not mean inconsequential. It is not that our work with adults, children and youth is insignificant; its significance rest in its contribution to the reign of God. Whether imagining an alternative model of faith formation focused on the adults of the parish or deciding on the best program for Eucharist formation or haggling over the budget for youth catechesis, we see beyond these activities—or, better perhaps, through these activities— the on-going expression of the reign of God already present in the life, death and resurrection of Jesus and yet waiting for fulfillment at the end of time.

## Questions for Reflection

- What words or phrases characterize your understanding of "kingdom" or "reign of God"? Is the image of the reign of God a life-giving or invigorating one for you? Why or why not?
- What difference would it make to how you think about your work as a catechetical leader to see it through the lens of the reign of God? What are the challenges to seeing your work through this lens?
- How might you help those who share your work—parents, catechists, youth leaders—to envision their activities through this fundamental focus or goal of catechesis— proclaiming the reign of God?

The ecclesial documents on catechesis written in the past thirty years provide a rich resource for those involved in catechetical leadership. Careful attention to these texts allows the reader to draw out core principles that give depth and meaning to the work of catechesis. These documents serve as an important perspective on the "mind of the Church" and as a way of recognizing and strengthening the connection between the day-to-day activities of catechesis and the broader mission of the Church.

This essay has attended to some of the core questions that one can appropriately ask these documents: questions concerning the nature of catechesis, the resources upon which catechesis draws, the characteristics of the learner, and the fundamental focus or goal of catechesis. Clearly there are other topics that can profitably be brought to dialogue with these texts: questions of methodology or the specifics of content, issues related to the formation of catechists and the role of families. A number of these topics are explored in other essays in this series.

What comes through clearly in these documents is this: Catechesis is an essential dimension of the life of the Church and crucial to the fulfillment of the Church's mission. As catechetical leader you walk in a solid line of those who have shared in the task of Jesus as first evangelizer, first catechist—proclaiming and living into the reality of the reign of God.

## Bibliography

Boyack, Kenneth, ed. *The New Catholic Evangelization*. New York: Paulist, 1992.

*The Catechetical Documents: A Parish Resource*. Chicago: Liturgy Training Publication, 1996..

Cowan, Michael and Bernard Lee. *Conversation, Risk, and Conversion: the Inner and Public Life of Small Christian Communities*. Maryknoll, NY: Orbis Books,1987.

Fowler, James W. *Becoming Adult, Becoming Christian: Adult Development and Christian Faith*. San Francisco: Harper and Row, 1984.

Marthaler, Berard L. *The Catechism Yesterday and Today: The Evolution of a Genre*. Collegeville, MN: Liturgical Press, 1995.

Regan, Jane. *Exploring the Catechism*. Collegeville, MN: Liturgical Press, 1996.

# 3
# The Processes of Catechesis
## Carl J. Pfeifer & Janaan Manternach

A few months ago, Jane, a long-time friend, was hired as a DRE in a nearby Virginia parish. She was excited, but understandably anxious. She invited us to lunch to talk about her new job and her fears.

"You know me," she began. "I'm a good volunteer, a kind of jack-of-all trades. I've been a catechist in a couple parishes over the last ten years. I love people and I'm a good organizer. But I have so little background in theology and catechetics. I'm excited about being asked to be a DRE, but I'm scared and feel inadequate. Right now I especially need suggestions on how to help the catechists be more effective and creative. I was a catechist for several years, but I don't feel ready to train others. What are some things you think I should stress with them?"

## Questions for Reflection
- How similar is your experience as a catechetical leader to that of Jane?
- What are some of the practical methods you have found most helpful as a catechist or religion teacher?
- What do you feel is the most basic catechetical process for helping individuals or communities grow in faith?
- What would you most stress with the catechists you work with about how to be effective and creative?

Jane's concern is understandable. Catechesis is a unique ministry. It involves teaching, but can also be like parenting, counseling, spiritual direction, and mentoring. Excellent textbooks abound, but they differ one from another in the way the themes and individual lessons are structured. Facilities for catechesis range from school classrooms, to offices, parts of a gym, a chapel, church, a room in a family's home, outside on a patio or on the grass under a tree. Parishes and schools differ dramatically in size, location, and spirit. Parishioners differ as to culture, nationality, race, educational background, socio-economic status, desires and expectations. Even nearby parishes in the same city or town may differ significantly.

So what can you and other catechetical leaders do to help yourselves and your catechists be effective in carrying out your ministry in the unique situations in which you find yourselves?

Perhaps the best way to explore that question is to take a few moments to reflect back on your own religious education. Jot down your answers to these questions:

- Which catechists or religion teachers stand out in your memory?
- Which ones most influenced you and your faith growth?
- What was it about them that makes them memorable?
- What about them and what they did would you most like to imitate or adapt to your own personality and ministry?

We will now share with you what we informally shared with Jane over several lunches—what we have learned from catechists who influenced us over the years, and from our own long experience in religious education. We will describe what we see as the most important "processes" for catechists to understand and work at doing well:

1) creating a caring environment,
2) preparing carefully,
3) engaging in the basic catechetical process, and
4) using appropriate methods.

## Create A Caring Environment

Know and love those you teach! Far and away the most important "process" for catechists is growing in knowledge and love of those they teach. Catechesis is relational—between catechist, individual learners, and the learning community. It is chiefly through personal relationships that the Holy Spirit, the Spirit of love and unity, acts and a relationship with the risen Christ grows. So it is vital to create a welcoming, caring social environment for catechesis.

Here are some practical steps you can share with your catechists to help them grow in knowledge and love of those they catechize.

(a) **Learn names.** This can be a challenge in once-a-week CCD/PSR programs. With larger groups we have found it helpful to use name-tags, or name-plates, at least for the first few sessions. We have also used games like this: one says aloud his or her name, the second gives her or his own name, and adds the name of the first one, the third gives his or her name and adds the previous two names—and so on until all are able to recall the names of all in the group. Most often, during our first meeting with a group, we take a Polaroid photo of each participant wearing a name-tag. We look at the pictures in between our meetings to refresh our knowledge of each one and to take a moment to pray for each of them.

**(b) Be available.** As your group arrives for catechesis, greet each one by name, comment on something positive about each, perhaps ask a question about a recent experience or event they may have been part of, and so on. After the session invite volunteers to help you rearrange the room, providing you additional time to chat with them and others.

**(c) Express your care directly.** Give honest praise for good insights or work. Gently encourage and help those who seem bored or struggling. Write caring notes on papers or projects they hand in. Express genuine interest in things you know interests and involves some or all, and real care and sympathy for those who may be hurting or suffering. Don't hesitate to laugh or stimulate laughter during catechetical sessions.

In short, make every effort to know and love those you catechize—individually and as a group. We recall a banner a parochial school principal hung in her office to remind herself and her teachers of the importance of their role. It read: "You are the Christ others know best." We firmly believe that to be true of catechists and their students.

**(d) Contact parents.** Try to meet, or at least call, the parent or parents of each young person you catechize—at least once a year, but preferably more often. Such personal contact can provide important clues into a child's personality, talents or problems which might never surface in your catechetical sessions. Talking with parents also can reveal important data about a young person's home environment, degree of parental support, and family makeup. We also send parents periodic letters, briefing them on what we are teaching and offering practical suggestions for follow-up at home.

### Foster a Sense of Community

Catechesis is not just about nurturing the faith of individuals, but about faith experienced and shared in community. Jesus promises to be with us when two or three gather together in his name. The Spirit of Jesus, the Holy Spirit, is a unifying force, continuing Jesus' efforts to unite people in faith and love. A catechist's task and privilege is to collaborate with the Holy Spirit in fostering a sense of genuine caring and community among those they catechize. They are called to be a community of disciples of Jesus. Catechists can help them become a learning community, helping each other grow in mutual respect, love, and a shared Catholic faith. In such a community all, including the catechist, are "co-learners" and "co-teachers."

We have found several effective "community-building" processes. One is to invite the group to create a name and symbol that will identify and characterize their group. Another is to invite them to formulate together a short list of "rules" to be observed when they are together. A third is to invite the group to choose several individuals to perform routine service-tasks, like being a catechist's assistant, time-keeper, media or computer expert, or attendance monitor. The roles can be rotated so that all have a chance to serve.

Besides these, and more important, is engaging the participants in common activities as a single group or in smaller groupings. Simple forms of "cooperative learning" are increasingly important in helping the participants to become closer to one another, forming a genuine learning community.

## Create an Attractive Physical Environment

We've learned through experience the importance and power of the physical environment as an expression of a catechist's care and an important influence on learning. In one dreary classroom that depressed us and our friends, we changed our attitudes and their capacity for learning simply by bringing in fresh flowers each time we met. Eventually we succeeded in having the room painted. We realize that many things may be beyond the control of catechists, and even catechetical leaders, but many are easily changed. Things like comfortable chairs, adequate and appropriate light, room arrangement that makes it easy to see and hear, and to work alone or together easily, can significantly help learning, praying, and working together.

Careful attention to the placement of visual images (photos, posters, sacred or secular art), symbols (crucifix, candles, palms, water, incense, colored cloth reflecting the liturgical season), can stimulate curiosity, create interest and focus attention, while visually communicating the catechetical content of a given session. Touches of natural beauty, like spring flowers and fall leaves, add to an atmosphere of peace and joy. Careful attention to the physical environment reveals a catechist's care and love for all participants and the "Good News" of Jesus Christ.

## Prepare Carefully for Catechetical Sessions

Effective catechesis rarely "just happens." Most often it is the result of careful planning. Such planning is an important expression of respect for and love of those you catechize. The fine catechetical textbooks created in this country are designed to help catechists become effective and even creative. The books facilitate but do not replace a catechist's personal planning.

We have long urged catechists, alone or in small groups (e.g., by age-level/grade-level) to prepare in three steps.

(a) **Long-range planning.** Early planning, ideally before the catechetical year begins, can sensitize a catechist to the major themes and topics he or she will explore in the months to come. First, it helps to take time before the year begins to do long range planning. Whether you design your own curriculum or use a commercial textbook, note down the year's major content themes and sub-themes, and the number of sessions. Examine one lesson or session plan to become familiar with its basic structure, components, and style. Check to see what supplementary materials are provided— e.g., for parents, for music and song, for duplicating, etc.

Second, plot out on a calendar how the year's sessions fit into the yearly calendar, the Church liturgical calendar and the parish calendar of ministries and special events. Sometimes a slight adjustment in logical order may make a session more relevant and meaningful in relation to a holiday, holy day, saint's feast, parish liturgical or social justice event.

Third, set up an empty box, drawer, or file in which to place photos or art works, magazine articles or newspaper stories, cartoons, graphics, etc., that you will now be alerted to notice because they could be helpful. Simply clip them out when you find them and place them in your drawer, box, or file for use later in relation to particular themes or lessons. These items can greatly enrich and personalize your catechesis.

**(b) Short-range planning.** Before each major unit, or each month, take a short time to do the same type of thing just described, but more sharply focused on the next several sessions. This will stimulate your mind to play with the themes, visuals, Bible stories you will soon be teaching. You will become more sensitive to noticing things or activities you might use in those sessions. This also allows you to schedule guest speakers and use of media, equipment or materials you may need.

**(c) Immediate planning.** A week or a few days before a given session, take some time to become thoroughly familiar with the topic and plan in your textbook for the upcoming session. Check through the resources you have gathered and stored earlier. Play out the session in your imagination. On a file card or sheet of paper write down a brief personal plan to take with you for use during the session itself. Also gather any equipment or resources and make any needed contacts.

## Questions for Reflection

What are some additional ways you have found in your own experience or observed in other catechists that you might now share with your catechists to

- create a caring social environment,
- foster a sense of community,
- create an attractive physical environment, and
- prepare carefully for catechetical sessions?

## On the Road to Emmaus and Back

After helping catechists develop the basic processes of preparing a learning environment marked by love and beauty, and preparing a personal "session plan," it is good to look at the dynamic process that is at the heart of catechesis. It is the core process by which catechists (and other pastoral ministers) can guide individuals and communities to grow in faith as Catholic Christians.  In our experience many catechists fail to understand this process and its importance even though they use textbooks or other resources that are based on it.  It is, for us, the most important catechetical process and catechetical leaders need continually to help catechists learn and use it more skillfully.

One of the best ways we have found to help catechists grasp this process is with a Gospel story.  Since at least the 1960's this story has become a focal point in helping catechists grasp the fundamental process of catechesis, and of other pastoral ministries as well.  We have personally used this dramatic story for three decades to help catechists get a better feel for and understanding of the goals, content, process and methodology of catechesis.

Unfortunately this story is not well known to many catechists. It is found in only one of the four Gospels and is read on only one Sunday (3rd Sunday of Easter, Cycle A) in the three-year cycle of the Lectionary for Mass. Yet it is one of the most exquisite stories in the New Testament.  For us it has long been most helpful in revealing the deepest "how to" processes of all catechesis. It is the story of two disciples on the road to Emmaus on the Sunday after Jesus' crucifixion—and what happens when a stranger joins them on their journey. We hope you find it worth reading carefully and prayerfully at this point and often in the future as you grow in your ministry as Catechetical Leaders.  As you read it slowly, highlight or underline anything that particularly strikes you in the story.

> Now on that same day two of them were going to a village called Emmaus, about seven miles from Jerusalem, and talking with each other about all these things that had happened.  While they were talking and discussing, Jesus himself came near and went with them, but their eyes were kept from recognizing him.  And he said to them, "What are you discussing with each other while you walk along?"  They stood still, looking sad.  Then one of them, whose name was Cleopas, answered him. "Are you the only stranger in Jerusalem who does not know the things that have taken place there in these days?"  He asked them, "What things?"  They replied, "The things about Jesus of Nazareth, who was a prophet mighty in deed and word before God and all the people, and how our chief priests and leaders handed him over to be condemned to death and crucified him.  But we had hoped that

he was the one to redeem Israel. Yes, and besides all this, it is now the third day since these things took place. Moreover, some women of our group astounded us. They were at the tomb early this morning, and when they did not find his body there, they came back and told us that they had indeed seen a vision of angels who said that he was alive. Some of those who were with us went to the tomb and found it just as the women had said; but they did not see him." Then he said to them, "Oh, how foolish you are, and how slow of heart to believe all that the prophets have declared! Was it not necessary that the Messiah should suffer these things and then enter into his glory?" Then beginning with Moses and all the prophets, he interpreted to them the things about himself in all the scriptures. As they came near the village to which they were going, he walked ahead as if he were going on. But they urged him strongly, saying, "Stay with us, because it is almost evening and the day is now nearly over." So he went in to stay with them. When he was at the table with them, he took bread, blessed and broke it, and gave it to them. Then their eyes were opened, and they recognized him; and he vanished from their sight. They said to each other, "Were not our hearts burning within us while he was talking to us on the road, while he was opening the scriptures to us?" That same hour they got up and returned to Jerusalem; and they found the eleven and their companions gathered together. They were saying, "The Lord has risen indeed, and he has appeared to Simon!" Then they told what had happened on the road, and how he had been made known to them in the breaking of the bread. (Luke 24:13-35)

This masterful story deserves reflection, prayer and study. You may find it helpful to read a good biblical commentary to flesh out some of Luke's subtle nuances. Here we will highlight those details in the story that reveal the core process of catechesis in the Church then and now. Our focus will be on what Jesus, our Mentor and Master Catechist, says and does—and how his words and actions impact the two disciples.

1) The two are apparently disillusioned with Jesus after his condemnation and execution on the previous Friday. It is now Sunday and they are walking away from Jesus and his other disciples, returning home to Emmaus and their previous way of life. Along the way, they converse intently about all that had happened to Jesus and to them, shattering their faith, hopes, and dreams.

2) Notice now what Jesus does. As a stranger, a fellow traveler, he walks with them, joining them on their journey. They do not recognize him.

3) Jesus, overhearing their words, sensing their sadness and pain, invites them into a conversation by asking a question about what happened—about their experience.

4) Jesus then listens, giving them an opportunity to share with him their experience. He listens with his heart as well as his ears as they pour out their story of frustrated hopes and loss of faith in Jesus.

5) When they have finished, Jesus chides them for their lack of faith, and tells the story of their faith community by recalling the passages about him in the Hebrew Scriptures. These texts provide a profound interpretation of Jesus' rejection and death. Jesus' story speaks directly to their story— to the very experience and events that the two had just shared.

6) The two disciples now beg the stranger to stay with them. Jesus accepts their hospitality, and joins them for a Eucharistic meal. His words and gestures recall those of their "last supper" with him the previous Thursday.

7) Now the disciples' eyes of faith are opened and they recognize the risen Christ as the stranger who was with them on the Emmaus road, to whom they had offered hospitality. Now the risen Christ disappears. They recall how profoundly his words, especially his opening the scriptures, inflamed their hearts. His words ignited the dying embers of their faith, which is now fully restored at the meal with Jesus. Joyfully they recommit themselves to Christ Jesus and his way.

8) The two then quickly retrace their journey, rejoining the community of disciples who announce to them what they, too, had just experienced: Jesus is alive and with us.

9) The story describes a journey—from Jerusalem to Emmaus and back to Jerusalem—a symbol of the disciples' continuing process of faith growth marked by more dramatic changes of heart. Today we speak of it as ongoing conversion.

## The Core Process of Catechesis

The above reflection on the Emmaus story reveals the dynamic process that is at the heart of contemporary catechesis (as well as of early Christian catechesis). It is a creative process of linking our human stories with Christ's story, and his story with ours. The core catechetical process nurtures faith by integrating daily life experience with Scripture and the Church's Tradition. This happens by bringing the light of Scripture and Tradition to bear on a human experience, event or natural phenomenon, which in the same process may provide new insights into that living Tradition and a deeper understanding of our sacred texts. When effective, the process leads to a deeper commitment to the risen Christ, to living as a disciple of Jesus, and a fresh awareness of his active presence in the Church, in people's daily lives, and in all of creation.

A first grader put it in words we will never forget. Her mother asked her at the end of her first year in the CCD program of a parish in Woodbridge, VA: "What did you learn this year in CCD?" Without a moment's hesitation, she told her Mom, "We learned that Jesus is alive, and he's right here in Woodbridge."

The Second Vatican Council [1962-1965] identified this process in more sophisticated language as a fundamental ecclesial process: "At all times the Church carries the responsibility of reading the signs of the time and of interpreting them in the light of the Gospel" (*Pastoral Constitution on the Church in the Modern World* #4; see also #10, 11, 44, 62). The terminology had been made popular by Pope John XXIII's frequent use (e.g., *Peace on Earth* #126) of Jesus' phrase "the signs of the time" (Matt 16:3). A slightly different expression of the same pastoral process is found in another Council document: "laying bare the seeds of the Word" in the "light of the Word" (*Decree on Missionary Activity in the Church* #11 and 15).

Both of the Church's two official catechetical "*Directories*" (1971 and 1997) consider this process as the heart of the Ministry of the Word, including catechesis. *Sharing the Light of Faith—National Catechetical Directory for Catholics of the United States* (1978) quotes the above Council texts and then applies them specifically to catechesis. "Catechesis recalls the revelation brought to perfection in Christ and 'interprets human life in our age, the signs of the times, and the things of this world'" (*NCD* #42; see also #33 and 46).

The Vatican's 1997 *General Directory for Catechesis*, which replaces the 1971 *General Catechetical Directory*, expands on the same process from the perspective of evangelization and the catechumenate—in accord with key encyclicals of Pope John Paul II. Woven through it are references to the Vatican II use of "signs of the times" (#31-32, 39, 108) and "seeds of the Word" (#38, 86, 91, 95, 200) in relation to the "light of the Gospel" or the "Word." Here is but one quote as an example of the *GDC*'s distinctive language about the basic catechetical process:

> pedagogical instructions adequate for catechesis are those which permit the communication of the whole word of God in the concrete existence of people. Being inspired by the pedagogy of faith, catechesis presents its service as a designated educative journey in that, on the one hand it assists the person to open himself to the religious dimension of life, while on the other, it proposes the Gospel to him" (#146-147; see also #153).

The language of the Council and the *Directories* describes a simple, but often challenging process: making connections between daily life and the Church's living tradition in order to discern God's Word and Christ's presence in both, and to commit oneself to a living Christian faith. The *GDC* stresses that "the relationship between the Christian message and human experience is not a simple methodological question. It springs from the very end of catechesis, which seeks to put the human person in communion with Jesus Christ" (#116). Just as happened in the Emmaus story.

## The Elements of the Process

The Emmaus story reveals the key elements of this process:

1) a human experience or event (the disciples' experience of Jesus' death, their disillusionment, and their journey with a seeming stranger along the familiar Emmaus Road),

2) an example of Christ-like attitudes or actions (the stranger's sensitivity, probing, listening, compassion, and care),

3) the faith community (the stranger's interpretation of the scriptures),

4) a liturgical symbol or ritual (the stranger's Eucharistic "breaking bread" with them), and

5) a lived response and creedal, doctrinal or moral beliefs (the two return to Jerusalem to bear witness to their faith and the "creed" of the Jerusalem community of disciples: "The Lord has risen indeed!"). The *NCD* singles out and explains these same elements as signs of God's Word. The Word of God is the unique source and content of catechesis. God's Word is discernible through signs that reveal "God's self-communication in the world" (#42).

These signs of God's revealing, saving Word are four: "biblical signs, liturgical signs, ecclesial signs and natural signs" (#42; #41-46). These, then, are the basic elements of the core catechetical process: biblical signs include any story, prayer or text in the Scriptures; liturgical signs include all that pertains to the Church's liturgy: symbols, rituals, gestures, feasts, prayers, seasons, sacraments; ecclesial signs include creeds, doctrines, Church teachings, and the witness of saints and other admirable Christians. These three signs comprise "the light of the Gospel," and the "Catholic Tradition." Natural signs include any human experience, event, natural phenomenon, the entire created world—"the signs of the times."

Recalling Vatican Council II, the *NCD* describes the catechetical process in now familiar terms: "examine the signs of the times and interpret them in the light of the Gospel" (#46; #33). Using slightly different terminology the *GDC* highlights the same "signs" of God's Word (#87, 95-96, 118).

A simple diagram may help visualize the catechetical process.

This dynamic process of "reading the signs of the times" and "interpreting them in the light of the Gospel" has been at the heart of contemporary catechesis since shortly before Vatican Council II. It remains central to contemporary catechetical theory and practice. Terminology differs from author to author, textbook to textbook, and even in the two official Directories. Perhaps the most popular term and fullest analysis of the process has been the "Shared Praxis" approach, particularly associated with the work of Thomas Groome. It has been variously called the "Discernment Process," "Faith Process," "Catechetical Process," and still other terms.

The sequence of steps or movements used by various catechetical experts and textbook authors to engage children, youth, and adults in this process vary in name and number (typically 3, 4, or 5). But the fundamental process of nurturing faith in individuals and communities is rooted in an understanding of catechesis as a form of the Ministry of the Word which embraces both daily experience and the Church's rich tradition of faith in a creative, dynamic dialogue.

You and your catechists will notice that contemporary catechetical textbooks are designed to facilitate and guide this very process. Lesson plans typically begin with a life experience common to children and youth of different ages, as well as adults. That experience is then linked with one or more signs of Catholic Tradition that relate to that life experience—e.g., a related Bible story, liturgical ritual, symbol or prayer, a Church teaching, or the example of a saint. The lesson typically then engages the participants in discerning how the life experience and the selected aspect of Catholic faith illuminate one another and invites them to live their faith. Unfortunately many catechists tend—because of limited time, or failing to recognize human experience as an important sign of God's Word—to skip the experiential part of their catechesis. Both the *NCD* (#176) and the *GDC* (#152) stress the importance of human experience as a vital sign of God's Word and presence.

This process can also begin with some aspect of Catholic Tradition rather than with a life experience (*NCD* #176; *GDC* #118). What is vital is that the selected human experience and aspect of Catholic tradition do genuinely intersect. Only then can the two signs of God's Word, of Christ's presence, and of the Spirit's guidance, illumine and enrich one another. This same basic process is also at the heart of the way the Scriptures took shape over centuries, how doctrine develops in the Church, and how individuals or groups grow in spiritual discernment.

Perhaps an example will help. We were asked one year to be catechists for an 8th grade group. In that parish, eighth grade was the year to study the Creed—which many of the youngsters knew by heart. Their 7th grade catechist had warned us that this group felt they already knew all they needed to know about their Catholic faith and its teachings.

After getting acquainted with our 8th graders, we began the year with a relatively old rock song by Cat Stevens, "On the Road to Find Out." They did not know it, but some of them had heard of Cat Stevens. The song expresses a young adult's search to make sense out of life's puzzling journey. We all listened to the song once. They liked it. We then gave them each a copy of the lyrics. As they listened again to the song, they were to mark any words that spoke to their own experience, anything that touched them, moved them, or raised questions for them. Those who wished shared some of their reactions. We then mentioned that we are all—young and old—on "the road to find out." From time to time we grapple with experiences and issues we don't fully understand. We asked them to write down some of the questions they have, some of the things they would really like to find out. When they finished, we asked them to hand their papers to us— but only if they wished. We promised not to show them to others.

Their questions were surprisingly profound, like, "What is God like?" "Why is there so much hatred and violence?" "What will happen when we die?" "How will the world end?" "Why are there so many poor people, especially children?" "Why do so many marriages break up?" As we studied their questions during the week, we realized that many related directly to parts of the Apostles' Creed, and others readily fit with other Catholic teachings related to creedal affirmations.

Each week we explored one belief expressed in the Apostles' Creed in relation to one of their questions. Sometimes we drew on Bible stories or quotes in the process. Other weeks a sacramental ritual or liturgical symbol or prayer seemed more helpful, or the story of a saint.

We all enjoyed our year together "on the road to find out." They got into the process and learned much together—about life, about the Creed, and about what it might mean to put the two together.

## Questions for Reflection
- What strikes you most about Jesus' actions and words in the Emmaus story?
- How does that story help you better understand the process of catechesis?
- How well do you understand and involve all the participants in the basic catechetical process?

## Making the Process Work

As that example suggests, integrating life experience and Catholic tradition to nurture faith does not just happen by simple juxtaposition of a life experience and an aspect of our Catholic faith. Active involvement is required. Over the last thirty years catechists have identified four processes or strategies that make possible faith growth using the basic catechetical process. These active, engaging processes are named differently from author to author, textbook to textbook. They may be coalesced into four dynamically interrelated "moments." These critical strategies relate to both the life experience and the aspect of Catholic Tradition under consideration in any catechetical session. The order in which we present them is not meant to indicate a particular sequence.

(a) **Reflection or thinking.** Catechesis is for faith growth, not just for information. It involves thinking, probing, exploring the signs of God's Word and their connections. Critical thinking (appropriate to one's age) is vital for ongoing growth in understanding, acceptance, and commitment. While it is valuable to learn a creed, Bible text, sacrament, commandment, or prayer by heart, grappling with its meaning for day to day living in today's world, is needed for faith growth. Ultimately faith faces mystery. The real risk of religious education or catechesis is to leave young and old with a sense that they now have all the answers, the whole truth. Faith opens us to God, who is always attracting us to probe deeper, to come closer, yet remains always beyond and "Other." This is what the two disciples on the road to Emmaus were doing—pondering, probing, trying to find some meaning in the horrible events of Jesus' arrest, trial, condemnation and execution as a criminal. They were reflecting on their experience.

We were reminded of this dynamic one bitterly cold evening as we waited with a stranger for a Long Island commuter train. As we chatted, he confessed: "When I graduated from grade school, I received a gold medal for being the best religion student. From that moment on I never set foot into a Catholic Church again for many years."

Noticing our surprise, he continued: "As a kid I had many questions. My parents divorced. I was not happy. But any time I tried to ask a question in religion class, our religion teacher said, 'That is a good question, but we have to move on. There is so much material still to be covered'" The gold medal became for me a sign of her and the Church's lack of understanding and compassion. She filled us with ideas, but had no time to care about or deal with my disturbing questions about my life and about God."

We never forgot his story. It reminds us of what the great theologian, Karl Rahner, once said, that questions are a sign of God's transcendent presence in our lives. If ever we believe, or teach that we know all about God or life, we may be bereft of the wisdom that God continues to reveal in us and in those we catechize.

So we often ask our students—about the meaning of their experiences or stories, and about aspects of the Church's faith tradition—not only "What do you think?" but also "Why do you think you think that?" It is by way of such critical and reflective grappling that participants can come to appropriate not only what they believe but, with God's grace, what the community believes as well.

**(b) Dialogue or sharing.** No one of us or those we catechize can hear all the nuances of God's Word in daily experience and the Church's living Tradition. God's Word invites us to community, to a shared faith. Each of us experiences and hears God's Word uniquely, so we all have something special to share with others. The Holy Spirit enlightens and inspires each of us differently. Each is given special gifts, not just for oneself, but for the benefit of the community.

It almost goes without saying that catechesis which welcomes and invites sharing about personal and religious experiences must make every effort to develop a high level of trust among participants. In this regard what was said above by way of creating a caring community and environment should be recalled. Moreover, catechists should be encouraged and trained to employ a variety of sharing styles. Large group discussion, small group work, turning to one's neighbor, or even "sharing" one's thoughts on a piece of paper with oneself are all viable options. Obviously, no one should ever feel forced to share and the climate should always be such that a participant can take a "pass" at any time.

The two Emmaus disciples each pondered the mystery of Jesus' apparent failure. They shared their questions, feelings and insights—so intensely that the risen Christ readily picked up in their words the profound sadness and disillusionment that wrenched their hearts and shattered their lives. After they came to trust the stranger and his questions they shared their experience and troubled thoughts with him. In response he shared with them his profound insights into the Scriptures. That dialogue touched a spark of hope in their hearts and brought them to "see for themselves." This led to further dialogue with the disciples in Jerusalem.

Once we were called upon at the last minute to lead an adult catechetical session on prayer. The regular catechist was ill. Instead of lecturing about prayer, we sat with the group in a circle. We listened to a recording of several Psalms. We then asked the group if they resonated with any of the prayers they just heard. They began immediately to talk quite openly about their own prayer lives, sharing experiences and insights. We shared with them as members of the group. At the end we closed with a few minutes of shared prayer and two of the Psalms they found most meaningful. It was a marvelous experience of the power and richness of sharing personal faith in dialogue with the Church's tradition.

**(c) Prayer or Praying.** Prayer is the third of the vital processes or strategies that give life to the basic process of integrating daily experience with the Church's faith tradition.   Fr. Gerard Sloyan, one of our chief catechetical mentors, often said that the very purpose of catechesis is to help people to pray.   Learning to pray includes but is far more than learning traditional Catholic prayers like the Our Father, Hail Mary, Glory Be, Apostles' Prayer, Act of Contrition, the Rosary, etc.   Prayer needs to rise up out of each person's experiences which reveal God's loving presence or disconcerting absence in their life.   That prayer in turn needs to be brought into conversation with the Church's rich prayer tradition.   Both fonts of prayer— personal and communal—need to be integrated in the catechetical process.

One Sunday morning we decided to teach our third graders the ancient "Jesus Prayer," which is repeatedly recommended in the Vatican's *Catechism of the Catholic Church* (#435, 2616, 2667-2668). We sat on the floor in a circle with the children.   We asked them to relax, to close their eyes and to become conscious of their breathing as they inhaled and exhaled more slowly and deeply.   Then we invited them to silently pray the name "Jesus" with each breath cycle. They did this until we closed the prayer with an "Amen."

The following Sunday one of the boys arrived early, as we were preparing the room for our session.   He was excited and eager to tell us something. "Do you know what?" he asked.   "No, what?" we responded.   "That prayer we said last week sitting on the floor. . . . We kept saying "Jesus," "Jesus," "Jesus" as we breathed.   You know you can also pray it when you're walking!"   We were silent, awed at the wisdom of a third grader.

Our task is not only to share traditional prayers but to encourage those we catechize to pray out of their own experiences, in their own ways, drawing on the Church's rich tradition of various styles of prayer.   It was the prayerful meal ritual in their Emmaus home that opened the eyes of the two disciples to Jesus' risen presence.

**d) Action or Doing.**   Catechesis and the basic catechetical process are meant to nurture Christian faith, which includes responding to God with our heads (beliefs, truths), our hearts (trust, love), and also with our hands (doing, action, lifestyle).   Some of this active response to God's Word can take place in the actual catechetical experience, e.g., writing to an elderly family member or neighbor, creating book marks with Bible messages to give to friends, neighbors or those in nursing homes, planning a food collection for the needy, or writing to public officials regarding social justice issues. Other active responses outside of catechetical sessions might include tutoring slower students, visiting the sick, helping out at a food kitchen for the poor, helping with chores at home.

In any event the action facilitates and flows from the process of integrating life experience and the Church's faith tradition. After their meal with Jesus and coming to recognize him, the two Emmaus disciples rushed quickly back to Jerusalem to witness to Jesus' resurrection.

One Sunday with fourth and fifth graders the textbook theme was on a social justice issue grounded in the Work of Mercy, "Feed the hungry" (see Matt 25:31-46). We began our session with a surprise snack of M & M's which we knew the youngsters liked. We gave each a paper plate with one or more M & M's on it. We had calculated this beforehand to reflect actual food distribution worldwide. So most received one piece of candy. Several received two or three or four. And one received 24 M & M's. Needless to say there was considerable unhappiness and overt claims of unfairness, bias, and favoritism. Finally, the "rich" boy decided that he would share his green M & M's since he didn't like green ones. However, all except him felt the whole procedure was unfair.

We led them to reflect on and talk about the experience. We shared with them the statistics of global food distribution upon which we based our distribution of M & M's. Then we looked at the story of the Rich Man and Lazarus (Luke 16:19-31), talked about it together, prayed, and decided to take some action. They each wrote a letter to the mayor urging him to find a way to do something to remedy hunger, especially of children, in their city. Then they decided to start food drives in the several schools they attended.

These four strategies—reflection, dialogue, prayer and action—are basic processes needed to make the core catechetical process of "reading the signs of the times and interpreting them in the light of the Gospel" effective in nurturing faith growth in those we catechize.

This is facilitated when we recognize and consciously foster the relationships among the four strategies. Dialogue leads to critical reflection and action is best conducted in a prayerful context. Critical reflection probes more deeply into what one has shared in dialogue with oneself and others, as well as, one's actions and the actions of the communities with which one is allied. Action, in turn, leads to further reflection and conversation. We may pray for the strength to do more or for God's forgiveness for having fallen short of the mark, and so on. The four processes are dynamically interrelated and in practice continually overlap one another.

## Questions for Reflection

- How comfortable and effective are you with these four strategies?
- Why do you feel these strategies are important in effective catechesis?
- What are some ways you have found to help learners think more

critically, share more honestly, pray more sincerely and act more faithfully?
- How can you help catechists become convinced of and skilled in these four catechetical strategies?

## Methodological Processes

Obviously, as our examples above reveal, the catechetical process and its four strategies are normally carried out effectively through a variety of methods. The modern "catechetical movement" began at the start of the 20th century with the discovery of the importance of creative, engaging methods in catechesis. American catechetical leaders soon focused on such methods to involve students in learning the catechism. For example, Fr. Aloysius Heeg, S.J., of St. Louis, popularized flip-chart paintings of Bible stories, which for decades were found in the classrooms of almost every parochial school nationwide. He told us once in the 50's: "If you want to be effective religious educators, you need to do three things: 1) use pictures, 2) tell stories, 3) and ask questions." We continue to follow his wise advice. We are equally grateful to the Franciscan nun who taught us theology through children's literature, especially Winnie the Pooh. One implication of the Incarnation is that the "stuff" of religious education is all around us.

More recent studies by educational and developmental psychologists like Jean Piaget, Erik Erikson, Lawrence Kohlberg, Carol Gilligan, and James Fowler have reinforced and expanded this insight. Catechists need skills and age- appropriate methods of actively engaging participants across the life span in the basic process of faith sharing and growth. Good textbooks are designed to be age- appropriate and to provide a wealth of tips and techniques to help catechists be more creative, imaginative, and inter-active. But catechists often need encouragement and guidance in using them. The *NCD* (#176) and *GDC* (#148- 162) explore various aspects of catechetical methodology.

We have found in Harvard psychologist Howard Gardner's theory of multiple intelligences a helpful framework for, and basic check-list of, catechetical methodology. Gardner's claim, based on intensive scientific study, is that everyone has seven intelligences—seven distinct but comple-mentary ways to learn, seven "smarts." It is important to employ all seven intelligences in our catechetical sessions—both to be holistic in our ap-proach and to provide participants with an opportunity to learn using the "intelligence" that comes most naturally to them. As a catechetical leader you can help your catechists learn concrete methods for engaging each of the seven intelligences.

We'll briefly sketch each intelligence and suggest several ways catechists might stimulate that way of learning. A great value of this multiple-intelligence theory is that it helps us look at catechetical methodology from the side of the learners:  How do they best learn?  What methods can I employ to engage the various intelligences?  What methods will help assure optimal learning—so that each will have an opportunity to learn through her or his best way of learning?  Gardner's multiple-intelligence theory of seven "smarts" can help catechists respond to those questions.

**1) Linguistic (Words).**  This intelligence is most at home with words—speaking, writing, reading.  Even though not everyone learns best through words, most catechists tend to teach as if they did.  While God's Word is not limited to words, words are important in catechesis.  The Bible and the Creeds are made up of words.  It is important to be able to verbally articulate one's faith and express it accurately.  But some words are more effective than others in catechesis.

Except for the learning of technical terms and definitions, verbal catechesis is most effective when the language used is concrete, poetic, imaginative—more like the language of love than of science.

Poetry and children's literature are effective with people of any age.  In almost every catechetical session we read aloud a carefully selected piece of children's literature that is relevant to the lesson's theme.  We also invite participants to write, for example, a story, a description of a personal experience, a reflection on a Scripture text, a story of their own, a poem, a doodle, or their response to a question.  And we give them plenty of opportunities to speak.

A 17th century French Bishop advised his catechists to use the language of the Bible and that of ordinary people.  The two are very similar:  simple, concrete, imaginative, and readily understood.  Catechetical language is also moving—the language of love, of musical lyrics.

Jesus was a master of such language, and is our best model.  He told stories (parables) which are remembered and speak to people even to this day.  He spoke the language of the people, of daily experience, in beautiful and compelling images.  He asked questions that pierced to the heart of human experience.  He summed up his profound teachings in creative, challenging, easily remembered aphorisms and stories.  In these ways catechists, too, can effectively speak to and engage the linguistic/verbal intelligence of those they catechize.

**2) Logical-Mathematical (Numbers/Order).**  At first glance it would seem that this intelligence or way of learning has a quite limited role in catechesis.  It relates to the ability to use numbers, calculate, do mathematics, engage in scientific thinking and experimenting.  It is a way of learning that thrives on patterns, routines, order, rituals.

Catechists can engage students in using this intelligence by maintaining a certain amount of predictable routine and order in their sessions. Certain rituals, like snacks at the start of classes that follow Sunday Mass, small gifts or treats on birthdays or special occasions, celebrations of Church seasons (like Advent wreaths, Lenten acts of compassion), regular prayer moments (e.g., for student's intentions, for people in need). Catechists need to be alert for any sign that a routine or ritual has become boring and meaningless, but need to maintain some routines and rituals for those who learn best through this mathematical/logical intelligence.

Some aspects of catechetical content also appeal to this way of learning. From the earliest days of the Church, Christians have reasoned about the mysteries of faith. Early on they spoke of "faith seeking understanding," and made use of logical reason to define and protect from heresy their most cherished beliefs. As a result we have creeds, doctrines, reasoned explanations, and catechisms. The great Summas of Thomas Aquinas are monumental examples of logical-mathematical intelligence put to the service of Christian faith. Logical thinking is one approach to understanding better our faith in Christ. It has a place in catechesis today, especially for those whose logical-mathematical intelligence is strong.

In addition, the Bible has many numbers whose special religious significance can be explored (e.g., 3, 7, 12, 40, 50; also the ages of the patriarchs). Likewise, Catholic lists of "seven" are abundant: sacraments, capital sins, last words of Jesus, etc. Some biblical themes can be traced through their numerical patterns, e.g., the Israelite's wandering in the desert, Jesus' retreat in the desert, and Christian celebrations of Lent are linked by the number 40. The number 12 suggests links between the Tribes of Israel and the Christian Apostles. Explore the symbolism of these biblical and traditional numbers—perhaps in the form of games. It can be a fun way of engaging participants in probing the meaning of the realities symbolized and connected by numbers and logic.

**3) Musical (Music, Sound).** Many people enjoy learning through music. They have a sensitivity to sounds, tones, rhythm, melody, and musical phrasing. They are attuned to words put to music, songs, and hymns. Musical intelligence is both common and important, yet is often neglected in catechesis, even though liturgical and devotional music have a rich tradition in Christian faith. St. Francis Xavier often composed simple melodies to make basic Catholic truths easier to remember. Famous theologian and catechism author, St. Robert Bellarmine, took popular love songs and rewrote the lyrics to convey religious truths. Catechists today, and their students, can well imitate such effective catechesis.

We almost always build some music or song into our catechetical sessions, no matter for what age, but especially with teenagers. Instrumental music can create a desirable mood for a given lesson or for prayer. Many contemporary songs, including rock and rap, have deep insights into life's mysteries, often expressing the innate yearnings of the human heart. We invite those we catechize to bring in CD's or audio-cassettes of songs that are popular at the moment and which they feel speak to life's deeper realities and Catholic faith. We often distribute the lyrics and ask participants to underline or circle words that particularly speak to them as they listen to a song. Gospel music provides rich resources for remembering and probing biblical stories or passages more deeply. Hymns sung at Sunday Eucharist can help link catechesis and community worship. Prayers like the Our Father and Hail Mary, the Magnificat, the Peace Prayer of St. Francis and St. Richard of Chichester's Christ-Prayer ("Day by Day," Godspel) have been put to music. As St. Augustine said centuries ago, "Whoever sings, prays twice."

**4) Visual-Spatial (Pictures, Color, Environment).** Centuries ago one of the early Church's most famous catechists, St. Cyril of Jerusalem, wrote that "faith through seeing is stronger than faith by hearing." From at least the time of the catacombs, visual images provided one of the major media of catechesis. Shrines, churches, and cathedrals visually portrayed the main events of the Bible, the Creeds, and the lives of saints and other great Christians. The *Catechism of the Catholic Church* not only includes several works of Christian art but repeatedly points out the importance of visual images in the Church (#476-477, 1159-1162, 2129-2132, 2500-2503, 2513).

"Through sight to insight" has become not only a catchy contemporary phrase but a dominant way of learning in our visually saturated culture. Unfortunately—despite the insights of catechetical experts like Pierre Babin—the visual media are probably less used in everyday catechesis today than in the days of Fr. Heeg a half-century ago.

It is important for catechetical leaders to help catechists become more conscious of and skilled in visual communication. Visual learning begins with the look and feel of the place in which catechists and participants gather and in the demeanor and attire of the catechist. (See the section above on environment for some general suggestions.)

We normally set up a small table or desk, covered with an attractive cloth, perhaps with a pillow or stand on which to place the open Bible. We place beside the Bible a candle or two and flowers. This visually expresses reverence for the Bible and God's Word and can become a focal point for prayer.

We often place a carefully selected print or slide of a photo, painting, poster, or symbol where it will be immediately visible as the participants enter.  It can visually attract them to the theme, Bible story, or liturgical ritual that is the session's focus.  It can also be used during the session to engage our friends in reflecting, sharing, and praying about the visual's silent messages.  Because contemporary media saturate us all with visual images, we often find it better to focus on one carefully selected visual at a time, or two complementary or contrasting images.  It is important to give people time to look at and really see the photo or art piece or symbol.  We draw out their perceptions by inviting them to tell what they see, how the visual makes them feel and why, what it says to them.  Sometimes we ask them to write a brief caption to succinctly express their insight about the visual.

Usable visuals can be found in newspapers, magazines, art galleries, libraries, from the homes of friends, parishioners, or the participants themselves.  Book stores often have tables full of "sale books," filled with excellent sacred art of biblical stories or people at reasonable prices (at least for a parish or school).  Ads and cartoons are often marvelous media for probing life's values, experiences, and foibles.  Many families have photos or videos that may be useful for catechesis.

At times we also use media equipment like a slide projector or overhead projector.  We use newsprint and colored markers, the chalkboard, videos of movies or TV programs.  Except for very short videos, we select only a segment or two that most illuminate or has the power to elicit questions or comments on the focus of a given session.

We have found creative drawing or painting an excellent activity with children, youth and adults.  Not only does it provide those gifted with visual intelligence an avenue of expression, but can be an excellent catalyst for sharing and discussing insights.  We were confirmed in our appreciation of the value of drawing in a seventh grade class in a nearby parish.  One of our students did not speak up or ask a question almost all year.  But during a session on Pentecost we invited them all to draw the Pentecost event.  He proceeded to draw the most insightful, perceptive, thought-provoking picture of the inner meaning of Pentecost that we have ever seen.

Making "collages" or "story-boards" is a simple, self-revealing and group-sharing visual method we use occasionally.  All that is needed is a stack of magazines, scissors, and glue.  We invite participants, either individually or in pairs, to quickly page through one or more magazines, select and cut or tear out visual images (and sometimes words) that resonate with a given topic or theme (like "What does love look like?" or "What does sin look like?" or "What do I really want out of life?" or "What brings out the meaning of this Bible story or saying?" or "What is prayer to you?").  After 5-10 minutes they choose from their selected images, and glue/paste them onto a piece of poster board.  When they finish, we invite them to show their visual story and talk about its meaning for them.

Often "a picture is worth more than a thousand words," as Confucius observed long ago.  Part of our problem today is that we are so bombarded by visual images that catechists often need guidance in finding and using visuals effectively in the process of nurturing faith sharing and growth.

**5) Bodily-Kinesthetic (Body, Movement).**  This intelligence or way of learning works through physical, bodily movement.  Some people learn best by using their hands, feet, or whole body.  Almost all of us need some periodic physical activity to enhance the other ways of learning—periodic breaks, changes of position or place, stretching.  Such physical breaks or changes tend also to raise the interest level in a group.

Creative ways to engage this bodily-kinesthetic in catechesis are relatively easy to implement and are often fun.  Some have already been mentioned in relation to other ways of learning:  writing, singing, drawing, cutting, pasting, making collages.

With those we teach we often create gestures to enrich the praying of prayers like the Our Father and Hail Mary.  Dramatizing Bible stories, playing charades, role-playing personal or typical experiences can be very effective.  One of our groups of seventh-graders created a highly imaginative and symbolic physical dramatization to experience what they were learning about monastic communal prayer.  We ourselves were part of a group of adults who created an unforgettably creative and profoundly symbolic dramatization of the first creation story in Genesis 1.  We remember happily our fourth graders acting out the powerful children's book, *The Legend of the Blue Bonnet* by Tomie dePaola.  The pastor liked it so much he invited the fourth- graders to reenact it as part of his homily at Sunday Eucharist.  We have often invited groups to express their understanding of, for example "Church," without words, using only their bodies.

Dance adds further dimensions of expression and learning to bodily movement.  But some groups, especially at certain ages, may be hesitant or embarrassed to dance in a catechetical setting.  Catechists may need at first to prepare some individuals or groups to dance, perhaps beginning with simple movement or gestures.  Sometimes one or more who are comfortable with and skilled at dance can lead the others, making dance more comfortable and acceptable for the others.

The traditional Catholic sense of sacramentality encourages a wide variety of physical signs, symbols and gestures to express God's graciousness and our own faith. This is evident in liturgical worship and can become more common in catechesis.  For example, catechists, parents, or children can bless other persons, animals or objects, normally with a sign of the cross or "laying on of hands." Gestures like standing, kneeling, sitting, bowing may deepen prayer. Adaptations of the liturgical "sign of peace" can express and nurture caring and community.

Then there are a wide variety of projects and crafts that engage individuals or groups in creative physical activity. We often use household aluminum foil as a more readily available modeling medium than clay. For example, we've asked children, youth, and adults to take a foot-square piece of aluminum foil and shape it into a symbol of themselves before God in prayer.

Church seasons and feasts lend themselves to physical learning: making Advent wreaths and crosses, creches and candles, sun-catchers and luminaria, etc. We enjoy asking our friends to each find a small stone and paint on it, for example, a brief quote from a Psalm, and then take it home to place in their room. The list of physical projects and crafts is almost boundless. Catechists can draw on their own creativity as well as that of their students.

**6) Interpersonal (People).** A vital intelligence or way of learning is through interaction with people, sharing, talking, creating, working together. People-smart persons are particularly gifted with the ability to sense other people's strengths and weaknesses, feelings and desires. They pick up moods and personality clues that enable them to understand others and to look at life through their eyes. Blessed with sensitive insight into others, they can be compassionate toward others or skillfully take advantage of them. Interpersonal "smarts" is particularly valuable for Catechetical Leaders whose ministry involves relating to diverse individuals and committees.

Catechesis can involve and nurture interpersonal intelligence. Small groups often learn more by studying and working together because they can compensate for individual weaknesses by sharing individual strengths. "Cooperative learning" not only facilitates learning Catholic beliefs, but also fosters Christian "people skills" or virtues like insight, sensitivity, and compassion, mutual respect, and the ability to cooperate and collaborate. And getting people to work together is likely the best way to build community—always an intention of Christian catechesis.

Almost any catechetical activity that individuals can do by themselves, can also be done—and sometimes better—when done collaboratively. For example, the whole group (or small groups) can explore together a piece of art, a photo, a biblical story, a contemporary issue, or a Church teaching. One strategy is to ask questions of the whole group before inviting responses by name from individuals. Individuals can share with the whole group something they have written or crafted. Using dialogue and discussion, story-telling and poetry-reading are other ways to employ this intelligence. Sometimes giving public expression to an insight helps insure that it is actually and accurately learned and understood.

People—young and old—can also help one another directly as helpers, tutors, or mentors. On suitable occasions it is good to invite an older group or class to share what they learned the year before with a younger group or lower grade.

Naturally there needs to be a balance between individual and cooperative activities. But a valuable goal for any catechist working with people of any age is to foster a learning community in which all are and see themselves as "co-learners" and "co-teachers"—including the catechist. That ideal may be a real challenge in our individualistic culture, but it is in harmony not only with this interpersonal intelligence, it also exemplifies the New Testament ideal of a "community of disciples" filled with and inspired by the Holy Spirit. The Spirit of the Risen Christ is with us always but particularly "where two or three are gathered" in his name.

**7) Intrapersonal (Self and Interior Reflection).** The intrapersonal intelligence is an important intelligence or way of learning. We and those we catechize live in a culture that is not only individualistic but often superficial. The speed, complexity, noise, and rapid change of modern life militates against quiet reflection on life's deeper, mysterious, and enduring realities. The young in particular easily become addicted to noise and the ceaseless flow of rapidly changing images.

We all need to develop some skill at introspection, being still to reflect on who we and the world are and are becoming. Some are particularly drawn to introspection, trusting most what they learn themselves, tending to silence, self-analysis and solitude. Catechetical leaders have the task of helping catechists develop this capacity for interiority in themselves and in those they catechize. Catechists need also to become sensitive to those whose tendency to quiet reflection and solitude is creative and fruitful, or excessive and a cry for help.

Healthy introspection and reliance on one's own insights is a long cherished aspect of Christian spirituality and catechesis. It is all the more important in catechesis since it is often given little attention in secular education. We try in every class to have moments of silence for prayer and reflection. We introduce those we catechize—of all ages—to prayer forms like meditation, centering, contemplation. We allow time for pondering a question by inviting them to think a while in silence. We remember with delight a third grader's response after a quiet time to our question, "Why do you think God created you?" "Well," he said reflectively, "God wouldn't have made me unless he really loved me."

## Enhancing All Seven Intelligences With Electronic Media.

The rapidly increasing availability of electronic media, particularly computers, makes possible a whole new range of possibilities for catechetical methodology. Careful, creative use of computers, with the rich array of software and access to the Internet, can enhance each of the seven intelligences or ways of learning in the catechetical ministry. The electronic media open up a world of words, visuals, music and song previously unknown or inaccessible. To manipulate computers to access these vast new resources requires exercise of mathematical sequences and logical links as well as physical activities involving keyboard and mouse. Encourage your catechists to explore together how any of the methods we have suggested could be enhanced by use of these new media. In many cases students who are growing up with the computerized electronic media are more able than older Catechetical Leaders, catechists and religion teachers to suggest and design new methods or enhancing older ones. Catechetical and educational journals like *The Living Light, The Catechist's Connection, Religion Teacher's Journal, Catechist, Today's Catholic Teacher*, and *Momentum* provide helpful ways to use the electronic media for fostering faith growth through catechesis.

## Questions for Reflection

- Which of the seven intelligences best reflects your personal way of learning?
- How can you discover students' dominant ways of learning?
- With what methods are you most confident and successful?
- What methods do you need to develop most?

## Conclusion

These are the main ideas we shared with Jane—our friend and newly appointed DRE. They center on the creation of a caring, attractive environment, commitment to careful preparation, growing skill in the basic process that is at the heart of catechesis, and expanding catechetical methods to meet the dominant "intelligences" of those we catechize. We feel these are the key processes that, with the help of God's grace, make for effective catechesis. We wish you well in your challenging, but so crucial and rewarding, vocation as a Catechetical Leader.

## Questions for Reflection

- What have you found most helpful in this essay?
- What do you not understand or disagree with in the essay?
- What do you need or desire to find out more about?
- How can you translate some of these key insights into catechist training and formation?

## Bibliography

Official Church Documents

*Catechism of the Catholic Church.* Rome: Libreria Editrice Vaticana, 1994.

Congregation for the Clergy. *General Directory for Catechesis.* Rome: Libreria Editrice Vaticana, 1997.

*The Catechetical Documents—A Parish Resource.* Chicago Liturgy Training Publications, 1996. Helpful Resources: Books

Darcy-Berube, Francoise. *Religious Education at the Crossroads.* New York: Paulist Press, 1995.

Durka, Gloria. *The Joy of Being a Catechist—From Watering to Blossoming.* New York: Resurrection Press, 1995.

Groome, Thomas H. *Christian Religious Education—Sharing Our Story and Vision.* San Francisco: Harper & Row, 1980.

Manternach, Janaan & Carl J. Pfeifer. *Creative Catechist—A Comprehensive Illustrated Guide for Training Religion Teachers.* Mystic, CT: Twenty-Third Publications, 1991.

Manternach, Janaan, with Carl J. Pfeifer. *And the Children Pray—A Practical Book for Prayerful Catechists.* Notre Dame: Ave Maria Press, 1989.

Nuzzi, Ronald. *Gifts of the Spirit: Multiple Intelligences in Religious Education.* Washington: National Catholic Educational Association, 1996.

Pfeifer, Carl J., and Janaan Manternach. *How to be a Better Catechist—Answers to Questions Catechists Ask Most.* Kansas City: Sheed & Ward, 1989.

Pfeifer, Carl J., and Janaan Manternach. *Questions Catechists Ask & Answers that Really Work.* Kansas City: Sheed & Ward, 1993.

Treston, Kevin. *A New Vision of Religious Education.* Mystic, CT: Twenty-Third Publications, 1993.

*Helpful Resources:* Video

National Conference of Catechetical Leadership. *Echoes of Faith.* Allen, TX: Resources for Christian Living, 1997

Helpful Resources: Periodicals

*Catechist.* Dayton: Peter Li Education Group

*The Catechist's Connection.* Kansas City: National Catholic Reporter.

*The Living Light.* Washington: United States Catholic Conference.

*Religion Teacher's Journal.* Mystic, CT: Twenty-Third Publications

*Today's Catholic Teacher.* Dayton: Peter Li Education Group

# THE PEOPLE OF CATECHESIS

## PART TWO

# 4
# The Parish and
# Family as Catechist
## Michael J. Corso

Then his mother and his brothers came; and standing outside, they sent to him and called him. A crowd was sitting around him; and they said to him, "Your mother and your brothers and sisters are outside, asking for you." And he replied, "Who are my mother and my brothers?" And looking at those who sat around him, he said, "Here are my mother and my brothers! Whoever does the will of God is my brother and sister and mother. (Mark 3:31-35)

"Who are my mother and my brothers and sisters?" What is a family anyway? This question is as apt today as when Jesus first asked it. On the one hand, we want to uphold the ancient wisdom of a family being comprised of a husband and wife and their children. Even today, in the wake of controversies stirred up by television celebrities and polarized by politicians, the consensus of sociologists and psychologists is that children benefit most from homes where both father and mother are present. Whole families do not guarantee whole children, but it seems to increase the likelihood that children will grow up relatively secure and healthy.

On the other hand, we must recognize that families always have and continue to come in every shape and size. The United States bishops recognize that "the Church itself is no stranger to changes in family definition" (National Conference of Catholic Bishops, *A Family Perspective in Church and Society*, Washington, D.C.: USCC, 1988, #19). In truth, there are as many relational configurations of families as there are families. Even brothers and sisters are not born into precisely the same family, as the very presence of older siblings changes familial structures and dynamics. There are "nuclear" families, families with children and a single parent, blended families, families with grandparents who take care of grandchildren, and foster families. We must be as flexible in our definition of family as Jesus was—not because it is the most progressive or liberal stance, but because it is the most realistic one. The United States Catholic bishops provide a definition which maintains the real meaning of family and yet is suitably broad: The family is "an intimate community of persons bound together by blood, marriage, or adoption, for the whole of life" (ibid.)

Our own families of origin have played a significant role in our call to become catechetical leaders. We are formed (and sadly sometimes, deformed) by the environment we grow up in. Some respond to their parents' vision for them, others bristle at parental expectations. Your faith may have come to you by way of your family or in reaction against it. Your call to be a catechetical and pastoral leader likely indicates that you have been formed by a community of faith—in family or parish or both—and have also appropriated the community's faith for yourself.

## Questions for Reflection
- What are your earliest memories of faith? What relatives in your family of origin do you recall being especially inspired by?
- What relationship do you see between the faith you personally profess now and the faith you were raised in?
- What is your view of the best working relationship between families and parishes? How do they actually support one another in your particular community?

## A Family Orientation for Practical Reasons

You may recall that the scene above from Mark's Gospel follows one in which Jesus' family "went out to restrain him, for they were saying 'He has gone out of his mind!'" (Mark 3:21) There seems to be evidence that Jesus' own relatives did not accept who he was or what he had to say. What, after all, are we to make of the man whose response to a would-be disciple asking to first go bury his father was, "Follow me and let the dead bury their dead!" (Matt 8:22, see also Luke 9:60) A Jesus who in Matthew's Gospel claimed, "Whoever loves father or mother more than me is not worthy of me, and whoever loves son or daughter more than me is not worthy of me" (Matt 10:37). A spiritual master who said,

> Do you think I have come to establish peace on the earth? No, I tell you, but rather divisions. From now on a household of five will be divided, three against two and two against three; a father will be divided against his son and a son against his father, a mother against her daughter and a daughter against her mother (Luke 12:51-53).

At first blush, Jesus' preaching sounds decidedly anti-family.

Yet it was this same Jesus who gave Jairus and his wife back their daughter (see Mark 5:22-24; 35-43) and who returned a dead son to his widowed mother (see Luke 7:11- 13). It was this miracle worker who raised Lazarus at the bidding of his sisters Martha and Mary (see John 11:1-44). It was this very Jesus who insisted that caring for aged parents with one's financial resources takes precedence over donations in support of religious structures (see Mark 7:8-13). And Jesus, too, who taught us to call God our Abba—our Father (see Matt 6:9-15).

If anything it should be clear that there is no simple answer to questions such as: What is a Christian family? How are we to educate so as to sponsor families in faith? What programs should catechetical leaders promote and support in order for families to grow spiritually? How is our catechetical ministry to families effected by divorce, separation from extended family, and over-programmed children?

We can not possibly address all these issues here. Many questions can only be answered by catechetical leaders themselves working in and among the local faith community. In this essay, I argue for an approach to catechesis and religious education that is fundamentally family oriented. Before I make my case on philosophical and theological grounds, let me do so on purely practical grounds.

As Dr. Jane Regan's article "Principles of Catechesis from Ecclesial Documents" makes clear, in the great majority of Church documents on catechesis catechetical and pastoral leaders are being encouraged in no uncertain terms to make adults the primary focus of their educational efforts. The recently published *General Directory for Catechesis* states clearly: "Catechesis for adults, since it deals with persons who are capable of an adherence that is fully responsible, must be considered the chief form of catechesis. All the other forms, which are indeed always necessary, are in some way oriented to it" (#59). In 1998, the United States Catholic bishops discussed a draft of a national pastoral plan specifically on the importance of adult catechesis and education.

The Good News of Jesus Christ, despite the injunction to become like little children, is primarily intended for an adult audience. The message that we must take up our cross and follow Jesus must be aimed at those mature enough and experienced enough to know the full implications of that momentous life changing decision. We can, and do, socialize and inculturate children into Catholic Christianity. However, the Gospel call to *metanoia*, to life-long transformation and conversion, must be made to adults who "are capable of an adherence that is fully responsible."

What then is a catechetical leader to do? Church documents and the Good News itself increasingly call us to focus on adult catechesis and yet the majority of our existing efforts are child centered. We ourselves see the wisdom and the need for greater education among adults and yet we know parents would not sit still if we scaled back our current children's programs. One way out of this dilemma is to get at the adults through the children. This is certainly one possible, though somewhat surreptitious and potentially incomplete approach.

Another approach, one that hopefully is in place implicitly if not explicitly, is to have our children's programs be adult-oriented. Childhood catechesis should set people on a journey of faith that will continue their whole lives. The truth that being in relationship with God through Jesus Christ and in a Christian community is an ongoing and life-long experience should be regularly reinforced. Programs should be open-ended. Although milestones may be marked along the way, there really should be no equivalent of "graduation" in a religious education program.

I believe the beginning of a practical and concrete response to these competing concerns is to take a family approach to religious education. For example, instead of registering children for religious education, parishes should register families. Include in whatever formal agreements you have with the family, an invitation that parents assist in their child's class several times during the year. Likewise, parents can constantly "home school" their children in faith, not only by the atmosphere of the home, but by often reviewing their children's experiences in the formal catechetical programs of the parish or school. You might also invite parents, as part of a family approach, to attend a monthly adult faith class themselves. Be sure to invite all adults in the parish to the adult meetings and keep educational content more or less "kid-free." Look for textbooks and curricula that are family structured and oriented, or at least that have "family pages" which enable parents to actively participate at home in the formal catechesis of their children. Find or create activities with instructions that say "Have your child research the life of Saint. . ." rather than "Help your son or daughter research the life of Saint. . ." The difference seems subtle but could be significant.

Instead of a "Children's Liturgy" have a "Family Liturgy"— either a full liturgy or at least a Liturgy of the Word. Using different terms is an important beginning. Send families forth at the end of liturgy with ways of continuing the patterns of praise and thanksgiving begun in church. I have often marveled at the success and simplicity of the Advent wreath in my family. It is a way of continuing in our home the action of the parish community. It connects us during the week to that Sunday space and time when we are part of something larger than ourselves. It is a ritual we perform as a family, not as parents helping children, or children participating in an otherwise adult mode of prayer.

I am certain with just a little effort and imagination, people can create family activities and rituals just as simple and successful. Our parish community began one Lent with a large bowl of sand in front of the altar at our Family Liturgy. After the liturgy, each family was instructed to take home a zip lock bag full of sand, place it in a small container or bowl, and use it as a candle holder during Lent. We invited them to light the candle and have it be the center piece for their family prayer during the Lenten season—whether a simple grace at dinner or a more involved evening prayer. We provided a booklet of prayers and suggested scripture readings, many focusing on the desert like experience of these forty days. The idea was that the sand, having come from the larger assembly, was connecting them with that community as they prayed in their homes.

Then, on Passion Sunday came the announcement: "Please bring the sand you received at the beginning of Lent, now enriched by your family's prayers, back to our Family Liturgy next week." On Easter Sunday, we invited the families to add the sand to the pots of the lilies that surrounded our baptismal pool. The voiced hope was that the many prayers they said as a family and the love they shared in their homes might blossom in our community in a greater love for God and one another.

In addition to family education and family liturgy and rituals, service and outreach opportunities can be family friendly. For example, if there is a service component to your confirmation program, have parents engage in the service with their child—not as chaperone or supervisor, but as active participants. Be sure that the same service opportunities are open to all members of the parish—single, married and without children, those with grown children, families with children in Catholic schools, etc. Hopefully taking a family approach—where family means anyone who is someone's son or daughter—is a practical way of bridging the gap between the call for adult catechesis and the reality of many parish and school programs focused on children.

## Questions for Reflection
- What would be the response in your community if you shifted from a child emphasis to a family oriented approach?
- Is such an approach valid? Is it practical in your community? What other ways do you imagine being able to balance the call for increased adult education and the responsibility to formally educate children in faith?
- Create a ritual for families that connects their home to the larger faith community.

## A Family Orientation: Philosophical and Theological Reasons

The reasons we might focus the efforts of our catechetical leadership on families go deeper than it being a nifty way to educate adults and children without necessarily doubling our efforts. Catechesis that is family oriented rests on two foundational truths: first, the nature of the human person points to such an approach; second, the nature of Christian faith strongly suggests the same.

First, a family oriented approach is a human approach. The human condition is, quite literally, inherently relational—everyone is someone's daughter or son. Moreover, the human propensity for relationship extends far beyond the bonds of parent and child into all of life. We are created by God for relationship, for friendship, companionship, partnership. Soon after God creates the first human being, God says, "It is not good for the human to be alone" (Gen 2:18). A family approach to catechesis, therefore, seems eminently suited to the human condition.

We are "we" before we are "I" or "you." Intersubjectivity precedes subjectivity. Such an approach maintains, with the Jesuit philosopher Bernard Lonergan, that the person is not the primordial fact. What is primordial is the community. It is within the community through the intersubjective relations that are the life of the community that there arises the differentiation of the individual person. (Bernard Lonergan, *Philosophy of God and Theology*, London: Darton, Longman, and Todd, 1973, 58-59.) I become myself only in relationship. And my family of origin provides me with the most primordial and formative relationships I will have.

Moreover, within a family, the individuals grow and mature as a result of their developing physical, intellectual, moral, social, and spiritual capacities and their interaction with adults and siblings at various other places on the developmental spectrum. The work of developmental theorists such as Piaget, Erikson, Kohlberg, Gilligan, and Fowler has shown us that human maturity occurs in a series of sequenced stages and that those stages unfold as a result of the challenges posed by the encounter with others further along in the sequence. Fowler, in particular, has increasingly applied his faith development theory to family systems and the effects of the "cog-wheeling" of the generations. (See James W. Fowler, *Faith Development and Pastoral Care*, Philadelphia: Fortress Press, 1987.)

It follows that if we are to educate persons in Christian faith, we must do so in a way that acknowledges their families, communities, and the social systems of which they are a part. We must move away from a kind of "rugged individualist" approach to all forms of education, and embrace the truth that human beings are relational. To effectively form, inform, and transform persons we must engage families. Some of the most well received and successful work we have done at my parish, St. Ignatius Church in Chestnut Hill, Massachusetts, have been programs that relate to and engage the whole family whatever its configuration.

Christian faith itself is relational and, therefore, ideally nurtured by family catechesis. Christian faith is relational for at least three reasons.

(1) The very God we profess belief in is a community, a family; God—Father, Son, and Spirit. Although theologians must work out the overly male imagery that comprises Trinitarian doctrine, we must never lose sight of the deeply relational truth about God in this formulation. Speaking more generically about Creator, Redeemer, and Sanctifier or more abstractly still about the First, Second, and Third persons of the Trinity can help us grasp certain truths. But it also runs the risk, not only of depersonalizing God, but of failing to recognize that the persons of the Trinity are related as the members of a family.

"As" is significant. We would do well to remember the Thomistic principle that everything we say positively of God we say by way of analogy. This helps temper the maleness of much of our God language, too. God is beyond every human category, gender included. As the *Catechism of the Catholic Church* states: "God transcends the human distinction between the sexes." (*CCC* #239) In truth, saying God is our Father no more means God is masculine, than saying "God is my rock" or "my fortress" means God is composed of stone. God language is always poetic, it is meant to conjure images. According to our Bible, God is father, mother, warrior, shepherd, eagle, hen, shield, and so on. The more images we employ, the closer we come to understanding who God is for us.

The same is true when we refer to the second person of the Trinity as "Son." The masculinity of Jesus notwithstanding, "Son" is a way of talking analogously about the relationship between the first and second persons of the Triune God. It is like the relationship between a father and son. So we profess belief in a God who is within the Godhead relational and always turned toward us in relationship—what theologians call the "immanent" and "economic" Trinity.

(2) Christian faith is relational because God calls us into relationship, into covenant. And God's view of us is frequently familial. "When Israel was a child, I loved him, and out of Egypt I called my son" (Hosea 11:1). For Christians, this call is effected in and through Jesus and the Holy Spirit. Paul writes:

> So then, brothers and sisters . . . all who are led by the Spirit of God are children of God. For you did not receive a spirit of slavery to fall back into fear, but you have received a spirit of adoption. When we cry, "Abba!

Father!" it is that very Spirit bearing witness with our spirit that we are children of God, and if children, then heirs, heirs of God and joint heirs with Christ. (Rom 8:14-17)

God has no grandchildren. No one is born a Christian. We become Christian by our baptism. We are "born again" as sons and daughters of God, as members of God's family. So our faith calls us to relate to God as Abba—a familial term.

I did not fully understand the significance of calling God Abba until I became a father, a daddy, myself. I had bought into a kind of overly romanticized version of a God who was "Daddy." God the warm fuzzy. God the comfortable chair. Until, that is, my daughter called me "Daddy" and I saw in her eyes not only that I was someone to cuddle, but someone awesome, all powerful, someone able to pick her up and hold her in the palm of my hand. It continues to be a humbling experience.

We are to relate to God as Abba not as an adult connotes that term but as a child does. Yes, God loves us, yes, God is a prodigal parent who will forgive us, and yes, God is fearful and awesome and almighty. Our faith calls us to be in relationship with God, and one of the richest metaphors for that relationship is from Jesus himself. His disciples asked, "Lord teach us to pray." Teach us how to relate to God. "He said to them, 'When you pray, say: Father, hallowed be your name. Your kingdom come'" (Luke 11:1-2).

(3) Christian faith is relational because if God is like our loving parent, then we are siblings. "Whoever does the will of God is my brother and sister and mother." In his Epistles, Paul repeatedly refers to his fellow Christians as brothers and sisters. In many Christian communities today, members still greet each other as "brother" or "sister." In the Catholic Church, those titles have typically been reserved for vowed religious. However, it would surely be a boon to religious education and faith formation if we all got into the habit of calling each other sister and brother. Think of the message this sends, think of the powerful lesson it would communicate, think of what it teaches!

## Questions for Reflection

- What is your understanding of the relational nature of the human person? Do you agree or disagree that "we are 'we' before we are 'I' or 'you,'" that intersubjectivity precedes subjectivity? What are the implications for religious education in your context?
- How do you understand the familial terms used in Trinitarian

theology? What is their practical significance for catechetical leadership?

- What would be the reaction in your community if you began to model the habit of calling everyone brother or sister? What might happen in your community if everyone used such language?

## Faith Is a Language

There is in fact a third reason for adopting a family approach to catechesis. Besides such an approach being indicated by the relational nature of the human person and the relational nature of God and of Christian faith, it is suggested by the nature of catechesis itself. According to the *General Directory for Catechesis*, catechesis "transmits the words and deeds of Revelation; it is obliged to proclaim and narrate them and, at the same time, to make clear the profound mysteries they contain" (#39). Notice, explicitly stated—what we already know implicitly—that catechesis "transmits," "proclaims," and "narrates." In other words, catechesis is a way of talking, it is a language.

Religion is a language, broadly understood. That is to say, religion is a symbol system, a way of communicating to one another about our experiences of God, of transcendence, of human love and community. As such, the language of faith embraces all the "trappings" of Christianity-songs and scriptures, symbols and sacraments; prayers, parables, and proverbs. The language of faith includes acts of contrition as well as the Acts of the Apostles. For Catholic Christians steeped in their tradition, it comprises the Rosary and first Friday Mass and Benediction. All are part of the "language" of faith.

We have spiritual experiences and religion is a way of expressing and talking about those experiences. The language of faith, like all language, is learned principally in the home. And language is first learned not by being formally taught, but by immersion. It is actually quite stunning to realize that in just two years a human being has in place most of what he or she needs to communicate effectively. No less may be true of the language of faith.

Conceiving of religion as a language, suggests that catechesis is the learning of a language, and for at least four reasons. First, as with language, we are "genetically" predisposed to the language of faith. Developmental scientists tell us that infants are born with brains that are open to learning language. The human brain is both hard-wired for language acquisition, and also flexible enough to learn whatever language it finds itself born into. Similarly, I believe the human person is born open to God, open to the divine. There is a kind of hard-wiring that makes us by nature spiritually oriented. In the words of St. Augustine, "Thou hast made us for thyself alone." Yet there is also a marvelous flexibility that allows children to unfold this spiritual predisposition into whatever faith community they find themselves born—Christian, Jewish, Muslim, Buddhist, etc.

Second, just as language acquisition and development can be stunted and stymied despite an inborn predisposition, spiritual growth can be similarly hindered. There are tragic but instructive stories and subsequent studies of children who were abandoned or locked away and so never exposed to language. In many cases, depending on the age the child was discovered and returned to more normal surroundings, language failed to develop as it should. In a similar way, the human spirit is harmed, though not irreparably, by a lack of exposure to religious "language" (again I use the term here in its broadest sense). In the *Declaration on Education*, the Second Vatican Council stated: "Since parents have conferred life on their children, they have a most solemn obligation to educate their offspring. Hence, parents must be acknowledged as the first and foremost educators of their children. Their role as educators is so decisive that scarcely anything can compensate for their failure in it" (#3). These are some of the strongest words in the Council documents.

More positively, it is the interaction between the naturally open child and parents already speaking and living a Christian life that lays the groundwork for religious language that will grow and develop as its own throughout the child's life.

> Children perceive and joyously live the closeness of God and of Jesus made manifest by their parents in such a way that this first Christian experience frequently leaves decisive traces which last throughout life. This childhood religious awakening which takes place in the family is irreplaceable. (*GDC* #41)

Moreover, just as every parent need not have a degree in English to teach their children the English language, every parent need not have a degree in theology to communicate their faith. Children learn the language of faith simply by being around adults and older children who are "using the language"—attending church, praying in the home, reading scripture, reaching out to those in need, working for justice, and so on. As long as we continue to baptize infants, a family oriented approach which takes the profound influence of the family on the growing child into account is mandated.

Third, just as language is first learned in the home and then more formally and methodically studied in school (remember diagramming sentences?), so, too, the language of faith is learned first in the home and then later studied more systematically in formal religious education. But catechists are not the principle teachers of religious language. They simply help to understand and gain mastery over a language of Christian faith that hopefully is already in place.

No doubt some will need remedial help, and for others the language of Christian faith may be a "second" language. The ideal is that catechesis and religious education be a reflective activity—studying and breaking open experiences and the symbols for talking about those experiences that are already part of the language previously procured in the home and in the wider community. The *GDC* maintains that faith

> is deepened all the more when parents comment on the more methodical catechesis which their children later receive in the Christian community and help them to appropriate it. Indeed, family catechesis precedes . . . accompanies and enriches all forms of catechesis. (#226)

Fourth, although language is learned in the family, the language is not the family's language. The language is the symbol system of a larger community. Catechetical leaders are accountable to that larger community and must exercise care over inappropriate or even harmful use of the language. They have a responsibility to nurture an orthodox Catholic Christian appropriation of the language of faith.

Of course we need various "dialects" and "accents" within Catholicism. And families will have a word or two unique to them (usually a child's mispronunciation that "sticks"). Differences may occur as a result of geography (notice the difference in "dialect," for example, between midwestern Catholicism shaped by its proximity to the Bible Belt and Boston Catholicism influenced by old New England formality), or ethnicity (notice the different "accents" among Irish Catholics, Italian Catholics, and German Catholics), or education (the Catholicism of an adult with a Master's degree in Theology may have a slightly different "syntax" than the Catholicism of an adult whose last formal training in religion was at age thirteen). Such differences make our language richer not poorer. The language we teach and learn, however, cannot stray too far from our Church's "mother tongue" or it runs the risk of becoming unrecognizable.

In short, catechesis should focus on families because faith is a language and language is learned primarily in the home. Catechetical leaders should support families, giving them the resources to speak the language of faith to one another and with the larger community. In addition, parish and school catechesis should review in a formal way the faith language that is being learned in the family. Providing leadership and support in this regard involves noticing two significant components of language, and by analogy, faith.

First, religious language provides us with a vocabulary for talking about our experiences of mystery, love, awe, and transcendence. By language, we enter into a conscious relationship with God. We are convicted by an experience of God's justice and righteousness as we express that experience in language. We encounter the transforming power of God's mercy and forgiveness. We are moved by the story of Jesus and fall in love with God in and through him. In some way or other, we come to know the love of God for us. And just as in human love, we seek to express ourselves, to communicate that love, to avow it in word and symbol and sacrament. We search for a vocabulary that will help us convey the experience of being loved by God without restrictions or qualifications or conditions. Christianity provides one such vocabulary.

Christians claim that Jesus himself is such a word of faith. In Christ Jesus, God avows God's love for humanity and in our response to Jesus we avow our love for God. In that radical re-orientation of horizons that is Christian conversion, "Jesus" is the name of the one who is present. Christ, the Christian tradition, its sacraments and doctrines, provide Christians with the words and actions for expressing the love of God they have experienced—a vocabulary of faith.

But there is more to the Christian "language" than being able to label previously unnamed experiences of transcendence. Language provides us with not only a vocabulary, but also a grammar. Christianity is not just a set of terms for talking about spiritual encounters or conversion, but affords us a logic, a syntax for understanding and communicating those experiences in a coherent way.

Just as children begin to name their experiences of the world, so too children of God begin to name their experiences of God. But the words children are given to name the world are not their own, but a community's. And the words that are given are not just a vocabulary, but exhibit a grammar, a pattern. "Daddy" is already a noun, "eat," a verb, "beautiful," an adjective. At first the grammar is hidden, later it is disclosed, eventually it will be rigorously studied.

Christianity, too, contains a grammar given by a community by which we can not only name the experience of the Spirit, but discern that the experience of the Spirit is patterned. For Christians, that pattern is the "Way" of Jesus of Nazareth. It is the "logic" of self-surrender and self-donation. It is the life-long pursuit of habits of discipleship—prayer, charity, service. Christ is, therefore, the "grammar" of God's self-emptying to be among us and Jesus Christ's dying to redeem and liberate us. Christian conversion is meant to be a transformation into that self-emptying, paschal pattern.

The effects of Original Sin in us tempt us into a pattern that is self-seeking, rather than self-emptying. We form habits that indicate we think equality with God a thing to be grasped at (the "original" sin of which all other sins are copies). In Jesus, we are confronted with a human person who lives life in an entirely different pattern. And Jesus' life reveals the very pattern of the divine life. The very nature of God—both within the Godhead and in relationship to us—is one of loving self-donation.

It seems that the best way for Christians and Christian communities to celebrate, learn, and appropriate this Christ-shaped pattern and its attendant vocabulary is by way of family catechesis. The language of faith will only flourish if it is a regular and habitual part of a person's life. Faith must be spoken, day in and day out, if it is to be truly effective and formative. The family is the foremost locus of such catechesis. "It is, indeed, a Christian education more witnessed to than taught, more occasional than systematic, more ongoing and daily than structured into periods" (*GDC* #255). One acquires the patterns of Christian life in much the same way one acquires a grammar—tacitly.

What then is the role of the catechetical leader and the catechetical team of a parish or school in such a relational or family-centered approach? Catechetical leaders must make certain that they and the catechists in their care are well versed in both the vocabulary and grammar of the Catholic Christian "language." First and foremost, they must speak the language in their own lives. Wilkie Au's article the "The Person of the Catechist" offers some concrete advice on how to nurture catechists in their own faith lives. In addition, catechetical and pastoral leaders must be students of the language of Christian faith. They do not need doctorates in theology, but they should be "well read," "articulate," "eloquent," and "fluent" in Christian faith. They should be capable of providing resources and support to families as they attempt to talk the "talk" by walking the walk of lived Christian faith. All of this is to support in a more formal and structured way, the more informal and implicit catechesis that is already taking place in the Christian home.

## Questions for Reflection

- I have used the analogy that religion is like a language— comprising both a vocabulary and a grammar. What do you find helpful? What gets in the way of your understanding? What would you add?
- What do you see as the practical implications of conceiving of

catechesis as language acquisition?
- In your own community, how, concretely, would you implement such an approach?

## Mediating Meaning

Religion is like language because it is a way of communicating meaning. The human person craves meaning. We look at clouds and see castles and dragons. By nature, we want all of life to be meaningful. We ask "Why?" almost as soon as we are able. This profound desire for meaning is a central characteristic of the human condition. Meaning leads us to truth and goodness and even love. Lovers say to one another, "You mean a lot to me." Ultimately, meaning leads us to God.

Christianity is pregnant with meaning. Meaning is embodied in many ways, only one of which is linguistic. Christian meaning is carried in human intersubjectivity, in art, in symbols, in language, and in the lives and actions of persons trying to live as Christians. No single carrier of meaning is sufficient. Catechesis, therefore, must support families across a wide range of such embodiments of the meaning of faith for life. Let us briefly examine the several ways the meaning of Christianity is mediated and consider the implications for family catechesis.

First, Christian meaning is communicated intersubjectively. Faith, as the expression goes, is "caught, not taught." Here we see most powerfully the importance of nurturing entire families in faith. Christian meaning is communicated in loving tones of voice, in the unspoken air of confidence in the face of adversity, in the fundamental trust in the goodness of creation. Christ is encountered in the peacefulness of the Christian home, in the embrace of the Christian parent who forgives a misdeed, in hands held around a Christian table as grace is spoken, and in the manner with which Christian spouses try to settle their disputes. As Gerard Manley Hopkins has expressed it: "Christ plays in ten thousand places, lovely in limbs, and lovely in eyes not his . . ."

Catechesis supports such an embodiment of the Christian Gospel by sponsoring marriage preparation programs, by holding discussions on Christian parenting and appropriate forms of discipline, by inviting professionals to speak to the community about end of life issues. Anything that enables families to live Christ-shaped lives, embodying the Gospel to one another in their day-to-day human interactions, should be considered an important component of family catechesis.

In our parish, we are planning a seminar for parents using the frequently over-looked book by Sidney Craig, *Raising Your Child, Not By Force But*

*By Love* (Philadelphia: The Westminster Press, 1973). Dr. Craig provides a most welcome corrective to other so-called Christian approaches to child raising which seem to focus heavily on the proverb "Spare the rod, spoil the child," while completely neglecting Jesus' admonitions to "turn the other cheek" and to "forgive as God has forgiven you."

Second, Christian meaning is communicated artistically. This includes, but is not restricted to, having in the home works that portray scenes from the Gospels, or depict Jesus living, crucified, or risen. The meaning of the Gospel is mediated in works of art—narratives, sculptures, paintings, songs. Such artistic carriers need not always be explicitly Christian. Children's stories can be chosen so as to reflect Gospel values. Families can watch movies or television programs that stimulate faith-filled conversation. Music can be chosen that is peaceful and positive. As we enter into such works of art they enhance our capacity to grow, to be transformed.

Catechetical leaders should help people to have access to such artistic resources. They might hand out bibliographies of children's literature or suggest certain movies. Or perhaps sponsor a family trip to a nearby museum—so much art is inspired by faith. Perhaps the parish or school can begin a media library where families can check out music, books, or movies. Youth ministry programs might have a movie night where parents and older children watch and discuss movies such as *Entertaining Angels: The Story of Dorothy Day*, *Dead Man Walking*, *Romero*, *The Spitfire Grill*, or *The Mission*, to name just a few.

In addition, catechetical leaders should encourage the creation of artistic expressions of faith both in the home and by families in and for the parish and catechetical program. At St. Ignatius we sometimes conduct an "Arts in the Afternoon" program. Families are invited to come and create church banners, write scripts to enact for upcoming homilies, or to learn liturgical dance. One Advent, focusing on the reading that Jesus was "Emmanuel— God with us," we constructed a large stable mounted with a collage of parishioners' family pictures. When we placed Jesus in the creche, we had a powerful symbol that indeed God was with us!

Third, Christian meaning, Christian beliefs, are carried in symbols. Symbols evoke feelings and the symbols we create or appropriate are themselves evoked by feelings. One central symbol of Christianity is the cross. The cross is the image of the reality of Christ's following the pattern of self-giving to its inexorable conclusion, reminding us forever that our God suffers with us.

Christian homes should have crosses. If the crosses somehow have their origin in the parish community, it serves to connect the "domestic church" with the "local church." What a simple thing it would be to invite families to bring their crucifixes from home to Church—on Good Friday or the Feast of the Triumph of the Cross—for a special blessing. Imagine a table, draped in purple, covered with crosses, while the community extended its hands, invoking God's blessing on these symbols, the houses that would contain them, and the families that make these houses their homes.

Christianity also carries meaning in special symbolic actions called sacraments. By a sacrament not only is an image of reality present but the reality itself is present. Baptism not only symbolizes a person's entrance into the Body of Christ, it effects one's becoming a member of that Body. The Eucharist not only symbolizes Christ's body broken for us, it is Christ— body and blood, so "real."

Sacramental preparation programs ought to prepare, not just individuals, but the entire family. As a member of the family comes of age to receive a sacrament, the entire family should be renewed. Even Reconciliation, seemingly the most individualized of the sacraments, should begin with reflection on the experience of forgiveness in one's family and lead one back to reconciliation with the family one has sinned against—if my own experience is any indication.

Fourth, meaning is most commonly understood as being carried linguistically. So much of what we do and say as human beings involves words, and although above I used the notion of language metaphorically, here I intend it literally. Christian faith is rich in linguistic embodiments of meaning. These fall into three main categories: 1) technical theological language, such as creeds, dogma, and doctrines, 2) conversation, common sense, everyday language, and 3) narrative language, including poetry, myth, etc.

Doctrines employ precise and technical language to express common beliefs. Creedal formulations, defined dogmas, and explanatory treatises are examples of this kind of language. Doctrines are not a substitute for symbols. They answer the need to notice one crucial point within a community—a point that, if misunderstood, might lead one to misunderstand the whole story of Christian faith.

Family catechesis attempts to help people not "miss the point." Baptismal preparation and *RCIA* programs are wonderful opportunities to educate families about what they are professing when together they profess, "We believe . . ." and what membership in the community means to the entire family.

Christian conversation is reflected in the various transient and common sense expressions of belief. Conversation in this sense is the very fabric of Christian catechesis. Dinner dialogue about the meaning of current events in light of the Gospel, reflecting together on the Sunday homily on the drive home, and discussions about moral decision making informed by faith are all examples of this linguistic embodiment of Christian meanings.

Catechesis itself is frequently conducted conversationally. We may refer to or examine the technical language of this or that doctrine, but we typically do so in common sense terms. In fact, one of the aims of catechesis is to make the technical language of theology understandable in the common sense terms of a particular group of people. A parish program which sponsors faith sharing communities encourages Christian conversation. The option to be part of an intergenerational small faith community makes such programs especially family-friendly.

The Christian community also says what it means in commonsense terms through stories, Gospels, narrative. While ordinary language and conversation is transient, the written word or word meant to be learned "by heart" is more permanent. In narrative, linguistic meaning overlaps with artistic and symbolic meaning. Its intention is to evoke feeling, to point toward decision, to foster conversion. The Gospel is its prime example. Christian catechesis, in its most artistic moments, is narrative in this life-changing sense.

Family oriented Christian catechesis should make frequent use of other models of education that wed the artistic to the linguistic. Drama, poetry, fiction, and parable are just a few such media for the message of Christianity. Families, and the parishes that nurture them, should work diligently to expand their commonsense "vocabulary" and practice a repertoire. For example, at St. Ignatius, we frequently employ drama at our family liturgy as a reflection on the readings.

Moreover, catechetical leaders and catechists who promote family catechesis must pay careful attention to the "colors" and substance of their words, the tones with which they speak, the perspective within which they frame their words. Their God-language, their person-language, the questions they ask and encourage, the kinds of discussions they entertain, everything about the way they use words, should at least approach the care that the poet takes with words. Maria Harris writes:

> Our thinking and our knowing in all human endeavor is shaped by the metaphors we employ. It matters which words we choose when we teach and when we teach others to teach. The metaphors we choose can catalyze or paralyze the capacity to perceive and receive what is there, no matter how plain or abundant the evidence. It is not that any of us willfully refuse to look; it is that if we do not have the appropriate language, we cannot see. And the reason the point is crucial is that words not only can paralyze, they can redeem. . . . People are moved by experiencing their imaginations

touched by someone or something that excites them into hoping and acting. When the word is made flesh, redemption is at hand. It is the vocation of the teacher to give flesh to language and to make metaphor incarnate (Maria Harris, *Teaching and Religious Imagination*, San Francisco: Harper and Row, 1987, 20).

Catechists should be taught that their words must be carefully crafted. The way they explain doctrine, the conversations both formal and informal they carry on, the narratives they employ, the stories they tell can either make redemption and liberation more accessible or less so. Effective and appropriate use of the many linguistic carriers of meaning at a catechist's disposal can prompt conversion, while an insipid and impoverished use of the preeminent medium of human communication can lead to a corresponding apathetic response to Christ Jesus and the Good News he proclaims. And while it is not the catechist who redeems but Christ, catechists either realize Christ in language or they do not.

Likewise the Christian family should speak to one another, and all they meet, in language patterns that reflect their discipleship to Jesus. We think in language and are powerfully shaped by it. Christian parents must be aware that their words can form or deform children. While renouncing physical violence in their methods of discipline, they should also renounce violence in their voices. Moreover, God's name and the name of Jesus should only be used in meaningful and prayerful ways. By these linguistic habits, families learn deep respect for themselves, one another, and God.

The fifth embodiment of Christian meaning is its incarnation in human life. Incarnate meaning combines all or at least many of the other carriers of meaning— intersubjective, artistic, symbolic, linguistic. It is the very meaning of a person's life, the sum total of his or her actions and words. Incarnate meaning is Christianity's most powerful expression. The most convincing theological argument for Christianity is not a treatise but a saint. Incarnate meaning is witness, living discipleship. It is the compelling testimony of a genuine apprentice of Jesus Christ.

Catechesis which takes a family approach does everything possible to foster families that can witness to one another. Witness is perhaps the most meaning-full and effective of all the carriers of Christian meaning. In *Evangelii Nuntiandi*, Paul VI writes, "Modern man listens more willingly to witnesses than to teachers, and if he does listen to teachers it is because they are witnesses" (#41). It is through witness that catechetical leaders, catechists, and family members most effectively realize Christ.

The relationships nurtured in the family are fundamental to education for conversion and towards the reign of God. In the Christian family one hopefully learns what it means to have a nurturing father, a prodigal mother, a true brother and sister. In this context, Jesus' insistence that if we ask, we will receive comes into sharper focus—"Is there anyone among you who, if your child asks for bread, will give a stone? Or if the child asks for a fish, will give a snake? If you then, who are evil, know how to give good gifts to your children, how much more will your Father in heaven give good things to those who ask him!" (Matt 7:9-11)

Catechetical leaders, besides making plain their own discipleship to Christ and fostering families that can witness the Gospel to one another, should draw on the incarnate meaning present in Christian community. They should provide opportunities for families to hear Christian doctors and lawyers and butchers and bakers and candlestick makers testify to the challenge of living a Christ centered life in their work and family life.

I recall being personally moved in an adult education course on the role of the laity in the church by a woman who owned and operated a card store. Taking her faith seriously meant not carrying certain lines of cards that were fairly popular, but offensive in the light of the Gospel. That decision meant her store made less money. For her the financial loss was more than compensated by the loyalty of customers who appreciated her willingness not to gain the world at the cost of her soul.

Nor must catechetical leaders be restricted to the local community or even to the living. Witnesses abound. The incarnate meaning of Christianity can be transposed through books, plays, and movies, to the lives of Christian saints both past and present, famous and not so famous. Nor need such a transposition be restricted to non-fictional or even explicitly Christian accounts. The efforts of a fictional character to follow Christ or to lead a heroic, good, and truthful life can be an aid to Christian imagination, dialogue, understanding, judging, deciding, and even loving. Such education includes catechists' sharing biographic, autobiographic, and fictional accounts of both the struggles and triumphs of trying to live a Christ-shaped life.

Finally, catechetical leaders, catechists, and parents should reveal themselves as witnesses, as persons in solidarity with the poor, as professing belief in Christ, as seeking to understand and embody the truth they find in Christianity, and as persons of prayer and worship. Pastoral leaders must know Christ, practice Christ, and live Christ. They must make themselves available as those engaged in the ongoing struggle toward mastery of the Christian life. Accordingly, students will learn not only from what catechists say, but from who catechists are and how they live their lives as disciples of Jesus Christ.

## Questions for Reflection

- We have been discussing the various embodiments of Christian meaning in family and catechetical settings— intersubjective, artistic, symbolic, linguistic, and incarnate. Which embodiments of Christian meaning are already prominent in your community? How might you build upon what is already present?
- Take some time in your community's worship space. What does the artwork there teach? What meanings do the symbols convey?
- Consider the public witness of your parish staff and catechetical team. What does it communicate to families about the Gospel?

## Family Faith Formation

We have already seen that Christian faith, though personal, is never individualistic. Persons do not emerge *ex nihilo* to climb the ladder of faith formation on their own, encountering others who have made a similar solo journey only when each arrives breathless at the top. We are born into families which in turn are parts of extended families. Families belong to constellations of friends, to school systems, to civic communities, to nations, to churches. We have seen that the person is not the primordial fact. What is primordial is the community.

In addition, families and communities have a heritage. We each shape our own life, but only in interaction with the traditions of the communities in which we happen to have been born. These traditions themselves are but the deposit left to us by the lives of those who have gone before us. It is the task of catechetical leaders and their teams to make the rich treasure chest of the Catholic culture and faith accessible to everyone in the community.

There is dynamism that is set up by catechesis grounded in human family, community, and tradition. The origins of a relationship with God begin with the cradling environment of the parents' love into which infants are born. In a Christian family, love of God and others supports a system of values by which the children will be taught and raised. The children are simply immersed in that love and those values and, at first, accept and live by them without seriously questioning their validity.

Children will be taught to view the world in certain ways, to trust or distrust people, to believe that there is more to the world than meets the eye or that "seeing is believing." As the children grow, they will learn that some behaviors are acceptable "in this family" and other behaviors are not. They will be taught day after day, explicitly and implicitly what is right and true and good. As they mature and develop, questions will emerge, beliefs long held become understood, raising still further questions. Eventually, they will be faced with the realization that they can decide for themselves what to make of themselves. They can accept and appropriate the faith, and values, and beliefs espoused by their parents, they can reject them entirely, or they can blend them with other credible, authoritative positions and their own experiences into a stance uniquely their own.

How can catechetical leaders support families as they create an environment that facilitates a positive outcome for their children? How do they help families form an ongoing relationship with God in Jesus Christ by the grace of the Holy Spirit? How can catechetical and pastoral leaders give access to the conversion to Christ that is the aim of Christian religious education? I believe one way they can provide such access and increase the likelihood of genuine relationship with God and neighbor is by developing programs with the following five characteristics of Christian family and community life firmly in place: (a) Loving Discipleship, (b) Responsible Solidarity, (c) Faithful Belief, (d) Intelligent Theology, and (e) Attentive Prayer.

**(a) Loving discipleship.** "Jesus called the crowd with his disciples, and said to them, 'If any want to become my followers, let them deny themselves and take up their cross and follow me.'" (Mark 8:34, NRSV). Christian faith fundamentally involves being a disciple of Jesus Christ. In addition, it involves carrying one's cross. It is an apprenticeship to a pattern of living that involves self- sacrifice. As such, the decision to follow Jesus is an act of charity, of love, of self-donation.

More accurately, it is a decision to respond with love to God's having first loved us. "In this is love, not that we loved God but that God loved us and sent the Son to be the atoning sacrifice for our sins" (1 John 4:10). God avows God's love for us in the life, passion, death, and resurrection of Jesus. We respond to that love by acting— by deciding to follow Jesus, his program, his Way. Discipleship is the appropriate answer to the question of how we will respond to the love of God in Jesus Christ.

Family catechesis, then, must encourage and nurture discipleship to Jesus. It does this by proclaiming the Gospel—announcing the Good News that God loves us. Obviously, this will take on many forms depending on curricula, programs, activities, and so on.

Moreover, catechesis tells the story not just in words but also in deeds. The proclamation of the Gospel can be spoken much more loudly in actions than in words. The deeds of genuine disciples of Jesus are what inspire our admiration and fire our hearts to want to follow as well. Christian catechesis and teaching is concerned with the pattern and way of Jesus Christ as it is lived. The story must be repeated, yes, but it must be repeated as performance and not just as a recitation.

Christians accomplish this most readily by apprenticing themselves to those who are already Jesus' disciples. Effective family catechesis employs apprenticeship as a means of religious education. It involves mentoring both within the family and without. What this looks like from community to community may differ. One community may have a big brother and big sister program. Another may make use of prayer partners or spiritual directors. A third may have regular witness talks given by senior members of the community.

Besides the catechetical apprenticeship of Christians to those more experienced in discipleship and faith (including the saints), there is the apprenticeship of all Christians to Christ. In the words of John Shea, Jesus Christ is *"The Spirit Master."* Thus, "apprenticeship to Jesus would include the disciple [student], a contemporary master [catechist], and the inspired witness of the Original Master. In and through the interaction of these three the spirit of the Original Master is present and active." (Shea, *The Spirit Master*, 143.) Ultimately, it is Christ, present and active in our lives, who is our teacher, it is in his footsteps that we dare to follow.

In addition, the call to follow Jesus is a call to become part of a community of disciples. The response of Christian discipleship requires Christian community. Many are called; a few follow. But the few are some and not one. From the beginning, there is a community of disciples gathered in the Spirit (see Acts 2:1-4 and 10:44-48). As love is only present in community, Jesus' presence seems to depend on at least a minimal presence of community (see Matt 18:20). Eventually the some can grow into many as discipleship to Christ in the Spirit is fostered, nurtured, and reinforced in community.

Here again we see the wisdom of parishes and schools adopting a family centered approach to religious education and catechesis rather that a child/individual approach. Families are built-in communities—they are the Body of Christ in and of themselves, a domestic church, but also and always in relationship to the larger faith community. Are there any apprenticeship models of education in place at your parish or school? If so, how can you expand on them? If not, what can you do to create such a model?

**(b) Responsible solidarity.** "Then the righteous will answer him, "'Lord, when was it that we saw you hungry and gave you food, or thirsty and gave you something to drink? And when was it that we saw you a stranger and welcomed you, or naked and gave you clothing? And when was it that we saw you sick or in prison and visited you?'" (Matt 25:37-39) The commitment to take up one's cross and follow Jesus is a commitment to solidarity with the oppressed of this world. The follower of Jesus recognizes a mandate to value the other not only over the satisfaction of oneself but at the cost of oneself. Jesus' "passion and cross invite and can enable disciples to see life from the perspective of the poor, the outcast, the maltreated, the powerless, the oppressed, the enslaved, the reviled, and all who suffer. It at once challenges Christians to act on their behalf and empowers them to so act." (Groome, *Sharing Faith*, 439.) Both the Hebrew and Christian scriptures make clear that the will of God is biased in favor of the widowed, the orphaned, the alienated. Christ makes manifest that the price of such commitment may be one's life.

The question posed by Christ crucified—initially answered by the decision to follow him—becomes a question for deliberation and action. The question is posed now by discipleship itself as Christ's love continues to unfold in the life of the apprentice: How do I responsibly enact my decision to follow Christ? How do we, as apprentices to Jesus, act to bring about God's will on earth?

The answer involves being in solidarity with the oppressed. In order to turn and follow Christ one must take up one's cross and follow. Taking up one's cross puts converting Christians in communion with all others on the *via dolorosa*- -those whose crosses have been freely chosen and those whose crosses have been unjustly imposed. Genuine discipleship issues forth in solidarity. Solidarity is a deepening of the realization that the neediest among us reveal Jesus on the cross—hungry, thirsty, alienated, naked, unjustly condemned. And if we are converted to Christ, crucified with Christ, then in Christ we suffer in solidarity with all victims.

More than just responsible obedience to a divine decree, Christian faith requires that care of the alienated become the "preferential option" in one's deciding and acting. Solidarity is, therefore, not some extrinsic addition to the Christian life of discipleship but intrinsic to what it means to be a responsible follower of Christ. As the Roman Synod of bishops wrote in 1971,

> "Action on behalf of justice and participation in the transformation of the world fully appear to us as a constitutive dimension of the preaching of the Gospel, or, in other words, of the Church's mission for the redemption of the human race and its liberation from every oppressive situation" (*Justice in the World* #6).

Solidarity is neither a linguistic nicety nor a juridical mandate. It should be who Christians are. Solidarity is a of reality as embodied in and lived by the Christian family and faith community. It is conveyed in Paul's notion of the Body of Christ. It is attested to whenever Christians pray, "Our Father . . ." It is prayed for by Christ when he prayed, "That they may all be one.

As you, Father, are in me and I am in you, may they also be in us" (John 17:21). According to Matthew's Gospel, solidarity with those in need is the surprising criterion for inheriting the kingdom prepared from the foundation of the world (see Matt 25:31-46).

Family oriented catechesis will create opportunities for families to stand in solidarity with one another and those less fortunate than themselves. Families must be nurtured and encouraged to make responsible decisions in the light of Jesus Christ and, with God's grace, for Jesus Christ. To that end, Christian catechesis must include participation in Christian service not as extra-curricular, but precisely as integral to the curriculum Christi.

> "As the Church, in imitation of Christ, must constantly seek to be more sensitive and responsive to the needs of the poor among us, so too must each Christian family see Christ in those who are less fortunate and, at cost to its own convenience and comfort, strive to be Christ to them, in the parish, the neighborhood, and the larger communities of the nation and world" (*TTJD* #50).

Sara Little is correct that "we are more likely to act our way into believing than to believe our way into acting" (Sara Little, *To Set One's Heart,* p. 27). Families must be provided with opportunities to try on Christ, to imitate his Way, to carry the cross in solidarity with the suffering. The values held by the Christian community and distilled in doctrines cannot be fully understood unless they are acted out. Merely assenting to a value gives one no practical insight into its meaning. One thinks of Jesus' parable of the two sons in which the first son said he would not tend his fathers vineyard and later did, while the second son said he would and did not (see Matt 21:28-31). Likewise, some family members may act themselves into a decision for Christ. What opportunities for service and solidarity exist as part of your catechetical program? Are they integral to the curriculum or added on? Are they activities in which the entire family can participate?

**(c) Faithful belief.** "If you confess with your lips that Jesus is Lord and believe in your heart that God raised him from the dead, you will be saved. For one believes with the heart and so is justified, and one confesses with the mouth and so is saved" (Rom 10:9-10). In addition to following Christ and being in solidarity with those he loves, Christians are called to belief and faith in Christ.

We encounter Christ and are transformed. Christians make him the center and shape of their life. They follow Jesus lovingly in the way of the cross. Next, love for Christ reveals the value and dignity of the human person. Converting Christians commit themselves to the other, especially in situations where the other's value has been diminished. Then, among the values discerned by love for Christ is the value of believing the truths taught by him and the tradition which bears his name.

The realization that Jesus is the Messiah and the Son of the living God does not necessarily precede following him (see Matt 16:15-16). Typically one finds oneself already following Jesus because of the priority of community. God draws us to acclaim Jesus by creating us in and for community. Christian families provide the context in which Christians, by following Christ and loving others precisely because they are in a Christian family, come to believe. One decides to believe as a response to the love of Christ witnessed by and embodied in others—those principal others being one's own family.

Catechetical and pastoral leaders, then, must provide a forum for families to articulate what they believe as a result of their following Jesus. Christian service should always include prompt communal reflection on that service. Moreover, families should have meaningful access to the central affirmations and teachings of the Church in order to probe the congruence between what the Church has come to affirm as true over time and what each family and family member has come to affirm true as a result of their own experience.  Such conversations are much truer to life when they are intergenerational and family oriented.

Are there opportunities in your faith community for what the universal Church professes to be put in dialogue with the beliefs that grow out of contemporary Christian living?

**(d) Meaningful and intelligent theology.** Discipleship, solidarity, and belief are not the whole of the Christian story. They are, however, primary—both temporally and in importance. They combine to create living Christian faith. But the community of Christ's disciples has never been content simply to live their faith.  From the beginning they sought to understand and to mediate that understanding to others. The author of 1 Peter writes: "Always be ready to make your defense to anyone who demands from you an accounting for the hope that is in you; yet do it with gentleness and reverence" (3:15-16).

Such effort continues to this day.  So besides Christian religion there is reflection on religion, besides faith and belief there is the meaningful community's wish to embody belief and the intelligent community's desire to understand their faith.  Such is the task of theology—to bring faith to understanding and to express faith in an intelligible way.

The life of discipleship, solidarity, and belief in Christ raises questions: "Who is this Christ we follow?"  "Why does following him involve care for the poor?" "What does it mean to profess that Jesus is Lord and Savior?"

Our desire to be loved unconditionally finds an answer in the love of God in Jesus Christ. Now our desire to know seeks to give a reason for the hope that is in us.

Theology is both an effort to understand Christian belief and the attempt to embody Christian belief in a way that is understandable. This latter task of theology to mediate the meaning of God's love is part of the task of religious education. Christian religious education attempts to embody Christian belief in meaningful, appropriate, and creative ways for a particular group of people at a particular place and time. It does this as we have said above—intersubjectively, artistically, symbolically, linguistically, and incarnately.

Besides the various meaningful embodiments of belief, there is that effort to understand belief more conceptually and systematically which we call theology. On this view theology is a second order activity. Christian theology is reflection on conversion to Christ. Without conversion there can be no theology.

Questions for both understanding (What? How? Why?) and judgment (Is it true?) must not only be posed by catechists, but must arise out of participants' own desire to understand and know. The questions which most engage participants are their own questions. Catechists, then, must not simply answer their questions, but help guide people to answer the questions for themselves, intelligently and rationally. Questions matter more than answers, norms and rules, because without the questions the latter do not make sense. Only by starting with questions can participants develop their mind and come to their own and "owned" faith. And if they possess a well-trained mind, they will be more likely to greet the illuminating power of Christian teachings.

In order for families to realize Christ, they must come to understand and judge the truthfulness of Christianity for themselves. Family catechesis explores with participants the possibilities and probabilities of Christ's significance in their common lives. Catechetical leaders and catechists must repeatedly ask participants what they have understood and if what they have understood is true. They must help participants discover the further relevant questions that they themselves may not see. In the teaching-learning dynamic, catechists and teachers must check their own understanding and their own attention to relevant questions. In their lives, catechists and teachers must reveal the truthfulness of a life in Christ by every aspect of who they are.

In order to facilitate the kind of active questioning, understanding, and judging that helps families and participants to appropriate Christ, catechetical leaders must make every effort to create in their programs an atmosphere and a community of discourse. Through dialogue, families can test and try out their questions, understandings, and judgments against the questions, understandings, and judgments of others. Such dialogue is more than just alternating talk. Sara Little writes, "Teaching takes place in a context of mutuality. Dialogue is therefore not a method, but an attitude appropriate for all teaching—it can occur when no word is spoken, so certainly it does not refer to discussion" (Little, *To Set One's Heart*, 89). Dialogue is a way of respecting families and participants as subjects and active agents of their own learning. Guiding and norming all such dialogue, sometimes implicitly, sometimes explicitly, should be the mind of Christ.

What programs are in place in your community that enable families to "do theology" with one another? How do you foster an atmosphere of dialogue that permeates the entire community? What would be the advantages of such an atmosphere? What would be its drawbacks?

**(e) Attentive prayer and worship.** "You know [the Spirit of truth], because it abides with you, and it will be in you. . . . On that day you will know that I am in my Father, and you in me, and I in you" (John 14:17b, 20). The Christian community is composed of those who love and follow Christ, who assume responsibility for the poor whom Christ loves, who believe the truth about God revealed by Christ, and who seek to meaningfully embody and intelligently understand that belief. The Christian community is also those who attentively pray through, with, in, and to Christ.

Conversion to Jesus Christ, the centering of oneself on and patterning of oneself after Christ in the Spirit, resolves itself in worship of Christ and the God revealed in Jesus. This involves not just mindful attentiveness, but embodied attentiveness. As Christ is incarnate God, so the Christian community's worship of Christ is an incarnate worship. Christian worship is sacramental, physical, earthy.

Family catechesis should make full use of the profound sacramentality of Catholic Christianity. One of the most wonderful things about Catholicism and one that makes it particularly suited to family modes of catechesis is that it is so exceptionally sacramental. There is so much in the material world that can be a window onto the divine: water and oils and bread and wine, rosaries and scapulars and statutes and medals, relics and incense and ashes and palms. It is a very sensual religion. Catechetical leaders should take care that families have an opportunity to both experience and learn about the significance of the various accouterment of Catholicism.

Obviously the quintessential celebration of the sacramentality of Catholicism is its Eucharistic liturgy. Every effort must be made to make families feel at home at Sunday services. I am reluctant to endorse architectural solutions which for the sake of quiet cut families off from the rest of the congregation. Although I appreciate the need to maintain a prayerful atmosphere, I am concerned about what this teaches, not only the children, but the adults as well. Remember Jesus' response to the disciples who spoke harshly to the people bringing their children to Jesus? Is a glass room any less deserving of Jesus' critique?

Catechetical and pastoral leaders must think creatively in order to accommodate all at the table of the Lord. I believe the ideal solution, resources permitting, is to have a full fledged family liturgy. This sends a clear message about the importance of family life to the overall life of the community. It affirms one of the truths with which we began this essay: that we are all at some time in our life or another a member of a family. Moreover, it symbolizes the truth that Christians are brothers and sisters in the Lord gathering whenever possible to pray "Our Father . . ."

Short of a family liturgy, a family liturgy of the word is a viable option. There are many good resources for conducting effective and prayerful services. Whatever such a solution involves by way of logistics, it is of paramount importance that families not be dismissed as if the rest of the community were glad that they were going. On the contrary, they should be sent forth to hear the Word of God as Christian families and to have it affect there lives in such a way that when they return the entire community is up lifted.

Nor should experiences of prayer and worship be restricted to Sundays. House liturgies are a wonderful opportunity to build intimacy and community within and among families. Family retreats, days of recollection, and evening prayer are just a few of the ways catechetical leaders can foster attentive prayer and worship. It almost goes without saying that catechetical and pastoral leaders should foster and provide the necessary resources for families to have a rich and meaningful prayer life in their homes.

What opportunities exist in your community for families to celebrate and worship together on Sundays? Are they adequate? Can they be improved upon?

## Summary

We began by suggesting that taking a family approach to catechesis was both pastorally and theologically well founded. While Church documents and our own intuition continue to point to the importance of adult education, the reality is that many of our programs are focused on children. Family catechesis is an attempt not just to bridge the gap, but to completely shift the ground. Whereas child oriented (and for that matter adult oriented) approaches take as their participants individuals—albeit in groups—a family centered approach attempts to honor the truth written in both our Scriptures and in our natures that we are relational. We are all brothers and sisters.

In an attempt to further ground as well as illuminate the implications of such an approach, we held that faith was a language, a way of talking about spiritual and ultimate matters—complete with a vocabulary and a grammar. We went on to look at the intersubjective, artistic, symbolic, linguistic, and incarnate ways the meanings of that language could be embodied catechetically and in family friendly ways. Lastly, we looked at five key characteristics of Christian family and community life to explore ways that catechetical leaders might nurture and support loving discipleship of Jesus, solidarity with the poor, faithful belief in the truths of community, intelligent and meaningful theology and dialogue, and attentive prayer and worship.

Ultimately it is you, the catechetical leader—in concert with the catechetical team and pastoral staff—who must discern how God is directing you to guide and nurture the community entrusted to your care. A community of diverse ages and various gifts and talents. A community of sinners and saints. A community, no doubt, of widely different temperaments and opinions about how catechesis should be conducted. A community not unlike a human family.

## Bibliography

Chesto, Kathleen O. *Family-Centered Intergenerational Religious Education*. Kansas City, MO:  Sheed & Ward, 1988.

Craig, Sidney. *Raising Your Child, Not By Force But By Love*. Philadelphia: The Westminster Press, 1973.

Eipers, Carol M. *Table Talk:  Story-sharing for Families*. Kansas City, MO: Sheed & Ward, 1997.

Groome, Thomas. *Educating for Life:  A Spiritual Vision for Every Teacher and Parent*. Allen, TX:  Thomas More, 1998.

_____. *Sharing Faith:  A Comprehensive Approach to Religious Education and Pastoral Ministry*. San Francisco:  Harper SanFrancisco, 1991.

Harris, Maria. *Teaching and Religious Imagination:  An Essay in the Theology of Teaching*. San Francisco: Harper and Row, 1987.

Little, Sara. *To Set One's Heart:  Belief and Teaching in the Church*. Atlanta, GA:  John Knox Press, 1983.

National Conference of Catholic Bishops. *A Family Perspective in Church and Society:  A Manual for All Pastoral Leaders*. Washington, D.C.: United States Catholic Conference, 1988.

_____ *To Teach as Jesus Did (TTJD)*, Washington, D.C.

United States Catholic Conference, 1968.

_____ *Sharing the Light of Faith*, the National Catechetical Directory for Catholics of the United States (*NCD*). Washington, D.C. United States Catholic  Conference, 1979.

Shea, John. *The Spirit Master*. Chicago, IL: The Thomas More Press, 1987.

VerEecke, S.J., Robert, George Drance, S.J. and Michael J. Corso. *Ritual Plays: Engaging Communities in God's Word*. Loveland, OH: Treehaus Press, 1996.

# 5
# The Participants in Catechesis
### Michael P. Horan

## Who Are the Participants in Catechesis?

### Questions for Reflection
- When you think of "the participants" in catechesis, who comes to mind?
- Imagine the person(s) you think of as participants:
  What do they learn?
  How do they participate?
  What are they bringing to catechesis?
  What do you hope they will take away?

Who are the participants in catechesis? This question may have yielded a brief and easy answer if the question had been posed at the beginning of the twentieth century. In the era when Dwight Eisenhower was President of the United States and Pope Pius XII was pope, a ready answer to the question would have been: The participants are children who attend Catholic schools or Catholic after school or Sunday programs. We can imagine that the answer might have named, as an afterthought, teachers (not yet called catechists) as participants in the teaching of religion. And no doubt, in our minds eye, many of those teachers would be women religious.

As Maria Harris has pointed out, the practice of religious education today reflects the more complex situation of our times (*Fashion Me A People*, p. 45-51). Harris shows that the participants are no longer just the children and their few teachers. Today we understand religious education to be a life long activity, with the entire community as the participant in catechesis (Ibid., p. 49-50). The centrality and importance of adult catechesis is frequently affirmed by the Magisterium of the Church (see, for example, *Adult Catechesis in the Christian Community* #4). In addition, the notion that every Christian and the whole community participates in catechesis has been and continues to be a central theme in Catholic Church documents since the Second Vatican Council. Catechesis is consistently identified as an activity that seeks to foster mature faith not only in individuals but in the community as well (see *GDC* #70 and *GCD-71* #21). Moreover, catechesis is often described as a task of the entire Church, an "essentially ecclesial act" (*GDC* #78).

Why do contemporary theorists and official Church documents emphasize this point? Perhaps because today we live in a more complicated nation than the one led by Eisenhower and we belong to a more complicated Church than the one headed by Pope Pius XII. Within our Church, the event of the Second Vatican Council and the subsequent development of documents by the Vatican and the American bishops have profoundly influenced contemporary practice in various facets of Church life. Among these facets is catechesis. A brief review of catechetical directories yields insight about the complex features of the ministry of catechesis, and specifically helps us name the many participants in catechesis in today's complex milieu.

The publication in 1971 of the first *General Catechetical Directory* identified catechesis as a ministry of the Word. *Sharing the Light of Faith*, the National Catechetical Directory for Catholics of the United States (*NCD*), followed from the publication of the first general directory. *The National Directory* described the diversity of the nation's Catholic population and the complexity of defining the American context for catechesis (*NCD* #13-16). It also highlighted the growth in faith of the participants in catechesis, showing that catechesis is a lifelong activity, no longer exhausted by school settings nor confined to the service of children and young people (*NCD* # 173-175 and 177-189). The newly released *General Directory for Catechesis* addresses similar concerns in the context of a complex post- modern society, noting that catechesis is "an essential task of the Christian community" (*GDC* #171).

Catechetical directories and current practice help us draw two conclusions: First, that the participants in catechesis are not confined by age or by setting; in other words, catechesis is not just for children in Catholic schools or after school Church programs. Second, that catechesis is a task for the whole Church; that is, the People of God that form the Church.

This essay presumes that the community is the participant in the ministry of catechesis. The essay considers the participants from three perspectives: The participants in their identity as graced individuals (a theological perspective); the participants in their needs as disciples who are growing in faith (a faith development perspective); and the participants as they learn a rich content through different learning styles (a pedagogical perspective).

## The Participants in their Identity as Graced—
## The Theological Perspective

Recently I celebrated an anniversary marking twenty five years since my high school graduation.  It caused me to search out and find my yearbook and consider the memories as well as the people who had an influence on me during those important years.  One person was Sr. Rita Ann, who functioned as an inspiration to many of us.  She taught sophomore religion as we called it then, and she was a very effective catechist.  The integrity of her example, as well as her words, seeped into our thinking and our acting.

She was the teacher who encouraged us to engage in community service and justice works.  She also challenged our thinking, encouraging us to pursue conversations about religious topics and to find answers among people and among the sources in the school library.  The yearbook records an interview with Sr. Rita Ann.  When asked by the editor to name her favorite subjects to teach, Sr. Rita Ann identified "the students" as the most important subjects.

While that probably wasn't what the interviewer had in mind, Sr. Rita Ann's response contains a great wisdom that I now discern from my vantage point as a middle aged enthusiast of catechesis.  In doing the ministry of catechesis, the most important "subjects" that we ever treat are the participants with whom we work.  Educating in faith today demands of us profound respect for the individual knowing subject who seeks to know God, self, and others. That search may begin with life's ultimate questions or the circumstances of joy or suffering themselves that spark the questions.  It no longer necessarily begins because of strong ties to a faith tradition or a Church community.  In the contemporary world, there may be fewer societal pressures to be Christian or to be religious in any way; there certainly appear to be fewer cultural supports than in the era of our grandparents (see *GDC* #58).

One important factor, often affirmed but rarely explained, when considering the learners in their identity as Christians is to say that people are graced by God. This claim, we should note, is a central and traditional claim of Catholic theology—arising from our creation in God's own image and likeness.  But what does it mean to make such graced "subjects" the focus of catechesis?

In former generations, Catholics like those of my own era studied small catechisms in preparation for quizzing by the visiting bishop at confirmation.  We often memorized various aspects of the life of grace, especially kinds of grace.  We classified sanctifying grace and actual grace, and we learned that the effects of grace in the soul stand in contrast to the effects of sin (which was the diminishment of grace in the sinner). We studied human nature as the condition of humans apart from grace, serving as a reference point for speculating about the effects of grace on human nature.

Through those lessons Catholic children and young people focused attention on what Catholic theological tradition has long called "created grace." This term refers to the everyday effects of God's life in the human being. But there is another dimension to grace, also treated in Catholic theology and catechesis, that has been called "uncreated grace" to denote the very life of God in us. "Uncreated grace" refers to the life of God within the human being—there prior to our own efforts to respond to God. It describes but does not capture the spark of divinity that was there before the dawn of creation and which offers the very possibility for the effects of grace in our lives; it is the ground that makes us capable of receiving God's everyday grace in our lives.

The great theologian of grace in the twentieth century, German Jesuit Father Karl Rahner, was instrumental in crafting the Vatican II documents that have been programmatic for the Catholic Church today. In an era of interest in created grace, Rahner wanted to retrieve the idea of uncreated grace so that people would have an appreciation for the way God is active in human life among searching people and so come to realize the essential goodness of people. We are essentially good because of God's "original" grace.

For Rahner, the most important "subjects" in life's search were the seekers themselves, and he hoped they might begin their search with an examination of what it means to be a human being. The notion of uncreated grace was important to emphasize because God's life in us is a fact, a happy truth that is true regardless of our acknowledging God or our response through how we live. Our human nature is the forum through which God is known; it is in ourselves, foremost, that we find the reflection of who God is—and through such reflection come to know ourselves as graced people.

We may experience the world of grace without calling it by the name of grace or by acknowledging its divine Source. But the story of Christmas—the saga of God becoming human—is the sure sign of God's commitment to be known through humanity and a divine affirmation of who we are and how graced our human condition is. The Incarnation of God is the consciously known story, the pinnacle moment of God's constant unseen or dimly recognized activity in human history.

Rahner showed that the signals of our humanity function as the preamble to our explicit knowledge of God and God's grace. These signals of God, unique to us humans, are found in our capacity to question, to love, and to hope. Before considering what this means for the participants in catechesis, let us notice each of these signals of our graced humanity.

Human beings are different from other creatures because of our ability to think into the future. When we awaken each morning we begin a process of internal questioning. What must I do today? Whom must I contact? What plans are there for this evening? These questions only scratch the surface; we often move quickly into the why and wonder questions: Why can't people get along better? I wonder whether a better job will come along? What is the meaning of this relationship anyway? Is the effort of this job, this commitment worth it? Is this where I should live/work/stay? And beneath these questions lies the most important, the deepest one: Who am I?

Although we never exhaust the questions of our lives, we learn fuller answers to them as we mature. But every question beckons us to go deeper toward another, and so our lives move forward not because we have found answers but because we are faithful to the questions. Our questions continually open up to others that are deeper and more complex. We never quite find adequate or exhaustive answers, but we do not stop questioning.

Human beings also love, and despite our disappointments and difficulties in family, friendship, or relationships of any kind, we continue to love even after disappointment. Our capacity to love, like our capacity to question, seems only to open us up to a wider and deeper horizon, inviting us toward more love. Our "supply" of love is not depleted by our loving; on the contrary, our capacity to love increases when we exercise love. With the first epistle of John, Christians affirm that God is Love, and therefore our experience of loving is a signal, a trace, of the experience of God, even if unnamed as such.

Our capacity to hope also signals our graced humanity, for we are creatures who can imagine, even conjure, the future. We plan and we worry about our plans, we daydream over them and sometimes we dread them. The future is a part of our thinking, for no matter what our disappointment or discouragement, no matter how daunting our setbacks, we have a capacity not only to imagine, but to invest in the future. Our capacity to hope is not exhausted by disappointment (indeed disappointment only occurs in the person who hopes).

What do such fantastic capacities mean for the participants in the catechetical enterprise? Many things! One suggestion would be that in the ministry of catechesis we need to do what the *General Directory for Catechesis* calls "evangelizing catechesis." For catechetical leaders this means helping people see and name more explicitly that God's life in us is available in our human experiences of questioning, loving, and hoping. Like Jesus, catechists ought to proclaim God's kingdom—God's activity in the life of the human being—and challenge people to recognize the kingdom of God already among us and help build the one yet to come (*GDC* #34). Catechists need to help people to see how God is alive and at work in the experiences of questioning, loving, and hoping, and then to discern how to respond as a person of Christian faith.

If all human beings are graced by God, the religious educator invites persons to understand and embrace this truth about themselves and others. The invitation takes many forms, hence the need to distinguish pre-evangelization and evangelization from catechesis. The *General Directory for Catechesis* reviews the structure of the baptismal catechumenate and characterizes the pre-catechumenate as that stage which is marked by an invitation to conversion of heart (*GDC* #88). But the situation in the Church today also demands that people be invited afresh into a community which is officially their own by baptism, but not their own by experience or commitment (see *GDC* #58).

## Questions for Reflection

* In what ways do you invite people to see and hear and experience God through the events of their daily lives? How can you do that more explicitly? More effectively?
* The ministry of evangelizing catechesis needs to be extended to every person and aspect in the life of the Christian community. In what ways do you do effective evangelization? How could you enhance this aspect of your ministry?
* How do you perceive the understanding of grace that is presented in this essay shaping your work as a catechetical leader?

Rahner's understanding of the participants' graced life presumes that people are already reflective and want to become more reflective. It further proposes that religious education fosters adult spirituality and serves the adult search for a deeper more authentic way of faith and life-long growth in holiness. And it insists that there is a compatibility between our human growth and our growth in the Spirit.

The effort to achieve the goal of all catechesis—to foster mature faith in all persons and in the Church at large—will necessarily be reached in a gradual and developmental manner. If our growth in the spirit of Christian faith is proportionate to (not in conflict with) our human growth, we need to understand what the social sciences and other disciplines can tell us about the process of human maturation.

## The Participants in Their Maturing Faith

### Questions for Reflection

Take some time to remember yourself and your life circumstances ten years ago.
- How do your faith questions and concerns differ from the faith questions and concerns you had back then?
- Have you ever experienced a "crisis of faith" in yourself or someone close to you? What was gained from it?

Let us consider the participants in catechesis as invited to mature in faith, asking first what a Catholic Christian vision of faith can offer to the person who desires to grow in living their faith.

### Faith as Intelligent Commitment

Theologians often distinguish between two dimensions of faith. "Faith" refers to both our sense of trust or commitment and to the object or content of our trust. Both dimensions of faith—the how and the what—are important to the maturing learner, and both dimensions are esteemed by Catholic tradition. If being fully human implies faithfulness to the questions of life, then Catholic tradition has much to offer to learners of all ages today. This is especially true when one notices the current promotion among some religious groups of a "blind faith" that demands surrender of the mind. Faith that is "blind" does not question; it relies on the word of some authority, and often is fueled by the belief that those who question are lost. In contrast to this submissive approach to faith, Catholic tradition emphasizes both aspects of faith: Faith as chosen commitment and faith as personal embrace of what we believe.

The content of our faith deserves reflection and analysis and study (*GDC* #51). Whenever we affirm our belief in God as Trinity or our belief in Jesus Christ as "God from God, light from light," we must ask ourselves what those affirmations mean, and then, what they mean for our lives now. Our human vocation to question will lead us to want to know more deeply the meaning of faith statements both in their internal reality and in their meaning for us as believers today. And when we ask about meanings we, the participants in catechesis, are doing theology. This theology may not be the formal kind associated with universities, but we need to make sense of our faith because of our human vocation as questioners.

For centuries Christian theologians have described theology as "faith seeking understanding." This phrase comes from the writings of St. Anselm of Canterbury (d. 1109), who encouraged his students to make faith intelligible. Anselm wanted the learners of his day to understand that faith statements cry out to be illuminated with reason and imagination; both reason and imagination are gifts from God that employ faculties of the mind. Without the activity of the intellect, faith claims and the traditional words of a community remain mere words which carry little meaning or inspiration for the believer.

The Catholic theological tradition has consistently presented the human desire—indeed, the demand—for understanding as part of our graced vocation rather than as a sad temptation. The Catholic tradition has consistently rejected fundamentalism as unhelpful to Christian faith because it denies the full exercise of our human vocation. Fundamentalism, as a reaction to contemporary culture, suspects, rather than respects, the mind as God's gift. Catholic Christians have a tradition of analyzing the meaning and demands of faith statements about God's revelation by the use of reason as well as by trust. But only in recent times have gains in knowledge from the social sciences helped to shed light on how we human beings grow in our capacity for trust and our knowledge of the truth of faith.

## Maturing in Faith

Here we will explore some selected theories and insights of the social sciences and the Church documents that aid us in answering the question: What is the process of growth in faith?

We begin with the stories of three people who currently have, or want to gain, a relationship with the community of faith. They are Juan, Linda, and Ben.

Juan is a fourteen year old student who lives in Baltimore, an east coast city that has a rich history of Catholicism. Juan's parents moved to Baltimore from Ponce, a fairly large town in Puerto Rico. Juan, who was born in Baltimore, attended the Catholic elementary school of his home parish. Upon graduation at the top of his class, Juan received a partial scholarship to a Catholic high school in the city. Juan has always considered his relationship with Christ to be a mainstay in his life.

Juan's life has not always been easy. Illness caused Juan's father to be out of work for more than a year, and finances have always been tight. The neighborhood is a challenge in itself. Many of Juan's peers have neither the desire nor the readiness for the kind of education that Juan now receives at the Catholic high school. At least his best friend has stuck by him. Juan and Eddie have been friends since first grade, and when they both chose the same high school, that seemed great for both of them.

When Eddie was killed by a drunk driver late last summer, Juan began a very difficult period in his search for religious answers. His parents agreed with Eddie's, that this must be God's will, difficult as it is to fathom. Juan's mother often quotes Juan's grandmother, who says that God's ways are not our ways. Juan isn't sure whether it is grief or shock or both, but he senses in Eddie's parents a numbness about Eddie's death. Juan himself found the "answers" spoken by many at the wake and even by the priest at the funeral not very helpful. Juan wonders whether there is validity to all the beliefs of the Catholic Christian community in which he once felt so at home. Juan wonders whether God "took" Eddie or whether there is another explanation. Certainly the kind of God these people worship—the kind who would take Eddie on a whim—doesn't appear to Juan to be worth his allegiance. And the kind of church that claims to accept God on these terms also seems childish to him.

Linda is twenty-four years old and is about to marry Rodney, a cradle Catholic. Before moving to Chicago for her work, Linda had a loose affiliation with the Baptist church in her hometown in Mississippi. But her father never really practiced any particular faith tradition. In meeting Rodney and his family, she has discovered a parish family as well, and is compelled to take another look. She has enrolled in the *RCIA*, despite the fact that she has already been baptized. There she finds a fascinating group of people of all ages, holding in common a real curiosity about the journey of faith.

The metaphor of journey has become very important to her lately, as Linda reflects on the surprising ways in which her own life parallels the Hebrew Scripture readings about a people who wander in hope of a yet unfulfilled promise. She finds in the *RCIA* group and in Rodney's faith a map, a point of reference that makes her glad for what she has found. She is confident that the journey is just beginning. She looks admiringly on the many members of the Catholic faith community who seem so deep in their resolve to live the gospel.

Ben, aged 71, joined the grief support group four weeks after Edna died. From the time of the diagnosis, Ben had held out hope that his wife of forty-nine years might be able to overcome the cancer. When hospice care came to their home, Ben began to be reconciled to the fact that Edna might not survive. He had always thought of himself as the strong one; in truth it was Edna, whose suffering somehow actually brought them closer together.

For Edna, the suffering began long before the cancer. Ben's drinking and his mercurial temper kept them from really getting to know each other for many of the early years of their marriage. When Ben finally joined A.A., he began to communicate his feelings rather than the end result of them. There was more to tell than rage, and with that new telling, Ben began to build a bridge toward Edna, a bridge that she had strained to construct so many years earlier. Now he wonders how he ever questioned God's will; whatever that phrase meant in his youth, it is now a more powerful and mysterious reality than his earlier concepts could catch. In fact, he looks back with some regret but also with a deep sense of gratitude for the reconciled years, the grace that Edna was in his life, and the real growth that came from his fidelity and care in her time of need.

The grief group that meets in the parish center each Tuesday has really helped Ben to express not only the grief but the joy at having known God through Edna, and having been loved by a God whose spirit whispers wisdom about life's paradox: That new life comes from suffering.

All three persons—Juan, Linda, Ben—possess faith, but in each case that faith is expressed differently and indeed it does not necessarily take the same shape in the life of the individual. Each deals with a different angle on the faith story of Christianity. Each relates to the Catholic faith community in a distinct way.

Theories of faith development can aid the religious educator in accompanying an individual on the "journey" of faith. Knowing something about the lives of the religious learners transforms the religious educator from "provider" of answers to "companion" on the journey of faith. But that journey can cover rough terrain, and the task of the companion may change along the way. At times the educator may be the  map reader, the guide, the one more in need, the one to provide sure footing, or the one to challenge the traveler to strain forward, beyond fear and fatigue. As we consider the process of growth in faith, certain assumptions need to be addressed.

Theories of faith development are built on the assumption that there are stages through which a person may pass, in a sequence that cannot be overlooked or short circuited. We will consider theories of faith development that flow from this assumption, as well as one which challenges the developmental view. The first two that flow from developmental assumption are the theories of John H. Westerhoff and James Fowler.

John Westerhoff, a religious education theorist, worked as a pastor and educator with a particular interest in how people become "socialized" into the community of faith. By this term "socialized" Westerhoff intends the process of coming to understand a culture. One who understands a culture understands the nuances—not only the surface meaning of the language, but also the subtle and nearly imperceptible forms of communication that help to share and to shape meaning. In the process, of course, those meanings and values are translated, interpreted, and expressed in new ways by a new generation.

For Westerhoff, the task of maturing in faith is at least a three step process. Westerhoff describes the life of a faith community and the life of the individual in a way which shows that the child who affiliates with the community of faith experientially encounters the meanings and values of the community.  This stage, called affiliative faith, occurs in the child or the newcomer to the community.  The second phase, searching faith, occurs in the adolescent or the person who needs to move away (either emotionally and/or physically) from the community's life in order to make sense of those meanings and values.  The person may need space in order to internalize and accept (or reject) the meanings and values of the community.  This move away from the community's activities and personalities, which often marks searching faith, is disturbing to others who may misread this move as an outright rejection of the Church.

Often searching faith functions as the preamble to the third phase, which Westerhoff calls owned faith.  At this phase the adult Christian can take responsibility for carrying the meanings and values to the next generation of Christians.  According to Westerhoff, the task of a faith community is to support all people in their life of faith, and to work to ensure that the community as a whole is faithful.  It is the community that communicates Christian meanings and values; whereas individuals assume various important roles in the group process of faithfulness to the Gospel (see "Formation, Education, Instruction," p. 578-591, especially p. 579-584).

Westerhoff's scheme offers a firm foundation for appreciating the role of the whole community in the process of introducing people to the life of Christ.  Westerhoff's work also draws attention to the power of liturgy as it forms a community's attitudes and as it subtly tells the story of Christianity.

The power of the catechumenate, the *RCIA*, has been revealed to many individuals and church communities that have welcomed people like Linda into their circle.  The liturgical rites and the faithful reflection that can accompany them have offered new life to many Catholic faith communities.  The meanings and values of Catholic Christianity have consistently been shared by symbols and gesture as much as by words.  The Catholic commitment to a sacramental faith has always invited the participants into a world of meanings and values that can be caught by the choice to participate.  This is especially true for active faith communities who welcome people like Linda into churches that have planned and developed a full process for their welcoming and growth.

Linda's affiliation with the community of faith seems new and exciting, and her admiration for the members of the community offer her a good starting place as she probes the meaning of Catholic Christianity for her life and her marriage.  The privileged vehicle for Linda's search need not be all words.  The community's actions speak more eloquently and often more honestly than the written or spoken words alone.

James Fowler's theory of faith development is more detailed than Westerhoff's; it also offers some interesting insights for catechetical leaders. Fowler's work is based in the work of psychological "developmentalists"— those who believe that we grow and mature in sequential stages. Fowler's sources include Jean Piaget and Lawrence Kohlberg, among others. Piaget was noted for his attention to cognitive structures, the increasing capacity of learners for knowledge, beginning with the sensory-motor level and progressing to abstract thinking. Kohlberg first examined structures of cognition as well, but with a view to cognitive moral development. Kohlberg went about the task of examining the ways in which people think through moral decisions in order to make judgments about actions. Kohlberg identified six basic stages or levels of sophisticated thought for arriving at conclusions about the morality of a particular action. More recently, Carol Gilligan has offered a helpful feminist corrective to Kohlberg's sometimes overly male categories. (Kohlberg used mostly boys and men as the subjects of his studies and drew generalized conclusions for all people—male or female.)

As a student of Kohlberg, James Fowler sought to consider whether there is a similar pattern to the ways in which people grow through their faith questions. He wondered if there is a shared pattern of stages, a series of steps that all people take on the faith journey.

Fowler, like others who promote a developmental perspective, claims that a stage of faith development cannot be skipped. His schema is based on six stages plus a pre-stage. In the earliest or pre-stage of primal faith, the infant learner acquires the capacity to trust in the trustworthiness of others and in one's environment. Primal faith is formed around the experience of the infant with caregivers.

This pre-stage operates alongside the first formal stage, known as intuitive-projective faith. In early childhood the imagination is not controlled or counterbalanced by logical thinking. Perceptions and feelings combine to offer a general intuition about trusting. Children watch adults carefully and they notice the symbols and gestures that will later be associated with a faith life. Both the pre-stage and the first stage are crucial to the faith development of the person in all subsequent stages.

In the second formal stage, termed mythical-literal faith, the child begins to hold in unity the narratives of family and community. The child can hear stories and re-tell them with an understanding of space and time. However, the child understands the stories and symbols of the faith community literally; the child can hear the stories of faith only on the level of a "once upon a time" tale. For example, God as Trinity may be apprehended by the child as God in three parts—in a very literal way.

During the third stage of synthetic-conventional faith, the young pre-adolescent or adolescent may be challenged to synthesize into a coherent whole the various messages about life that are transmitted by the prevailing culture, one's peer group, coaches and teachers, as well as one's parents or grandparents at home.  Young persons are trying to pull together these competing authorities and to synthesize them in a way that allows them to belong to the groups that sponsor the differing ways of thinking.

The fourth stage, termed individuative-reflective faith, is characterized by a move away from the locus of authority found in the home or the Church, so that the young adult can reflectively come to some authentic personal choices about God and faith.  People in this stage are less concerned about others' opinions of them.  This is the necessary stage before the adoption of conjunctive faith.

For Fowler, conjunctive faith, the fifth formal stage, is the faith of a mature person who can hold in tension the seeming contradictions that characterize life.  For the person of conjunctive faith, a "both-and" formula for life seems possible:  God is both completely beyond human experience and completely close.  The world is both holy and sinful.  The Church is made up of people who are at once wonderful and faltering.  Prayer is both a solitary activity and a communal endeavor.

For the person in other stages of faith, these pairs provide dilemmas, and the "both-and" formula seems fleeting or undesirable.  For example, the young person in synthetic-conventional faith may really be hoping to find the answer (either God is beyond our comprehension or completely close, but not both).  For the person of individuative-reflective faith, the fact that the Church is comprised of people who are at once holy and sinful may seem to be hypocritical rather than a natural condition of life.

But for the person of conjunctive faith, the apparent contradictions make sense in light of the experience of life as mystery.  The mature person understands that one cannot understand it all before immersing oneself in the mystery of life.  To the one who falls in love, or has experienced profound losses, or has known deep suffering as well as great joy, the notion of life as mystery seems more apt than strange.  To the one who has experienced many of these features of life's mystery, no explanation is necessary; to the one who has not, no explanation is satisfactory.  So the adult who embraces the conjunctive stage is alert to the paradoxes of life and faith.

Universalizing faith, the final stage, is achieved by those adults who offer self-giving love in order to overcome oppression and injustice, neither counting the cost nor compromising their passionate commitment.  These adults display remarkable detachment while also exhibiting passion for a hope yet unrealized. Society and the Church often experience these rare adults as revolutionaries or visionaries (see Fowler, *Stages of Faith*, p. 117-211).

Fowler's theory offers a way to give voice to some of our own best pastoral intuitions about the faith life of the participants in catechesis. We know intuitively that the faith journey has fundamental distinctions, points of uniqueness for each individual, yet the stories often carry a familiar ring, a signal of a shared quest.

The stories of Juan and Ben offer rich possibilities for understanding some of the many moments of challenge and growth in the life of faith as Fowler has described them. As you consider the stories of each person, perhaps you have identified other persons with similar circumstances or, more likely, similar questions. Juan's questions, like Ben's, are sparked by a death. But their faith responses to those events are quite different. While Juan finds in the events an opportunity to search for more adequate answers, Ben rests in the paradox of the paschal mystery, the truth of dying and rising. Here we may see traces of Fowler's stages in both Juan's confusion and reassessment of earlier "answers" and Ben's reconciliation with life's paradox.

What if our growth in faith is more mysterious, less predictable, and not as neatly sequential as Fowler or Westerhoff's schemes suggest? That is the question of religious education theorist Gabriel Moran, who seeks to soften the claims of developmental theorists about the invariant structures and unrepeated steps for the growth of the individual. In his book, entitled *Religious Education Development*, Moran affirms some of the basic ideas that we have seen in Westerhoff by claiming that the task of maturity occurs when the child moves from a stance of being "simply religious" to "acquiring a religion" to becoming "religiously Buddhist or religiously Christian," etc. (see p. 129-156).

Thus far we might recognize similarities to the schema set forth in Westerhoff's movements from affiliative to searching to owned faith. But Moran is concerned about the imagery of linear development that has been assumed by developmental psychologists. He proposes that the religious journey be conceived as an inward and complex journey. At various times and for various people in their uniqueness, religious development imagery may appear more like a circuitous route than a neat stairway. Moran wants to remind us that the twists and turns in the labyrinth toward owned and authentic faith may be radically different for each graced individual. For Moran, the task of human development ought to include religious development, and theories about psychological development which do not account for religious growth are impoverished.

For Moran, too, the task of religious education is much wider than incorporation into the meanings and values of a faith community as Westerhoff would describe it. The variety and diversity of world religions ought to offer the believer of any and every tradition a signal of the radical Mystery who is beyond our full knowing or naming. Moran's schema is designed with interreligious understanding as the foreground concern in the arena of faith growth, if not as his measure of faith maturity. Moran wants us to remember the uniqueness of the individual and the mystery of God even as we consider psychological theorists' wisdom about development.

In the final analysis, Moran shows the bias of the first world culture for the imagery of development as unbridled growth, with its accompanying assumption that everyone lives in conditions that encourage growth and progress. In fact, Moran reminds his readers that first world growth often occurs at the price of greed among North Americans and with the enormously high but conveniently hidden cost to other peoples and nations.

Moran's work helps to keep in perspective the worlds of Juan, Linda and Ben, but especially Juan and Linda. In the cases of these two younger believers, we may imagine that, in the course of their life spans, the United States will become more religiously diverse. The challenge of interreligious dialogue and, as Moran would have it, conversion toward a deeper expression of one's own faith by encountering the "other" faith, stands as a characteristic feature of life in the United States. This feature will influence the faith expression and the witness that Juan and Linda give on behalf of their adult faith. Their mission of both understanding and evangelization will be no easier than the tasks of previous generations of American Catholics who overcame the prejudice and misunderstanding of others.

Recent catechetical directories have incorporated faith development ideas in their discussion of the participants in catechesis. A unique feature of *Sharing the Light of Faith*, the *National Catechetical Directory for Catholics of the United States*, is its sustained attention to the image of the learners as maturing in faith. For *The National Directory*, mature faith clearly is not a theoretical matter or a detailed explanation of a concept. In chapter eight, the authors depict people of mature faith as friends of God, based in becoming more Christ-like (*NCD* #173). Consistent with Rahner's notion of the person, the Directory makes clear that human development and faith development are not separate realities but two features of the same process of human maturation (*NCD* #174). Without espousing or adopting any particular theorist of faith development, the writers of the *Directory* present growth in faith as a process that has shared patterns among participants.

The authors of the new *General Directory for Catechesis* offer extensive descriptions of learners in various age groups, even as they note the mystery of the gift of faith. The writers point out that people grow in stages beginning with infancy and lasting to old age and on into eternity. For example, the new *Directory* notes that various age groups have varying capacities for receiving catechesis and they call for an integration of the stages in the journey of faith (#171). But the *Directory* also notes that growth in faith is a mystery that cannot be fully comprehended (*GDC* #163). These two assertions expose one of the most challenging features of the Christian life, a feature which profoundly affects catechesis. On one hand, faith is a gift; on the other hand, this gift can be fostered by human cooperation or ignored by human indifference.

For those people who attend to the ministry of nurturing faith, what can we say about growth in faith? First, we can affirm that all human beings are graced by God whether or not they acknowledge God or God's grace.

Second, with Westerhoff we may note that the growth of an individual into a Christian faith stance invariably happens in a community of faith, where there are models of faith. These faith "heroes" provide examples of how to live a life of discipleship. At the same time, we might note with Moran that life in a religiously pluralistic society initially informs persons about the religious search in modes beyond creedal boundaries. In a world as diverse and complex as our own, people become interested in the faith search not exclusively in the context of Churches and communities.

Third, growth toward mature, conscious, and active faith, the goal of all catechesis, occurs in stages or moments; faith growth works in tandem with and not against the full growth of the human being in other aspects of one's life (physical, emotional, social, psychological, etc.). Like these other aspects, growth in faith generally does not occur all at once.

Fourth, the catechist's task in knowing the particular participants is to invite them into deeper faith, no matter what their level of commitment. This is true whether the catechist is understood as an individual or the whole community.

Fifth, learners in catechesis cannot be presumed to be evangelized. Sometimes the good news has not yet been received as good. Therefore catechists promote understanding not only of the content of the faith, but they offer examples of the faith journey. They offer initial proclamation of the Good News for those who have never heard it. They also offer to returning members of the Christian community, or to members in name only, an invitation to the community of Jesus Christ (see *GDC* #78). And they provide examples of mature, faithful people who question, love, and hope through the lens of Christian faith.

The path to "owned faith" (Westerhoff), or "conjunctive faith" (Fowler), or the point of "becoming religiously Christian" (Moran) may be both winding and confusing, with several stops along the way. Faith as trust and the content of faith may grow in proportion, as people learn new ways of imagining God at work in the world, specifically in the circumstances that most matter.

## Wealth of Content, Diversity in Learning

### Questions for Reflection:
- What do you think you have learned about the Christian life in the past year? How did you learn it?
- Make a list of the people in your own faith journey. Who taught you what you now know about the Christian life? What do you learn for your own ministry by reflecting on these people now?

In this section we consider the aspects of catechesis that comprise participation; these aspects constitute an expanded content for catechesis. Second, some features of the theory of learning styles provided by educational theory supply clues about the diversity in style by which people learn.

## Expanding Content:  What People Learn, How They Participate
In the first thirty years of the twentieth century, theorists and practitioners of Catholic religious education gave serious attention to the methods of teaching. Their interest, however, revolved around the use of texts with children, and, as a result their moves to professionalize the activity of catechesis, further emphasized the assumption that catechesis was directed to children. By the middle of the century, however, an interest in content replaced concern for method, and a new movement flourished. The kerygmatic renewal in catechetics—led by Josef Jungmann (1889-1975) and Johannes Hofinger (1905-1986), two Austrian Jesuits—promoted a use of the liturgy, Scripture, and life witness as essential elements of handing on the tradition of Catholic faith. This new movement emphasized the *kerygma*, the proclamation, rooted in the Bible, celebrated in the sacred liturgy and embodied in grateful service and life witness. It advanced many of the ideas that would later be associated with evangelizing catechesis.

For example, Josef Jungmann's programmatic work that set off the movement called for a content for catechesis that would be "whole souled" and integrated, unitary in its vision of the Christian life. Jungmann proposed that such a catechesis would lead people to gratitude for God's great love and such gratitude would fuel their desire to build the Kingdom of God (see Josef Jungmann, *The Good News Yesterday and Today*, 88; 112-113). Although Jungmann's assumed and explicit audience was children, he also understood that the population of adults who suffered from "unconscious

Christianity"—a condition brought on by familiarity with the loose elements of Christian culture, but without acceptance of the good news of salvation— was also in need of education.

Following the period of the kerygmatic renewal, catechetical leaders and writers on the subject promoted the "four signs" of catechesis as a way to both expand and summarize the vast, rich content entailed in initiation and formation in the Christian life. The four signs were the biblical, ecclesial, liturgical, and natural (experiential) dimensions of Christian faith. The four signs, revised and refined, became an integral part of the catechetical directory genre and its treatment of the content of catechesis. (See Mongoven, *Signs of Catechesis*, p. 9-24).

A new emphasis on expanded content can be found in the *General Catechetical Directory* (1971), in *Sharing the Light of Faith* (1979), and in the new *General Directory for Catechesis* (1997). Both foundational documents from the 1970's refer to the liturgy as an essential dimension of catechesis and to Christian witness in the world and service as desired aspects as well. The new *General Directory for Catechesis* echoes these references and integrates them with the work of evangelization and missionary activity (*GDC* #71, 85, 86). According to the *Directories*, participants are encouraged by effective catechesis to engage actively in these dimensions and to grow in faith and holiness through their participation.

To the question: "How do participants in catechesis actually participate?" we may answer: "In a variety of ways." Liturgy and worship, community service and justice, commitment to prayer and activity for the transformation of the world according to the values of the kingdom of God. All these are part of the participants' involvement, facets of "what they learn" in catechesis.

We have seen that a consistent effort in catechetical practice and theory in the second half of the twentieth century has been the expansion of the very notion of catechetical content. To claim that the whole Church catechizes, as proposed through out this essay, is a hallmark of this effort. But the whole Church is not monolithic in either its comprehension or interpretation of the Christian message, nor in the way it identifies itself as Christian in the world. The need for personal formation is connected not only to the interpretation of Church life, but it is bound up in public life, in the way that Christians live out the Gospel in many forums: politics, science, the world of the arts and mass media, and in other settings (see *ACCC* #22 and 27). Leaders' sensitivity is not enough; the participants in catechesis deserve real attention to the variety of "motivations of a socio-cultural, psychological, and pedagogical-pastoral nature" that cause people to move forward in, or to ignore, their faith journey. (*ACCC* #24).

What is true for adults can be said, with qualifications, of the whole Church. The children, young people, and elderly of the community do not generally occupy a place in the work force of society, nor do they typically exercise the same influence in the areas of politics or the arts. But, like adults in the work force, their motivations reflect a variety of stances and circumstances, as do their needs and styles of learning. If there is a shared pattern to growth in faith, there is rich variety in the expressions of faith and the settings in which faith is practiced. There is also vast diversity in the ways that people of all ages learn.

## Diversity in Learning Style

One area of educational research that helps to illuminate the great diversity among participants in catechesis is learning style theory. The term "learning style" refers to at least two facets of learning that aid catechetical leaders in knowing the participants in catechesis: 1) modality preference, and 2) cognitive style.

Modality preference refers to the preferred sense that an individual uses in learning. These senses include visual sense, auditory sense, and kinesthetic sense; whether by seeing, hearing, or moving one learns a variety of skills and gains an impression of a reality. Researchers offer many cautions in the process of identifying modalities. Chief among them is the exhortation that educators remember a simple truth: A preference is just that. Most people use all three modes, but prefer one in certain circumstances.

Because much of the research comes from schools, many of the subjects of research are children and young people (see Richard Coop and Irving E. Sigel, "Cognitive Style: Implications for Learning and Instruction," p. 152-161). Still the theory of modality preference enriches perspectives on the ways that members of a community "learn" through the modalities as they encounter various aspects of the content of catechesis. Some examples may illumine this point. Let us consider three aspects of content in the community's life: liturgy, service, and justice.

The movement and color and sound of liturgy affect people in different ways and to various degrees. The modality preference for the ways in which people "learn" through liturgy may account for some of the pastoral challenges that catechists face when some innovation or modification in liturgy seems "strange" to worshippers who do not like change and who register complaints after Mass. Leaders often account for strong reaction to innovation based on differences in theology or competing understandings of the Church. But perhaps some change has affected, among other factors, an individual's modality preferences in the circumstance of worship. One can imagine, for example, that inviting people to gesture the Our Father would impact kinesthetic learners somewhat differently than auditory or visual learners.

A second example is Christian service. In the case of service learning, those who learn kinesthetically find a way into the truth of the Beatitudes that will delight as well as challenge the learners by their actually encountering the very bodies of the poor and those who thirst for justice. They will learn the Gospel with their hands and feet.

A third example can be found in works of justice. The participants who prefer to process internally and verbally may participate in letter writing campaigns on behalf of political prisoners. In working quietly they will encounter in the written word a tool for their crafting a stronger understanding of their own Christian responsibility to work for justice and to respect life.

Related to modality preference is cognitive style, a term and a theory which are informed by psychological theory. Cognitive style refers to the style by which a person perceives, processes, and remembers information. A cognitive style helps to shape the ways in which an individual arranges data and forms perceptions about meanings and values. This branch of behavioral science is still in its early stage, but offers catechetical leaders some insight into peoples' processes for perceiving and understanding the Christian life.

One area of cognitive style studies is the Myers-Briggs personality profile, based in the psychoanalytical theory of Carl Jung. Jung believed that there resides in each person a dominant and a shadow dimension to conscious functioning. Four polar categories help to provide "types" by which a person functions in one's dominant mode. The polar categories are: introversion-extroversion (referring to the mode by which the person derives energy), intuitive-sensate (procedures for gathering information), perceiving-judging (operations for organizing the information and moving toward conclusions), and thinking-feeling (powers used to arrive at conclusions).

Many Church personnel have found the Myers-Briggs inventory of questions helpful in isolating individual "types" for the four polar categories. Once isolated and identified by type, individuals can know something about the styles that inform their own and others' approaches to tasks in ministry/work relationships. Since the Myers-Briggs typology relies on Jung's findings, the theory applies to adults, and therefore can be helpful to leaders who work with adult participants in catechesis. These would include catechists, *RCIA* candidates and team members, school faculties and Church personnel, among others. The Enneagram, developed by Richard Rohr and with roots in monastic spirituality, is another popular personality assessment tool.

In identifying the participants in catechesis, leaders can serve their communities well by integrating some insights from the world of learning theory. Among those insights are the following:

First, and most simply, not everyone learns the same thing in the same way. There are a variety of learning styles and ways of collecting, processing, sorting, and storing information. Because no two people are alike, no two people learn in like ways. We must employ, therefore, catechetical methods that take into account the infinite variety of participants in our educational programs.

Second, modality preference theory may enhance a holistic and integrated understanding of religious education, since the theory suggests that all people learn in many ways including kinesthetic modes. Implications for liturgical life, service activities, and ways to embody, quite literally, the content of Christianity are numerous.

Third, the process of learning, especially in the area of formation of meanings and values, escapes easy and sure measurement. Leaders must be patient with the participants who represent a variety of modalities and styles. Leaders cannot become focused on the outcomes of each moment in Church life, or try to assess effective catechesis using simple indicators.

Fourth, if catechesis is the work of the whole Church, then leaders can be hopeful that they need not be all things to all persons by themselves. The Church's current members offer a necessary and "built-in" diversity for new inquirers or newly baptized persons. Hopefully, even persons in very small Church communities can find a variety and diversity of style that would aid them.

## Questions for Reflection

The essay began by asking "Who are the participants in catechesis?" and pursued an answer by suggesting that:

> The participants are graced
> The participants mature in faith over time
> The participants learn a vast and rich content
> The participants learn according to different styles

Recall the person(s) you were imagining as you began reading this essay.

- What can you still learn from that (those) person(s)?
- What questions do you need to ask the person(s) as a result of reading this essay?
- Are there decisions emerging for you as a catechetical leader from your conversations with this essay?

## Bibliography

*Adult Catechesis in the Christian Community.* International Council for Catechesis, 1990.

Coop, Richard H. and Sigel, Irving E. "Cognitive Style: Implications for Learning and Instruction." *Psychology in the Schools* 8 (1971):152-161.

Fowler, James W. *Stages of Faith.* San Francisco: Harper and Row, 1981.

*General Catechetical Directory.* Sacred Congregation for the Clergy, 1971.

*General Directory for Catechesis.* Sacred Congregation for the Clergy, 1997.

Harris, Maria. *Fashion Me A People: Curriculum in the Church.* Louisville, KY: Westminster John Knox, 1989.

Jungmann, Josef. *The Good News Yesterday and Today.* Translated by William A. Huesman. New York: Sadlier Co., 1962.

Mongoven, Anne Marie. *Signs of Catechesis.* New York, NY: Paulist Press, 1979.

Moran, Gabriel. R*eligious Education Development.* Minneapolis, MN: Winston Press, 1983.

*Sharing the Light of Faith: The National Catechetical Directory for Catholics of the United States.* Washington, D.C.: United States Catholic Conference, 1979.

Westerhoff, John. *"Formation, Education, Instruction."* Religious Education 82(4): 578-591.

# 6
# The Person of the Catechist
## Wilkie Au

"Bishops Take Persons Over Methods, Tools" declared the headlines of an article in *The Tidings*, the official newspaper of the Archdiocese of Los Angeles. The article reported that the U.S. bishops at a synod emphasized that the "human and Christian qualities of catechists are ultimately more significant than their methods and tools." Though written over twenty years ago (October 28, 1977), the article expresses a perennial truth about catechetical ministry: as catechists, our actions speak louder than our words.

How we act and react directly influences those we catechize. As the saying goes, "values are caught, not taught." Or, put negatively, what we teach in words can be canceled non-verbally by our attitudes and behaviors as persons. Hence, the challenge of "walking our talk." This essay is about developing a spirituality, i.e., concrete and practical ways of living our faith, that can make us effective catechists and catechetical leaders and, at the same time, help us find our catechetical ministry to be a source of personal satisfaction, challenge, and growth.

At the 1977 synod, the bishops asked themselves, "What are the ideal qualities for which all catechists—laity, religious and clergy—should strive?" Before reading their responses, it might be fruitful to answer that question for yourself.

## Questions for Reflection
- As a catechetical leader, what qualities do you look for in catechists and hope to nurture in your own ongoing spiritual journey? List at least five.
- Why do these qualities seem so important to you? How do you imagine helping foster them in yourself as catechetical leader and in the catechists with whom you work?

## Qualities Delineated by the Bishops

**(a) Awareness that their catechetical involvement is a response to a call.** Whether salaried or volunteer, catechists must recognize that they have been given a share in the ministry of Jesus, who calls them to be his messengers today and relies on them to proclaim the Good News of God's reign. As messengers of God, catechists should be willing to give time and talent, not only to catechizing others, but to their own continued growth in learning, faith, and holiness of life.

**(b) Commitment to witness to the Gospel.** Communicating the Gospel message requires that catechists truly believe in the sustaining and transforming power of the Gospel in their lives. Such personal faith must be nourished through regular prayer—private and communal—and an ever-deepening relationship with God.

**(c) Commitment to be active members of the faith community, particularly the parish, and to share in its life of worship and service.** Since Vatican II, Catholics have been called to view the parish in a significantly different way than before. The call entails shifting from seeing the local church as an impersonal dispenser of the sacraments where people would go on Sundays "to charge up" spiritually for the week to seeing the parish as an affective network of people called to share their faith and lives with each other as the People of God. This shift invites greater personal participation in parish life.

**(d) Openness to grow continually in their knowledge of the faith, communication skills, educational methods, and understanding of how people grow and mature and of how persons of different ages and circumstances learn.** Evangelization and catechesis are concerned with a message. As the 1997 *General Directory for Catechesis* states, the catechetical message proclaims salvation as the central point of Jesus' Good News to us: "The message of Jesus about God is Good News for humanity. Jesus proclaimed the Kingdom of God; a new and definitive intervention by God, with a transforming power equal and even superior to his creation of the world" (*GDC* #101). As with all messages, the Gospel message is addressed to someone and by its nature, invites a response. The emphasis in catechesis is on effective communication, communicating the Good News of the Gospel to some concrete person or group so that it comes across as both "good" and "news." Therefore, catechesis is very much concerned with psychological, social, and cultural factors that influence effective communication.

## The Spirituality of Messengers

The ministry of the word takes many forms, including the catechetical and the theological. While the theological form is mainly concerned with "the systematic treatment and the scientific investigation of the truths of faith," the catechetical form is intended to make our "faith become living, conscious, and active through the light of instruction" (*Decree on the Pastoral Office of Bishops in the Church, Christus Dominus* #14). As catechists, we make faith come to life primarily by being messengers of God's word, bearers of the Good News of the Gospel. To do this, we need a spirituality that can keep us attuned to our identity, mission, and dignity as messengers of God. Four rhetorical questions once posed by Jewish thinker and Nobel prize winner Eli Wiesel provide the inspiration for such a spirituality:

- What could be more tragic than the person who forgets he or she has a message?
- What could be more tragic than the person who forgets what the message is?
- What could be more tragic than the person who forgets whom the message is for?
- And what could be more tragic than the person who forgets whom the message is from?

A practical way of staying alive spiritually as catechetical leaders is to reflect prayerfully and regularly, both alone and with colleagues, on the significance of your role as messengers of the Gospel. This essay is meant to provide some "food for thought" for your ongoing reflection.

## Catechetical Involvement is a Response to a Call to Ministry

The core message of the Bible assures us of the continuity of God's love. God's faithfulness endures forever. However, divine care takes on present reality only if Christians claim their call to continue the ministry of Jesus. Because a majority of Christians in the past were so often conditioned to think that the role of the laity is simply "to pray, pay, and obey," ministry seemed an alien category when applied to the life of ordinary Christians. Fortunately, much has changed in recent times. Lay ministry has now become a more familiar notion, as lay participation continues to expand in parishes and churches and laity perform functions once the sole preserve of priests and religious. This vibrant emergence of lay ministry in today's Church reflects a growing realization among Christians that ministry is an essential aspect of being disciples and not merely something reserved for a few. As Vatican II emphasized, the entire People of God are called to the service of Jesus Christ by embodying his caring presence and continuing his ministry of proclaiming the Good News to the world. Through baptism and confirmation, Christians receive the gift of ministry and are commissioned by the Lord himself to continue his saving presence to the world by acts of loving service (*Dogmatic Constitution on the Church* #30 and 33). This renewed realization of the gift of ministry invites catechists to keep explicitly in mind that their work has the special mark of a ministry and that it is done as a response to a call from God through a Christian community.

## Witnessing As Messengers of the Gospel

In John's Gospel, Jesus explains his ministry as doing "the works which the Father has granted me to accomplish" (5:36) He is the apostle—"the sent one" of God par excellence. His mission is to inaugurate and proclaim the Kingdom of God by preaching the Father's merciful love and saving intervention in human history. Thus, preaching the Good News of the Reign of God was Jesus' central and all-consuming concern (Mark 1:14-15).

Jesus' ministry—that is everything he engaged in to accomplish the mission given to him by the Father—can be viewed in three aspects: Jesus ministered:

1) By preaching the Good News of God's loving and powerful intervention in history (the kerygmatic—Word of God-aspect);
2) By forming a community that would embody and reflect the Good News in its way of life and activities (the koinoniac or communal aspect);
3) By doing works of love, service, and justice that would demonstrate in action that the Kingdom of God has indeed arrived (the diaconal—or service aspect).

These three aspects of ministry are reflected in Jesus' response to the disciples of John the Baptist. When they approached Jesus, seeking to confirm his identity as the Messiah, he told them: "Go back and tell John what you hear and see: the blind see again, the lame walk, lepers are cleansed, the deaf hear, the dead are raised to life and the Good News is proclaimed to the poor . . ." (Matt 11:4-5). Matthew's Gospel points to Jesus' works as evidence that the long awaited Messiah had arrived, initiating the Reign of God.

## Catechists Continue the Ministry of Jesus

Before leaving them, Jesus commissioned the apostles and the community he formed to continue his ministry. Just as he was sent by the Father, so he sent his followers to proclaim to the world the Good News of God's benevolent Reign over a Kingdom already begun but not yet flourishing.

Participating in the ministry of Jesus would thus mean sharing the same commitment and care of Jesus for announcing the Good News of God's Reign on earth.

Ministry, in its broadest scriptural sense, is any human activity engaged in for the sake of the Kingdom or, in the words of Jesus, "for my sake and the sake of the gospel" (Mark 8:35; 10:29). The three aspects of Jesus' own ministry mentioned above provide a useful framework for understanding how catechetical leaders and catechists can carry on the ministry of Jesus in their daily lives, as well as in their specific catechetical assignments. Corresponding to these three aspects, catechists can witness to the Gospel by proclaiming the Good News

1) through the language of their words
2) through the language of their relationships
3) through the language of their works.

**Proclaiming Through Words:** The kerygmatic dimension of ministry is not confined to a call to preach in any formal way. More broadly, it is a call to all in catechesis "to share the light of faith" (*National Catechetical Directory for Catholics of the United States*). To share one's faith within the given context of one's daily life is to be messengers of the Gospel in a real and concrete way. Thus, sharing the light of faith is not confined to their catechetical duties at the parish, but includes all that they do as spouses, parents, adult children, neighbors, and friends.

Parents minister to their children kerygmatically when they teach them how to pray or when they hand on their creedal belief. Husbands and wives minister to each other through their words of mutual reassurance during difficult times and by expressing love and joy, encouragement and trust based on their faith in a God who makes all things possible. Friends minister to each other when they supportively share their personal experiences of the presence and power of God in their lives. Adult children minister to aging and sick parents when they speak a tender word of trust in a God who always brings good out of everything. These are all examples of ways of caring for the Gospel message through our words. They continue Jesus' proclamation of the Good News that God is a loving Abba who is intimately and actively involved in our lives, to save us, to make us whole, to bring us to fullness of life.

**Proclaiming Through Relationships:** The relationships in our lives as catechetical leaders and catechists can also take on the nature of ministry. They can embody God's love, acceptance, forgiveness, care, and graciousness to God's people in such a tangible and obvious way that it is clear for all to see that God's Kingdom is here and that God's Spirit reigns in our lives. So too, parents minister relationally when their love and acceptance make it possible for children to believe in a loving, tender, and accepting God. Parents also minister relationally when their forgiveness enables their children to believe in a God who is freely forgiving of wayward children. Husbands and wives minister to each other in relationship when their intimate love deepens their understanding of a God who is Love. Old friends minister to one another by their loyalty throughout the years, enabling each other to believe in the abiding fidelity of a God who is called the Faithful One (Isaiah 49:15-16).

In the Gospel of Mark, Jesus provides a concrete illustration of what is involved in ministering to others relationally (1:40). A leper approaches Jesus, calling out for healing. Jesus attends carefully to what the leper is saying and doing. Moved with compassion, he reaches out to touch the leper in a way that brings him wholeness. In this episode, we notice a threefold dynamic that characterizes many of Jesus' interpersonal encounters:

1) Jesus is keenly aware of the needs of the people around him (awareness);
2) he lets what he perceives touch his heart so that he is moved with compassion (compassion);
3) moved with compassion, he reaches out to respond to the person in need (caring response).

Like the ministerial encounters of Jesus, our relationships become ministry when they are characterized by this threefold dynamic of awareness, compassion, and caring response. Seen in this light, the opportunities to share in the ministry of Jesus through our relationships, whether we are working at the parish, at home, at school, or at work are unlimited. When we relate to others in such a way, we are truly sharing the ministry of Jesus because by and through our actions the Risen Jesus continues today his ministry of freeing and healing people.

**Proclaiming Through Works:** Continuing the ministry of Jesus must also take the form of a "faith that does justice," a faith that is expressed in service, especially on behalf of the poor, the alienated, and the oppressed. In the parable of the Good Samaritan (Luke 10:25-37), Jesus challenged his followers to expand their understanding of "neighbor" to include those who do not share the same race, religion, culture, or class. Furthermore, he makes clear that Christian love of neighbor cannot stop with words; it must be shown in concrete acts of caring. Following the threefold dynamic of Jesus' own ministerial encounters, the Good Samaritan (truly a lay minister, as distinct from the priest and the Levite) saw the victim, "had compassion, and went to him and bound up his wounds, pouring on oil and wine; then he set him on his beast and brought him to an inn, and took care of him." The Good Samaritan is certainly a minister in the mode of Jesus; his loving service on behalf of an oppressed and needy neighbor is marked by awareness, compassion, and caring response.

Service to others takes on the nature of ministry when it is done for the sake of the Gospel and for the sake of Jesus, who identifies himself with the "least of these who are members of my family" (Matt 25:40). Works of service become the nonverbal proclamation of the Kingdom in our midst and the tangible witness testifying to the reality of God's Reign in the here and now. In brief, according to a scriptural understanding of ministry, we truly share in the ministry of Jesus when our lives continue to embody the care of God for others and when our words and manner of living contribute to the coming of God's Kingdom of peace and justice into human history until Jesus returns in glory.

## Ministry: Giving God a Face that Others Can See

We are called as catechetical leaders to model ourselves and nurture catechists who minister by giving flesh-and-blood reality to the ongoing compassionate care of God for all. Today God depends on us to embody the love of Jesus for others, as the following story emphasizes: A statue of Jesus wrecked by the shelling during the war stood just outside a small village near Normandy. Its hands had been totally destroyed. After the war, the villagers gathered around the ruined statue to decide its fate. One group argued that the statue was so badly damaged that it should be trashed and a new one erected in its place. Another group objected, arguing that the village artisan whose specialty was the restoration of damaged art objects could easily take care of the job. Finally, a third group voiced a proposal that ultimately carried the day: that the statue be cleaned up, but remain handless; and that a plaque be placed at its base with the inscription: "I have no hands but yours."

Similarly, the story of a young man killed in a drive-by shooting illustrates how ministry calls us to stand in place of Jesus for those who cry out for love and reassurance. The wounded man lay dying in front of the church, as a group of horrified parishioners gathered around him, waiting for the paramedics to arrive. As his life steadily slipped away, the young man could be heard over and over again crying out for his mother, seemingly to no avail. Suddenly, a woman broke through the crowd and bent down to cradle the dying man in her arms. Gently rocking him, she repeated in assuring tones, "I'm here, son. Everything's going to be okay." As the dying man breathed his last, she blessed him with the sign of the cross.

A few days later, the woman, filled with scruples, appeared at the door of the rectory. She wanted to confess that she had lied, that she was not really the mother of the young man who had died. She felt guilty for what she had done, even though at the time she felt drawn to do whatever was needed to comfort the dying man crying out for his mother. She left the rectory with peace of mind and a sense of validation, because the priest had reassured her that she not only had done nothing wrong, but, in fact, responded in a most Christ-like way. Following the example of Jesus, she had embodied the compassionate care of God for another.

Like the Samaritan woman, through whose words the whole town came to believe in Jesus (John 4), we are blessed, through baptism, with a share in the ministry of Jesus. As the *National Catechetical Directory* states, "All members of a community of believers are called to share in this ministry by being witnesses to the faith" (#204). Through our words, relationships, and works, we are called to proclaim the presence and power of God in the world today. Everyone Counts.

## The Story of *ish* ("Someone")

In Rabbi Lawrence Kushner's *Honey from the Rock*, we find a compelling reminder of how highly we must regard our vocation to be messengers of the Most High. Commenting on the Joseph saga in the latter chapters of Genesis, Rabbi Kushner illustrates how important a single ordinary person can be in the work of God. One of the most important people in the Pentateuch, the first five books of the Old Testament, according to Kushner, remains nameless. Known only by his deed of giving Joseph directions that were crucial to his finding his brothers, his name is quite secondary to the task he was sent to perform. Like a messenger sent by the Most High from another world to change the course of this one, his presence in the plot is awkwardly contrived. In a cameo role, he strolls across the stage of salvation history to deliver his sparse lines, only to disappear as quickly as he emerged, never to be heard from again. Perhaps he had a full life of family concerns and business interests. But so far as the Holy One is concerned, he had but one task: to be a messenger for the Divine. Who knows, perhaps he was pressed into the divine service, perhaps against his will or even without his knowledge. This person is a messenger who does not know he is a messenger. He was an important actor in the drama of salvation, but interestingly unnamed in the program. The Torah only calls him *ish*, "someone." Yet without him, the great deeds that God did for the children of Israel would never have occurred: they never would have stayed in Egypt, never have been freed, never have crossed the sea, and, indeed, never have come into being as a people (Kushner, 72- 73).

The significance of ish unfolds in the final chapters of Genesis which tell the story of Joseph, a favored and spoiled son. Joseph's grandiose dreams of his being set over his brothers in a privileged position provoked their wrath, just as his being their father's pet evoked their envy. When an opportunity arose, his brothers sold him to a caravan of traders headed for Egypt and what they hoped would be oblivion. Joseph's gift as a dream interpreter, however, eventually made the Pharaoh elevate him to second in-command of the realm, giving Joseph such power that he was able to manipulate situations so that his eleven brothers, along with their father, could escape a famine by settling in Egypt. "Clearly, the Torah means to teach us that it is all the doing of the Holy One" states Rabbi Kushner. "Event after event has the unmistakable mark of divine contrivance. But of all these scenes chronicling our descent into Egypt none seems more superfluous and dramatically unnecessary than the scene in Shechem" (Kushner, 72-73).

Having been sent by his father to check on his brothers who were supposed to be tending the flocks in Shechem, Joseph discovered upon arrival that they were not there. "A man (ish) found him wandering in the countryside and the man asked him, 'What are you looking for?' 'I am looking for my brothers,' he replied. 'Please tell me where they are pasturing their flock.' The man answered, 'They have moved on from here; indeed I heard them say, 'Let us go to Dothan.'" So Joseph went after his brothers and found them at Dothan (Gen 37:15-17).

Citing Ramban, a commentator on Genesis, Kushner suggests that the "man" (ish) was a messenger and his passing exchange with Joseph in the pasture was full of divine purpose. One of the greatest events in the salvation history of Jews might not have happened if it were not for the part played by "ish." "Indeed were it not for the man who 'happened' to find Joseph wandering in the field," writes Kushner, "he would have returned home. Never been sold into slavery. Never brought his family down to Egypt. The Jewish people would never become slaves. And indeed there could have been no Jewish people at all" (Kushner, 74).

Every catechetical leader and catechist is simply "ish," someone. No more or no less than the unnamed stranger of the empty pastures of Shechem, whose one-liner delivered in a cameo, walk-on performance, allowed God's purposes to be accomplished. This story supports the importance of every catechist's role in the work of God today. When it comes to our call to proclaiming the Good News of the Gospel and of sharing the light of faith today, everyone's simple and ordinary "one-liner" counts. Our "one-liners" in life—the daily opportunities provided us to give the living God a face that others can see—may seem small and unimportant. Yet, without them, the compassionate outreach of a God who cares will be handicapped, since the Risen Jesus "has no hands but ours."

In short, the call of catechists and their pastoral leaders to be messengers of the Gospel presents a lofty challenge, not unlike the role of angels! Unlike angelic messengers, however, human catechists are bound by the limitations of matter, i.e., our bodies and our material lives limit our time, energy, and resources. If we are to "walk our talk," striving to be effective messengers of the Gospel, we need a spirituality that can support us and serve as a guide or path. To be practical, such a spirituality must take into consideration the wide range of needs we have as human beings, must correspond to the concrete circumstances of our busy lives, and must sustain us in our catechetical ministry.

## Questions for Reflection
- What are some of your insights thus far for your own spirituality as a catechetical leader?
- Are there ways in which your own ministry is a source of spiritual growth for you? How so?
- What are the particular spiritual needs of catechists? How can you, as catechetical leader, help meet those needs?

## A Holistic Spirituality for Busy Catechists

A holistic spirituality is meant to be a way or pathway that leads to wholeness, holiness, and union with God. It should provide us with direction for life's journey. Like a map, however, a spirituality is useful for providing direction only if it corresponds to the actual territory we must travel. A spirituality that doesn't address the concrete areas where we feel stuck and lost will not have any kind of credibility today. A workable spirituality can serve as a map only if it matches our life situation.

Even more critical is our realization that a map is indeed necessary. And this realization comes only when we who trod the road to holiness are in touch with our struggles, our need for guidance in dealing with the perplexing obstacles that block our progress.

Martin Buber, the Jewish theologian, tells a story that brings this truth home nicely. Buber describes the encounter between a jailed rabbi and the chief jailer. The majestic and quiet face of the rabbi, deep in meditation, touched the jailer deeply. A thoughtful person himself, the jailer began talking with his prisoner and questioning him on various points of scripture. Finally, the guard asked the rabbi: "How are we to understand that God the all-knowing said to Adam, 'Where art thou?'"

"Do you believe," answered the rabbi, "that the scriptures are eternal and that every era, every generation and everyone is included in them?:

"I believe this," said the jailer.

"Well," said the rabbi, "in every era, God calls to everyone 'Where are you in your world?' So many years and days of those allotted to you have passed, and how far have you gotten in your world?" God says something like this: "You have lived forty-six years. How far along are you?"

When the chief jailer heard his age mentioned, he pulled himself together, laid his hand on the rabbi's shoulder, and cried: "Bravo!" But his heart trembled. (Martin Buber, *The Way of Man According to the Teaching of Hasidism*, p. 9-14)

Buber goes on to explain that God does not ask the question of Adam expecting to learn something new. Rather, God uses the question to confront Adam with the state of his life. God asks the same question of us today to jolt us into examining our lives and taking responsibility for our way of living. This decisive heart-searching is, according to Buber, the beginning of a spiritual way for human beings. So long as we do not face the still, small Voice asking us "Where art thou?" we will forever remain without a way to God, and to holiness, that is, without a spirituality. Adam faced the Voice, perceived how he was stuck, and discovered a way out. The question, "Where art thou?" is like the "red X" on the map of our lives. As on a map of a shopping mall, the "red X" marks the exact location of where we are standing. When we ascertain that point, we can then move ahead.

When pastoral leaders and catechists today face the question, "Where art thou?" they find their lives more complicated than ever. Often they feel buffeted by the pressures of life and torn by the competing values that lay unrelenting claims on their limited energy and resources. Inner voices flood their minds with quandaries and concerns: "I'd like to develop my prayer life, but I feel guilty when I take time away from the family." "I'd like to volunteer to help out at the shelter for the homeless, but my work schedule is so hectic these days." "How do I stay faithful to my responsibilities to my children and spouse and still get some time for myself? Is it being selfish to tell them that I just have to get away for a couple of hours and that they'll have to fend for themselves for awhile?" Perplexed by such inner pressures and questions, catechists often experience frustration, guilt, and confusion. They feel the need to clarify their situation and make good choices about how to spend their time and energy. They desire a spirituality that can help them make practical and realistic sense of how to live gospel values in the midst of busy lives.

Often in the past, spirituality was seen as an impractical, if not irrelevant, undertaking for ordinary Christians living in the real world of getting meals on the table and beating rush-hour traffic. This view of spirituality was colored by a one-sided approach that has plagued certain strands of Christian spirituality. According to this narrow view, spirituality was equated with the so-called "life of the soul," or the "interior life." The problem with this understanding of spirituality is that it makes the spiritual seem as if it were opposed to the ordinary aspects of our lives. If spirituality is exclusively concerned with developing the inner life or the spiritual soul, for example, then such important human concerns dealing with affectivity, sexuality, and whatever belongs to the life of the body seems irrelevant to holiness and spiritual growth. This ethereal view of spirituality was not earthy enough to be practical—and certainly not holistic.

Another unhelpful tendency of certain forms of traditional Christian piety was separating the sacred from the secular. According to this view, our encounter with God and the spiritual dimensions of reality is restricted to certain times, places and experiences that are explicitly "religious" or "churchy." This narrow understanding of spirituality severely limits our access to God, giving the impression that vast areas of our ordinary experience—like housekeeping, work and leisure, bringing up a family, earning a living, managing a business, running a parish religious education program—are irrelevant to our spiritual development.

Finally, some traditional forms of Christian spirituality made it seem that in order to be spiritual or holy, one had to be unconcerned about earthly affairs and concerned only about the world-to-come. It is not hard to see why Christians could get the impression that spirituality has nothing to do with real life. When the world is devalued as a transitory valley of tears, worldly affairs are judged to be of little or no consequence. Responsible involvement in political and economic matters loses all connection to spirituality. Once again, this kind of spirituality makes it difficult to see how we can integrate our faith with important aspects of human life.

In contrast to these one-sided ways of viewing spirituality, a holistic approach to Christian spirituality sees our entire life as the dwelling place and arena of God's Spirit at work. In other words, a holistic spirituality finds every human concern to be relevant because God's Spirit can be encountered in all aspects of life and not merely in such explicitly religious activities as prayer and rituals. A holistic spirituality stresses the fact that we live in a divine milieu and that every particle of the created universe can reveal the face of God, every bush can be a burning bush revealing God's presence, as was Moses' experience in the wilderness while tending his flock (see Exodus 3). A holistic spirituality attempts to encompass the whole of our lives, including our relationship with others, with our work, and with the material world.

Holistic spirituality is both a religious outlook and a way of structuring our lives in order to embody religious values. As an outlook, it asks the question, "How is God leading and loving me in the nitty-gritty aspects of my present life?" And as a life-structure, holistic spirituality deals with the concrete pattern of our lives. Viewing spirituality as a particular way of being in the world, a way of walking our talk, a holistic spirituality is concerned with helping us embody in a lifestyle the values that we say we hold, like the decisions we make about how we spend our money, time, and resources. Issues revolving around work and leisure, prayer and politics, sex and relationships all find a place in a holistic spirituality because it acknowledges that the transforming Spirit of Jesus moves in all these aspects of our lives.

"A place for everything and everything in its place" suggests a way of living a balanced Christian life and of achieving harmony. Yet to attain this balance, we need an overall perspective, a way of looking on our lives that provides a sense of the big picture. Only such a framework can serve as a spiritual map, a holistic spirituality to guide our daily practice of faith.

## A Gospel-Based Spirituality

The holistic spirituality I present here is based on the gospel loves as presented by Jesus. A compelling quality of Jesus' message was its absolute simplicity. When confronting the question set forth by a lawyer about which of the commandments is first, Jesus indicates that the greatest commandment is the twofold commandment of love: "You shall love the Lord your God with all your heart, and with all your soul, and with all your mind, and with all your strength . . . [and] you shall love your neighbor as yourself" (Mark 12:30-31). Cutting through the sometimes overwhelming weight of legalistic requirements, Jesus went right to the heart of the matter: loving is the core of authentic spirituality. Neither fulfilling the letter of the law, nor fasting and tithing, but simply loving God with our whole being and others as we love ourselves is the bottom line requirement for being a good Jew and ultimately a follower of Jesus. This truth, so starkly stated, must have been a refreshing moment of clarity for those perplexed by the intricacies of the Mosaic law. With equal force, it can restore perspective to our complicated lives today.

Because gospel love is multifaceted, it can encompass the complex dimensions of human life and at the same time provide a simple focus. Viewing spirituality from the point of view of gospel love thus allows us to construct an overview for monitoring the quality of our lives and making the difficult choices that competing claims force upon us. From the commandment of love, we can derive five distinct loves in scripture:

1) love of God, expressed through prayer, worship, and keeping the covenant
2) neighborly love, expressed through service and ministry
3) communal love, expressed through community
4) particular love, expressed through friendship
5) self-love, expressed through self-esteem

These five loves are distinct, but in reality interact and affect each other. For example, self-love makes it possible for us to love others, whether in friendship, ministry, or community. Yet, being loved by others also enables us to love ourselves. Similarly, when we love and appreciate our lives as gifts from a loving God, we find ourselves drawn in gratitude to love God. On the other hand, self-hatred provides no motive for loving God the creator. No one can authentically reach out to the other unless this reaching out is based upon a healthy acceptance and love of one's own self.

The holistic framework presented here is built around these five loves and their complementary opposites which must be included for a complete understanding of each love. We run the risk of misunderstanding each of the loves unless we see how that love might be completed and what its complement is. Thus, only in terms of its complement can each love be appreciated in its wholeness. In short,

prayer must be balanced by humor,
ministry must be balanced by leisure,
community must be balanced by solitude,
friendship must be balanced by generativity,
self-esteem must be balanced by self-denial.

## Defining the Elements of the Holistic Model Based on Love

What follows is a brief description of each of the elements as they are understood in this model. A fuller description of them can be found in *By Way of the Heart: Toward a Holistic Christian Spirituality* (Au, Paulist Press, 1989).

**Prayer:** the human heart in search of God.

**Humor:** a light-heartedness in our search of God, based on the realization that God is also in search of us and that our love for God is met with divine mutuality. As the *Catechism of the Catholic Church* states beautifully, "Whether we realize it or not, prayer is the encounter of God's thirst with ours. God thirsts that we may thirst for him" (#2560).

**Ministry:** loving others by embodying the compassion of God for those in need.

**Leisure:** down-time for rest, relaxation, and restoration. Community: loving others in a group (e.g., family, church, neighbors).

**Solitude:** time alone to "befriend" the self, to reflect on one's life and situation.

**Friendship:** loving other individuals in a freely chosen relationship marked by mutuality and reciprocity.

**Generativity:** a loving relationship that issues forth in life-giving ways for those around and that bears fruit for others, especially those in future generations.

**Self-Esteem:** loving oneself as someone of worth and taking care to live a healthy, satisfying, productive, and balanced life.

**Self-Denial:** possessing an inner freedom to say "no" to whatever in us, at a given time, hinders us from loving and caring for others.

This holistic framework can serve as a guide for achieving balance in our spiritual journey of love. It can be helpful by providing us with a bird's eye view of the five gospel loves and their complements that must in some way find a place in each of our lives. But discovering the proper place and balance of these loves will require individual reflection and discernment. Striking the right balance among the loves is not simply a matter of a 50-50 proposition. The process is much more fluid and requires constant and prayerful discernment. For example, when people are facing important life-choices, they may need more solitude for reflection than at other times in their lives. Or, people who are experiencing a set-back or failure in life may need to focus more on a healthy love of self grounded in God's unconditional love than on self-denial, which is also an important gospel value. And, people approaching retirement may need to deepen their appreciation of leisure and friendship. The proper balance among the gospel loves presented in this holistic framework will vary for people depending on their age and life circumstances. The proper balance can only be determined by persons' prayerful discernment at each point in their lives.

## Questions for Reflection

- How are the different elements of the holistic model of spirituality reflected in your life?
- Which love or element in the model do you have the most trouble or struggle with?
- How do you cherish the ordinariness of yourself? Do you reverence your body and get the exercise, rest, and nourishment you

need? How do you honor your humanity? Keep from imposing unrealistic expectations on yourself? Befriend your weaknesses as well as your gifts?

- How do you nourish others in your life and let yourself be nourished by them? What unrealistic expectations might you have of them?

## Obstacles to a Balanced Spirituality

Ministers in general, and especially lay ministers who have to juggle the responsibilities of family life with their commitment to serving the People of God, often struggle with finding a peaceful and harmonious balance in the midst of busy lives. Talk of stress, tiredness, and burnout is common in ministerial circles. Some of the factors that cause stress in ministry are systemic, e.g., the parish is short on funds and cannot hire the required number of people needed to get all the work done or cannot afford the supplies and equipment that would make the work easier to accomplish. Other factors that induce stress in ministry result from personal factors, such as codependency, an excessive sense of responsibility for taking care of the needs of others, or perfectionism, a compulsion to have to do everything flawlessly.

When ministers are overwhelmed and stressed out because of too much work, the serenity prayer provides sensible direction—"God, give me the serenity to accept what I cannot change, the courage to change what I can, and the wisdom to know the difference." Certain systemic factors that cause burnout may be beyond our control to change. We can press to have structures and policies changed so that the pace and volume of our work are more manageable, but there usually is a limit to the changes we can influence in the external world of budgets, hiring and schedules.

In the inner world of our own personality dynamics, we should observe what can be modified in our attitude and approach to work and ministry that might alleviate our stress and allow us to live more enjoyable and balanced lives. In *Urgings of the Heart: A Spirituality of Integration* (Paulist Press, 1995), psychotherapist and Jungian analyst Dr. Noreen Cannon and I address, from a psychological and spiritual point of view, some of the common culprits that cause us stress and imbalance: low self-esteem, codependency, and perfectionism. Awareness of how these factors contribute to our tiredness and discouragement in ministry allows us to experiment with new attitudes and approaches and frees us to minister in a more satisfying way.

**Low Self-Esteem:** A pervasive feeling of "not being enough" plagues people who suffer from low self-esteem. An exaggerated need to achieve at work may be an effort to compensate for an inner sense of inadequacy and to ease the pain caused by gnawing self-doubt. Deficient self esteem contributes to imbalance by fueling overwork and fostering an unhealthy tendency to identify our worth with our accomplishments. This temptation to equate our value with our achievements is reinforced by a society that is so oriented to tangible results and performance-based evaluation. When these secular standards are applied in ministry, however, burnout becomes a real danger. Because the results of ministerial toil are often intangible, a sense of uncertainty can plague ministers, causing them to question whether they are actually accomplishing anything at all. This kind of self-doubt can lead to an excessive and exhausting drive to succeed at all costs or to a demoralization that cripples people's capacity for effective ministry.

When we realize that low self-esteem is behind our tendency to over-work and is undermining the balance that we seek, there are two spiritual attitudes that can restore the proper balance between work and leisure. The first is an attitude of self-love. As Christians we are called to believe that it is God's love, not our own achievements, that establishes our worth. To awaken to the insight that God has already established our goodness is to diminish the need to prove ourselves. Those of us who do not feel securely established by God's love struggle to establish ourselves in others' eyes. Ironically, it may be more prayer and less work that we need. Prayer helps us find our identity before God and we discover anew that we are the apple of God's eyes. In prayer, our often shaky psychological identity is strength-ened by our theological identity as God's beloved.

The second attitude that can bring a graceful balance to our lives is trust in God's power working through us as we minister. St. Ignatius of Loyola's "Contemplation for Attaining Divine Love" offers a theological basis for such trust. For Ignatius, we live in a divine milieu because the presence of God pervades all creation. But God not only dwells in all things, God also continues to labor in all creation for our sake. In this final contemplation of his *Spiritual Exercises*, Ignatius asks us "to consider how God works and labors for me in all creatures upon the face of the earth . . . in the heavens, the elements, the plants, the fruits, the cattle. . . . [God] gives being, conserves them, confers life and sensation" (Ignatius of Loyola, *Spiritual Exercises*, #236). Because the mighty power of God is always preserving creation in being, ministers can trust that God is at work when they are at rest!

Ministry, for St. Ignatius, is primarily the action of God. We as human instruments are given a share in God's action through our call to ministry. At La Storta, about ten kilometers from Rome, Ignatius had a vision of himself being placed by the Father next to Jesus carrying the cross. This vision gave shape to his image of ministry: to minister is to be intimately juxtaposed with Jesus carrying the cross. It is to be invited by God to be closely associated with Jesus, who even now continues to work for the redemption of the world. In ministry, then, God is the principal worker and we are co-workers. God's sustaining action will not cease when ministers exercise prudent self-care by taking time off for leisure and solitude.

**Codependency:** The term "codependent" originally referred to persons who were so closely involved with an alcoholic or drug addict that their lives revolved around the addict's behavior. Today the term implies problems with a variety of issues such as setting limits, intimacy skills, and compulsive activity, usually in the form of "helping" others. Symptoms of codependency can appear in our lives, whether or not we are associated with an addict. The literature on codependency suggests personality characteristics that bear a striking resemblance to the caricature of the "good Christian": for example, compulsively putting the needs of others before one's own, an inability to say "no," and an excessive sense of responsibility for the welfare of others. Codependents have a way of getting into others' lives by making themselves needed, and then helping in ways that point to their own generosity and self-sacrifice. Others exists to make the codependent feel needed. Although codependents would be the last to see this dark side of their helpfulness, they relate to others as objects which they use to give themselves a sense of purpose and value. Another aspect of the dark side of the need of codependents to help others is that they do this in a way that makes others dependent on them. Genuine helping, in contrast to codependent helping, is not primarily self-serving but arises out of genuine empathy and compassion. Because it is a response to another's real need for help, not one's own need to be needed, it quietly enables those served to become healthier, more autonomous persons.

Codependents tend to be self-sacrificing, generous, other-directed and idealistic people. Since these are also characteristics of genuine Christian self-transcendence, codependency has often been confused with holiness. What distinguishes codependence from authentic Christian behavior is the compulsive quality of the codependent's relationship with others. For the codependent, giving is a "must" rather than a response of genuine compassion. Codependents do not give freely, they give because they "should." The "giving" of the codependent is often more a flight from self than the dying to self that characterizes true Christian service. Suffering from low self-esteem and feeling unlovable, codependents strive to overcome these painful feelings by proving to others that they are good and therefore worthy of love. In a culture that equates doing good with being good, codependents easily become addicted to helping others, thereby justifying themselves by good works.

Addressing the reality of codependency and how it affects our lives as ministers is a necessary aspect of developing a balanced, holistic spirituality. We must each discern the extent to which we are codependent and the degree to which we have relinquished control of our lives because of an unhealthy need to please others and to satisfy their expectations. People in ministry are constantly dealing with people's expectations. Not only are catechetical leaders often burdened by the diverse expectations of a broad constituency, these expectations are often conflicting. Interest groups in parishes and schools, for instance, may make contradictory demands on ministers. Striving to reconcile all these expectations will inevitably cause emotional strain. If catechetical leaders possess an excessive need to please or rely on the approval of parishioners for their self-esteem, then they will be even more in danger of living with a debilitating imbalance and burnout.

An integrated spirituality challenges us to make our way gracefully between the Scylla of narcissism, resulting from excessive self-concern, and the Charybdis of grandiosity, resulting from too easily dismissing our legitimate needs as human beings. When caring for others is not balanced with caring for self, ministering in a balanced and harmonious way proves impossible.

**Perfectionism:** A detriment to psychological and spiritual health, perfectionism must be clearly distinguished from the healthy pursuit of excellence that motivates many talented people. Appreciating our potential and taking genuine pleasure in striving to meet high standards is healthy. Demanding a higher level of performance than we can obtain smacks of perfectionism. Because our standards are beyond reach or reason when we are caught in the grip of perfectionism, we strain compulsively and relentlessly toward impossible goals and measure our worth in terms of productivity and accomplishment. Never feeling that our efforts are enough, we are unable to achieve a sense of satisfaction because we think that what we do is insufficiently good to warrant that feeling. In contrast, those who take pleasure in doing their best without needing to be perfect tend to be satisfied with their efforts, even when the results leave room for improvement.

When we are driven by a perfectionistic need to be flawless, we often feel anxious, confused, and emotionally drained before a new task is ever begun. We are motivated not so much by desire for improvement as by fear of failure. On the other hand, when we strive for excellence in a healthy way, we are more likely to feel excited, energized, and clear about what needs to be done. In general, the normal quest for excellence is growthful for us as individuals and benefits our ministry as a whole, whereas the compulsive drive for perfection easily leads to burnout in ministry. As catechetical leaders, we need to care passionately about doing things well, but we also need to know how to be gentle with ourselves when we fall short.

Striving for perfection, when it drives us to overwork and results in chronic fatigue, gets in the way of effective ministry. Ironically, when we strain to do everything perfectly, we undermine ourselves in several ways. First, severe and continual pressure leads to exhaustion, distaste for our work, and eventually to poor performance. To improve effectiveness, we who find ourselves working compulsively are challenged not to care less passionately about our work, but to relax our efforts and to be gently accepting of our limits in regards to time, talent, and energy. Second, perfectionistic tendencies impede our ability to collaborate with others in catechetical ministry. Already tired and cramped for time, we find that meetings, an essential component of collaboration, become a nuisance and collaborating with others undesirable. Furthermore, the need to have everything done perfectly makes us reluctant to delegate, because others may not meet our standards. This inability to trust others may isolate us so that we eventually operate as lone rangers rather than as collaborators. Finally, our perfectionism as catechetical leaders can have a negative impact on others when, like the Pharisees, we lay heavy burdens on those with whom we work. When our drive for perfection is externalized and imposed on others, we can end up putting unrealistic expectations on colleagues. If our coworkers are already perfection-prone and themselves given to overwork, what they need is not reinforcement of their compulsion, but help in understanding their limitations and accepting their humanity.

A self-absorbing pursuit of perfection has at times been fostered by a commonly misunderstood and misused exhortation of Jesus that as Christians we should "Be perfect as your heavenly Father is perfect" (Matt 5:48). Taken out of context, this passage has served as the basis on which Christians were urged to strive for individualistic moral perfection, to be flawless in thoughts, words, and deeds. Fear, hypocrisy, and legalism have resulted from the misconception that to be true followers of Christ required flawlessly embodying the perfection of God. Perfection, defined as being errorless, is a human impossibility. Yet, it has masqueraded for centuries as the nature of true Christian sanctity. When this biblical injunction is understood in context, a very different image of "Christian perfection" emerges.

This oft-quoted biblical exhortation is taken from Matthew's sermon on the mount. It is immediately preceded by a description of God, who "makes the sun rise on the evil and the good" (5:45) and castigates those who love only people who love them back. Thus, the context indicates that Jesus exhorts his followers to imitate God by loving indiscriminately. In other words, we are called to imitate God's all-embracing and inclusive love, a love that causes God to let the sun rise on the bad as well as the good and to allow the rain to fall on the upright and the wicked alike. Thus, this scriptural passage is not advocating the pursuit of perfection as a striving for individual moral perfection, but rather a lifelong stretching of our capacity to love as God does.

The Greek word used by Matthew that is translated "perfect" is the term *teleios*. According to exegetes, a thing is *teleios* if it realizes the purpose for which it was planned or created. Matthew 5:48 makes clear that Christian holiness consists in being Godlike; and the one thing that makes us like God is an unconditional love that indiscriminately embraces all people, no matter what they do.

In general, perfectionism is an obstacle to spiritual growth. By making us obsessed with being faultless and avoiding mistakes, perfectionism can so consume our attention and energy that we become narrowly focused on ourselves. Like a whirlpool, perfectionism can suck one into a hole of self-preoccupation. On the other hand, when our focus is kept on the ongoing development of our capacity to love God, others, and self—as outlined above in the holistic model based on gospel loves—the danger of self-absorption is minimized and our energies can be channeled into service.

## The Art of Loving:  A Life-Long Process

We are called to love God with our whole heart, soul, mind, and strength—with our whole being—and our neighbor as ourselves. We are called to do this as well as we can at each moment of our lives. To be holistic, our striving to unify the loves that make up a gospel spirituality must be characterized by several things.

First, it should be developmental. A developmental understanding views growth as a gradual process that should not run counter to either our human readiness to advance to the next stage or the rhythms of God's grace. Running ahead of ourselves or grace is not spiritually fruitful. A developmental approach reminds us that the process of growth is ongoing, with the dimensions of our struggle shifting with age and time. Because spiritual growth requires time, we need gentleness, patience and perseverance.

Second, it should be experiential. An experiential approach to spiritual growth allows for trial and error and leaves room for mistakes. The concrete balancing of love that Christians are called to possess is a complex matter. It cannot be resolved ahead of time by the abstract intellect alone. It requires learning by doing, and more often than not relies on an intuitive sense of what is right for a particular occasion or time. Thus, a holistic approach values the importance of harmonizing the head and the heart in learning and living.

Third, it should be integrative. A holistic spirituality is concerned with unified growth that does not develop the spirit and the mind while neglecting the body and the emotions, and vice versa. Neither does it cultivate independence at the expense of community nor group life to the detriment of individuality. A holistic approach to spiritual growth respects the body-spirit unity of the person at work, prayer, and in relationships.

Fourth, it should be transformational. A holistic approach to living out gospel loves aims for ongoing conversion of personal and social life. Growth entails continual change, not only in our thoughts, but also in our attitudes, feelings, values and behaviors. Holistic prayer, for example, is not effective if it does not make us become more responsibly Christian in our lives of work and love, prayer and politics, sexuality and social service. Based on gospel values, the understanding of Christian spirituality presented here is holistic in its concern for wholeness and balance. It encourages all of us—the *"saints and the ain'ts"*—to give each love its proper due and at the same time it challenges us to strike the right balance as we try to love as Jesus did in the nitty-gritty details of our daily lives as catechists.

## Questions for Reflection

- What are you taking away from this essay that is most valuable for your spiritual journey as a catechetical leader?
- What have you learned that may help you in mentoring the spiritual growth of other catechists in your care? Is there a decision emerging regarding your own spirituality? A next step in your spiritual journey?

## Bibiography

Au, Wilkie. *By Way of the Heart: Toward a Holistic Christian Spirituality.* Mahwah, NJ: Paulist Press, 1989.

Au, Wilkie and Noreen Cannon. *Urgings of the Heart: A Spirituality of Integration.* Mahwah, NJ: Paulist Press, 1995.

Borg, Marcus. *Meeting Jesus Again for the First Time: The Historical Jesus and the Heart of Contemporary Faith.* San Francisco, CA: HarperSanFrancisco, 1995.

Chittister, Joan. *Wisdom Distilled from the Daily: Living the Rule of St. Benedict Today.* San Francisco, CA: HarperSanFrancisco, 1990.

Hughes, Gerard. *God of Surprises.* Boston, MA: Cowley Publications, 1993.

Nouwen, Henri. *Reaching Out: The Three Movements of the Spiritual Life.* Garden City, NY: Doubleday & Company, 1975.

Svoboda, Melannie. *Traits of a Healthy Spirituality.* Mystic, CT: Twenty-Third Publications, 1996.

# THE
# REALITIES
# OF CATECHESIS

## PART THREE

# 7
# Qualities and Competencies
# of the Catechetical Leader
### Fran Ferder

It is dawn and the first snow of the season is softly embracing the campus at the University of Notre Dame. We stand in silence in front of the metal sculpture that draws us back again and again, each time our speaking schedule brings us to this place. Created by the artist Ivan Mestrovic, the sculpture is located at the end of the main quadrangle. It is an image, larger than life, of the Samaritan woman at the well conversing with Jesus.

Sometimes we look from a distance, commenting on the gentle intensity depicted in their interaction. On other occasions, we stand close enough to touch the reflective tilt of her head or the casual angle of his leg as it rests on the edge of the well. Each season seems to have its own way of transporting these two figures from another millennium into our own time. On a muggy moonlit night, when our only other companions are fireflies, it is almost possible to hear the voices of Jesus and the unnamed Samaritan woman as they talk in the semi-darkness.

But on this day, as the early morning light and snowflakes mingle, our attention is drawn to their faces. They seem more flesh than metal. There is a palpable energy in the frosty air around them. It is as though they have been here for 2000 years of nights, talking, listening, seeking, truth telling; so much so that the expression of countless seasons of intimacy has been molded into their faces.

## From Sculpture to Scripture

What does a metal sculpture on a Midwestern campus have to do with catechetical leadership? It proclaims the Gospel. It invites us to look beyond its metal outlines to a story— a story of the woman who is sometimes called the Bible's first catechist or first preacher. It offers us an image of a person who met Jesus, who came to believe in him, and felt called to tell others about his message. Ultimately, the sculpture reminds us that for Christians, all spiritual leadership begins with a personal relationship with Jesus. Like the Samaritan woman at the well, the effective catechetical leader is a person who has had a life transforming experience of God and is called to share God's message with others.

## Questions for Reflection

- Read the story of the Samaritan Woman (John 4:7-27). If you could place yourself in this setting, what questions would you want to ask Jesus? What would you want to ask the Samaritan woman?
- What adjectives would you use to describe the Samaritan woman? Which of them do you associate with catechetical leadership?
- Which of these qualities can you identify in yourself?

## A Woman, A Well, and the Word

Jesus and his disciples were returning to Galilee from Judea where the Pharisees were becoming increasingly hostile to Jesus. It would have been a journey involving no little distress. To complicate matters, they had to pass through Samaria, a country populated by people the Jews considered apostates. Jesus was tired. He sat down to rest by a well while his disciples went to the village to buy food. A woman came to draw water and Jesus asked her for a drink. It seemed a simple expression of need by a tired and thirsty traveler. But these were two people from vastly different worlds who normally would not have spoken to each other. She was a Samaritan. He was a Jew. She was a woman. He was a man, a rabbi. It was an unlikely occasion for a religious experience for many reasons:

Theological tensions among Jews and Samaritans were strong. Jews held the Samaritans in contempt and took great pains to avoid interacting with them. Respectful religious dialogue was not only difficult but forbidden. Gender inequities were deeply imbedded in the religious beliefs and cultural practices of the day. Jewish men did not speak to women in public. For a rabbi to do so would have been a great source of scandal to many. Fatigue, hunger, and involvement with other concerns would have further inhibited any meaningful conversation between Jesus and the Samaritan woman.

Still, these two people who chanced to meet at a well gradually transcended the barriers of religious tension, gender difference, cultural conditioning, and human limitation to engage in an interaction so profound that it continues to be a model for religious dialogue and human conversion some 2000 years later.

Although this Gospel story has been with us for nearly two millennia, the challenges faced by Jesus and the Samaritan woman parallel many of those faced by catechetical leaders, catechists, and learners today. Variations in theological perspective, different understandings of the roles of women and men, misunderstandings rooted in culture, and an exhausting list of personal distractions can pose tremendous challenges for contemporary catechetical leaders and those who wish to learn more about their Catholic faith. How did Jesus handle these tensions? What were his priorities as he encountered the inevitable obstacles to faith development present at any time in human history?

## Give Me A Drink:  Jesus, Initiator of Relationship

If we look beyond the individual encounters Jesus has with people in the Gospel stories and reflect instead on their collective significance, a clear pattern begins to emerge. Jesus centers his message in the context of relationship. He is constantly initiating interactions with others, and, we should note, this was most unusual for a teacher in his culture. He is seeking connections. He is offering the possibility of conversation, particularly with those who were the most excluded by the religious practices of his day. He places himself in the classroom of people's lives—weddings, funerals, cornfields, dinner parties, hillside gatherings, in the shadow of sycamore trees, and on the shores of a lake after a fishing trip. Often, having conversations with people seems, at least initially, to overshadow his interest in formally teaching them anything. He appears to know that communication elicits relationship. Relationship precedes conversion. Such is the case with the Samaritan woman at the well. It is this reality that forms the basic context out of which his teaching ministry emerges.

A profound commitment to relationships is visible not only in his teaching style, this same involvement in relationships also defines Jesus in terms of his personal style as a minister. From the very beginning, he chose not to "go it alone." Before Jesus healed a leper or cast out a demon, before he told a parable or multiplied loaves, he began to form a community of women and men around him. It is a simple fact that we dare not take for granted: The one whom Christianity claims as Lord and brother chose not to be a "solo savior," but entered deeply into the mystery of relationships and community himself.

This does not mean that he avoided solitude. Nor does it suggest that he did not encounter times of profound loneliness. The Gospel stories tell us that he frequently sought out times of solitude and prayer. But he never chose a pathway of isolation. Jesus was not a "spiritual lone ranger," who appeared mysteriously on the horizon of human history, and told people what they ought to believe and then disappeared.

Jesus' teaching style was solidly rooted in the reality of God's relationship with human persons. Much of the actual content of his teaching concerned the way in which people ought to live in their relationships with one another: "I give you a new commandment, that you love one another. Just as I have loved you, you also should love one another" (John 13:34). This ability to live in loving relationships was so important to the mission and message of Jesus that it was held up as the central identification mark of his followers: "By this everyone will know that you are my disciples, if you have love for one another" (John 13:35).

When the religious leaders of Israel voiced their dismay at his seeming neglect of some of the traditional practices of his Jewish faith, Jesus drew a connection between fidelity to the Law and fidelity to human relationships: "Do not think that I have come to abolish the Law or the prophets;" he told them, "I have come not to abolish but to fulfill" (Matt 5:17). Clearly, Jesus saw the ultimate fulfillment of the Law as profoundly connected to maintaining loving relationships with one's brothers and sisters.

What exactly does Jesus mean when speaking of bringing the Law to fulfillment? Or, to ask the same question from the perspective of today's catechetical leader, toward what end is our living and our teaching directed? On the one hand, it appears that Jesus wanted to return the Torah to its roots in the covenant between Israel and Yahweh, to re-ground it in its primordial setting of a loving relationship among the people and between the people and their God. The Gospels portray him as strongly opposing the practice of Pharisees who emphasized fidelity to every detail of the Law, sometimes at the expense of people. On the other hand, Jesus saw himself as completing the earlier covenant through his intimate relationship with the Abba-God of his life. Jesus experienced himself as "the beloved one of God." He, in turn, invited others to experience and affirm that same covenantal relationship of love in their lives. The *General Directory for Catechesis* (1997) affirms this when it describes the "very end of catechesis" as putting "the human person in communion with Jesus Christ" (#116). If this is the ultimate end of catechesis, how do we accomplish it as catechetical leaders? What qualities and competencies do we need to assist people in their search to experience communion with Jesus?

## Where Do You Get That Living Water?
## Sources of Catechetical Leadership

In considering the qualities and competencies of the catechetical leader, we must start where Jesus started. Jesus is the Master Catechist. Both our personal rootedness and our ultimate hope for others must be in relationships, on a personal relationship with a loving God, and on our lived relationships with one another as women and men who follow "the Way" of Jesus Christ. We derive the credibility, the energy, and the call to serve others in ministry from the grace and wholeness of these relationships in our own lives.  Like the Samaritan woman, we must meet Jesus at the well of our own lives even as we attempt to proclaim his message to others.  And, like her, we must tell the true story of our own journey to the God who already knows our pain and struggle, and offers us the possibility of healing.

Out of this process, genuine catechetical leadership receives its initial call.  Catechetical leadership is a vocation in the Church, a call from the Holy Spirit to serve the people of God through the ministry of sharing and nurturing the faith.  This call flows from the mandate given by Jesus to his followers to "make disciples and teach all peoples" (Matt 28:19), to "be my witnesses" (Acts 1:8), "baptize" (Matt 28:19), "do this in memory of me" (Luke 22:19).  As such, catechetical leadership is more than "a job" and must flow from one's own rootedness in God and relationship with Jesus.  The catechist must first be in touch with the "living water" of faith in his or her own life.  This presupposes a solid and consistent prayer life, one rooted in a contemporary understanding of Scripture, regular participation in the liturgical and sacramental life of the Church, and a healthy ability to move the vision of Christianity into the everyday places of one's life and relationships.

It is not, in the first place, a theological degree or a catechist training certificate that qualifies one to be a catechetical leader.  Thorough preparation, suited to one's catechetical responsibilities, is both necessary and vital to effective catechesis.  But it is not enough!  The kind of catechetical leader that enables others to experience communion with Jesus Christ is one who has such experiences of communion in his or her own life.

Imagine the following possibilities:  Jerry has a Master's degree in religious education and eleven years of experience in catechetical leadership in three different parish communities.  He can recite the Creed by heart, has committed to memory all the dogmas of the Church, knows the new Catechism well, and is able to lecture without notes on most of the official teachings of the Church.  At the same time, working with him is difficult for other staff members because of his controlling, abrasive style.  When things do not go his way, he resorts to verbal tirades, or withdraws in cold silence.  Although Jerry stresses the importance of personal prayer in his catechetical work, he rarely finds time for prayer in his own life.  It is difficult for him to enter fully into the worship experiences in the parish where he ministers because he is so often distracted by liturgical details and stressed about the perfect execution of the rituals he directs.

Susan became a catechetical leader by being a promoted volunteer.  She has very little background in theology, and no plans for future education.  She has taught in the religious education program for nearly twenty years.  She does not see the need to prepare as she considers religious education to be largely a matter of the heart and of telling people that God loves them. Susan loves all the participants in her program and feels that is enough. Although she occasionally uses a text, her classes are unstructured and focus primarily on the need to love one another. Hers is a very "touchy-feely" approach to religious education. Many on the staff appreciate her great love for others, but worry that the program she oversees in heavy on "fluff" and light on "stuff."

Teresa is a third catechetical leader. Although she is qualified to hold a position as Director of Sacramental Preparation in a large parish community, she is less experienced than Jerry, and is still completing her education. She has to spend extra time in preparation for the classes she teaches and continues to rely heavily on various outside resources as she undertakes her ministry responsibilities. Teresa is known among other staff members as a kind and prayerful person who takes her own spiritual growth seriously. She is someone others can readily turn to for understanding and help when they need it. Although she is careful about planning and preparation for sacramental functions, Teresa is most concerned about making these events prayerful experiences in the faith life of the community.

While Jerry might have more intellectual knowledge about the content of his Catholic faith than does Teresa, his ability to facilitate actual experiences of the Holy among those to whom he ministers is severely limited. Having knowledge about the Catholic faith is not synonymous with having a personal relationship with the living God. The ability to quote from a catechetical source by memory does not replace a prayer life. Teaching with eloquence about the Great Commandment does not release one from taking its practice seriously in one's own life.

While Susan may have great love for her students, this does not excuse her from the responsibility of updating herself theologically. There is a duty, not only to care for the participants and reveal God's love to them, but also to mediate God's revelation in Scripture and tradition in an intelligible and meaningful way. A holistic approach to religious education involves the head as well as the heart and the hands. In sum, catechetical leaders need to both know and live the gospel of Christian faith.

While the basic truths of the Catholic faith do not change just because a catechetical leader is difficult to work with or unable to articulate them intelligently, and the teachings of Scripture and tradition do not rise or fall according to the ability of the catechist to implement them in his or her own life, the person of the catechetical leader does have a profound impact on the health of the faith community. Often, the personal holiness and wholeness of the catechetical leader can help transform a faith community from one that "goes through the motions" of its religious obligations into one that is an alive and vibrant witness of the faith it professes to believe. Such a transformation presupposes that the catechetical leader is constantly striving to stay in touch with the living water of faith in his or her own life. This enables one to inspire others as well as educate them. Such inspiration is connected to the ultimate goal of catechesis—to stir hearts and move people to communion with Jesus Christ.

Grounding in a solid personal faith life requires ongoing nourishment. Making prayer a priority in one's life can be difficult in a world where so many demands are made on our time. Let us say, for example, that it is my turn to run the carpool for soccer practice. An aging parent needs my help cleaning the house. A friend's daughter is in the hospital. The children need help with their homework. The baby is sick. So is the baby-sitter. Groceries. Laundry. When the pressure is on it is easy to put personal prayer off "until tomorrow." Yet, creating time for solitude with God is as important to our spiritual wholeness as eating is to our physical wholeness. Most of us would not postpone eating "until tomorrow." The resultant hunger pangs or weakness would remind us that it is time to refuel our bodies. Is it possible that a different type of "hunger pang" is trying to get our attention when we neglect time for prayer? St. Augustine spoke of our hearts being restless until they find ultimate rest in God. Perhaps some of the restlessness that is almost epidemic today is symptomatic of the soul's starvation, a kind of spiritual hunger pang that occurs when the nourishment of prayer and solitude has been neglected.

Where do you get that living water? Where and how does the busy catechetical leader nourish his or her hunger and that of catechists? Perhaps some of the following practical suggestions might be helpful:

a) Make an appointment for prayer. Write it in your calendar and honor the time you set just as you would an appointment for an important meeting.

b) Select the days and the time each week when you are most able to keep the prayer schedule you set. Make sure the schedule you create is possible. Even fifteen minutes to reflect on the scripture readings for the day, or to sit in quiet solitude can be a vital lifeline to the "living waters."

c) Choose a "sacred place," a quiet setting where you are most apt to experience an environment conducive to reflection. It can be as simple as a pillow on the floor in the corner of a bedroom, or a chair by a quiet window. Some people find that their prayer time is facilitated by lighting a candle reserved only for this purpose.

d) Try to develop an attitude of prayer throughout the day. Let creation remind you of the God of the universe: Leaves falling. The sun low on the horizon in winter. The first hints of a spring thaw. A river. A mountain. A child riding a bicycle. An old man crossing the street with a cane. Even a phone call from a distraught parishioner can put us in touch with the Holy if we receive it with awareness.

e) If possible, find a good spiritual director and meet regularly.

f) Make use of opportunities for spiritual growth through participation in the liturgy and sacraments, attendance at religious education workshops, spiritual reading and retreats.

g) Try to create opportunities for regular prayer time and faith sharing with staff members where you work as a catechetical leader. This also helps build community among team members.

h) Talk to deceased friends and relatives who are part of the communion of saints. Catholics trust that companions on the journey of faith include all those disciples of Jesus Christ living and dead. Take time to recognize their continued presence in your life.

i) Talk to God in the "spare" moments. Make use of the informal transition times of the day to enter into these kinds of conscious contacts: Walking to the car. Pushing the grocery cart. Showering. Washing dishes. Waiting in line for the light to turn green. We believe that God is always present to us. Often, simply reminding ourselves of that reality can put us in touch with a transforming experience of the sacred. A simple trip to a well to draw water enabled the Samaritan woman to have an experience of God that changed her life. For her, an ordinary household task was transformed into an encounter with the Holy when she opened herself to receiving a thirsty stranger.

While the initial call to catechetical leadership is rooted in the Holy Spirit and in one's personal relationship with God, the exercise of all ministries in the Church depends upon a call from the community. No single individual, no matter how strongly he or she might feel called to minister in the Church, can self-appoint to a position of ministry. The call heard by the person must be presented to the Church community for verification and affirmation. For the catechetical leader, this call usually comes through the local parish, mediated by the pastor or pastoral leader. The local parish should have a process whereby qualified persons have their call to catechetical leadership tested either through a formal application or informal invitation process. Using professional language, a legal contract has also been enacted once a person is hired or chosen as a catechetical leader. Using the language of faith, we would say that the person selected has experienced a call from the Holy Spirit to serve in the ministry of catechetical leadership after having one's call examined and affirmed by a local community.

## Questions for Reflection
- What are the sources of living water in your life? What "well-springs" have you created for your catechetical team?
- What resources exist in your parish or school to help the catechetical team balance the spiritual, emotional, and intellectual dimensions of faith?

## I See You Are A Prophet:  Personal Qualities of the Catechetical Leader

Jesus was simply sitting by a well. He wore no trappings of honor. He did not hold himself above others. His was a quiet kind of leadership, one born of living in communion with Abba—God. He did not come to scold or correct, not even a woman who had been with five different husbands. Instead, he took her seriously. As they talked, he recognized truth and goodness in her. Jesus told her about the living water. It was revelation of the deepest kind, tapping into her profound thirst and awakened in her a desire for more. She saw in Jesus a prophet.

"Sir, I see that you are a prophet" (John 4:19). What did she mean? How was Jesus a prophet? How did he exercise prophetic leadership? In a world that often still identifies political and religious power as the capacity to coerce others into servility, Jesus offers an alternate way of human leadership. He rejects any form of authority that exploits or demeans people by treating them as anything less than persons—made in God's own image and likeness. Instead he calls his followers to become "servant-leaders" who reject the usual displays of position and privilege.

This aspect of Jesus' teaching was apparently one of the most difficult for the first disciples to understand or accept. It contradicted much of what their dominant culture had taught them about the ordering of society and religious institutions. It stood contrast to their expectations of how a messiah would participate in any political, priestly, or prophetic restoration of Israel.

In a scene all three Synoptics record (Mark 10:42-45; Matt 20:25-28; Luke 22:25-27), Jesus confronts the disciples' misunderstanding and shares his radical vision of leadership. The disciples have been arguing about who will hold the places of honor in the coming Kingdom. The response of Jesus varies slightly in each of the evangelists, but the underlying message is the same: Leadership is loving service, not the quest for dominating power. Over the centuries the argument that broke out among the original disciples has erupted again and again with predictable regularity. To the present time, the response to this argument has never changed: "The kings of the Gentiles lord it over them; and those in authority over them are called benefactors. But not so with you; rather the greatest among you must become like the youngest, and the leader like one who serves" (Luke 22:25-26).

Catechetical leaders are called to be contemporary prophets; persons whose power is expressed in loving service. We have already reflected on the importance of this service flowing from and being rooted in a personal relationship with a loving God, a relationship that is nourished by prayer and fed through regular participation in liturgical and sacramental experience. But what about some of the other qualities and competencies that enable effective catechetical leadership? After all, one can be a very prayerful and holy person, and not have other qualities and competencies for professional Church ministry.

For example, Louise is a genuinely religious person, in the best sense of that word. She has taken her spiritual growth seriously all of her life. She is prayerful, kind and generous. But Louise is a very shy woman who is not comfortable speaking in front of others, something a catechetical leader must be able to do with some degree of comfort.

Arthur is another example of a very sincere man who knows the content of Catholic faith well and is regarded as a man of justice and personal goodness. However, Arthur works best by himself and tends to become quite anxious when faced with the responsibility of group interaction. His anxiety is sometimes expressed by uncritically accepting the suggestions and opinions of others. Since catechetical leaders must work well in a team or on a staff, Arthur would be at a disadvantage in such a position, and so would his team!

Finally, there is Maria. Like Louise and Arthur, Maria is a prayerful woman who is knowledgeable in Catholic faith. Unfortunately, Maria's personal style tends to be authoritarian. She believes that people, young and old alike, will be compliant in practicing their faith if they are told what to believe and do with sufficient persuasion. A preference for literal interpretation of the rules makes Maria impatient with questions and not very tolerant of differences. Maria might help form very obedient Christians, but we would not likely find her sitting by a well speaking with reverent respect to a woman who had been divorced many times. And for someone "caught in adultery," Maria would have quite a struggle not to be among those throwing the stones.

We are now talking about some of the other qualities and competencies that are essential if one is to be the kind of catechetical leader who truly builds up the Christian community. It is not enough to know the teachings of the Catholic faith. It is not enough to be a good and sincere person. Nor is it enough to want very much to be a catechetical leader and to perceive in oneself a vocation to this ministry. Coupled with knowledge about one's faith must be a reasonable capacity to put it into practice in one's interpersonal relationships with others. There must also be a call from the church community which, with the catechetical leader, discerns the gifts necessary to fulfill that call. What are some of these gifts?

At the outset, we want to distinguish between a quality and a competency. Qualities are those internal dispositions of the heart that are a relatively stable part of the personality. Although a person can strive to attain certain qualities, many seem either inborn or formed very early in life in response to the environment. At other times, certain qualities appear to develop in an individual in response to particular life circumstances, or as a result of a powerful personal transformation or conversion experience. Qualities can be positive, negative, or neutral in terms of their helpfulness to the individual and their impact on others. Personality qualities are often used when we describe our experience of people: "He is really callous." "She is very sensitive to others." "They were so shy." "Both of them have a wonderful sense of humor!" These descriptions refer to just a few of the many qualities that might be used to characterize persons.

Competencies, on the other hand, are usually the result of specific education, training, practice, or innate ability. Often, competencies can be learned through hard work and experience. They are the skills an individual has in a particular area. They are the things we are good at doing. Put another way, qualities reflect the stance of the heart; competencies are a learned art. Examples of competencies include such things as public speaking, working with tools, riding a bike, or organizing a project. Sometimes, the line between a quality and a competency is not very clear, and sometimes a particular trait might be both. For example, being a good listener is usually regarded as a quality. Some people are just naturally good listeners. Still, most of us can develop greater competency in listening if we work at it.

In applying these terms to catechetical leadership, it is important to emphasize that some people are more naturally gifted for this ministry than are others. They possess many of the qualities that are associated with building and deepening community and inspiring others, qualities that cannot always be learned. While one can become competent in doctrine or correct teaching methods by obtaining a degree in religious studies, there is no academic program which can produce the quality of compassion in one strongly inclined to be judgmental. Nor can education alone change an abrasive personal style into a warm and caring one.

What are some of the personal qualities, those stances of the heart, that are associated with effective catechetical leadership? The following list is not meant to be exhaustive, but will serve as a starting place for discussion. Keep in mind that none of us will embody these qualities perfectly, and we do not need to in order to be effective catechists. But we do need to be people who possess some dimension of the following qualities, and are taking seriously the call to grow in each of these areas:

- Prayerful
- Respectful of the dignity of all people
- Compassionate
- Genuine—in the sense of integral
- Affectively engaged and connected
- Self-aware—having a realistic appraisal of one's gifts and limitations
- Truthful
- Centered
- Conscious of personal and interpersonal boundaries
- Committed to justice

**Prayerful:** Although already discussed above, prayerfulness is listed here along with other qualities of catechetical leadership because of its central importance to any ministry in the Church. The catechist who maintains a regular prayer life will be in touch with an energy source needed to be authentic as a minister and teacher of the Catholic faith. Being a person of prayer means practicing what one is teaching. It does not presuppose that one has achieved perfection in the spiritual life. It simply means trying to be present to the Holy in whatever way feels most true to one's personal prayer style. What is your preferred style of personal prayer? Why?

**Respectful of the dignity of all people:** Every human being is a son or daughter of God. As such, each one is an icon of the divine, an image of God their creator. Respecting some people is easy. They treat others well and act in ways that seem deserving of our respect. With others, it may be more difficult. This is when we are really challenged to remind ourselves of the sacred origins and destiny of the person. Respect for the dignity of others is manifested in ordinary acts of kindness, in trusting in their capacity for growth, and avoiding judgmental or negative attitudes. This does not mean that we should allow ourselves to be mistreated. Masochism is not a virtue! Someone once said that respect for the dignity of persons sometimes involves not allowing them to be less than they can be. Psychologists call this "tough love." For the catechist, it involves practicing the kind of inclusive love that Jesus practiced—inviting everyone to the table.

Respecting the dignity of people sometimes stretches us beyond our comfort levels, especially when dealing with those who are different than we are or who have ideas or values that are at variance with our own.

Identify some people or groups of people that fit in this category for you. What does it mean for you to honor their dignity? What are the actual behaviors of respect that you would hope to display toward those who are "other" in your life?

**Compassionate:** In Hebrew, the word "compassion" literally means "to have womb feelings" for someone. It involves tender care, doing whatever one can to facilitate the well-being of another. In his Gospel, the evangelist Matthew gives this familiar admonition: "Be perfect, therefore, as your heavenly Father is perfect" (Matt 5:48). In Luke's Gospel, however, this same admonition is given a different emphasis: "Be compassionate as your Father is compassionate" (Luke 6:36; JB). Being compassionate, having genuine mercy toward one another, is a Gospel mandate. Even in Matthew's version, the Greek word for "perfect" refers not to the avoidance of mistakes, but to the ultimate destiny of union with God—our life-long journey.

Notice that the Gospel writers do not say, "you must be correct" or "you must be right." For the disciple of Jesus, the Gospels suggest that it is more important to experience compassion toward one's brothers and sisters than it is to have the right answers to all of the questions of life. Ultimately, the test of the authenticity of one's commitment to Christianity is not so much the number of correct responses produced on a religion test, or the amount of material memorized from a catechism. Ultimately, the primary criterion of Christian discipleship is the love and compassion experienced and expressed toward all of God's sons and daughters.

The catechist does need to be concerned about teaching the content of the Catholic faith. But, when producing the right answers becomes more important than how one's neighbor is treated, genuine religion has become distorted and faith has been reduced to an intellectual commodity rather than a lived response of the heart to God.

## What Might Be Some Examples of Compassion at Work in the Classroom?

**Genuine:** Being genuine simply means being real. People who are genuine are not concerned about impressing others, competing with them, or being considered more virtuous, more important, or more knowledgeable than they actually are. Genuine persons are comfortable and at home with themselves. They are consistent in words, behaviors, and attitudes. Others do not have to worry that such a person will say one thing to them, and later say the opposite to someone else. They have personal integrity. Most of us can tell when we are in the presence of people who are genuine and integral. We are more apt to feel relaxed with them, and more at home ourselves. By contrast, we tend to be uneasy around those who seem to lack genuineness. We experience them as "phony" and insincere. It is difficult to experience trust with someone who does not appear to be authentic. People who are being true to themselves have a self-confidence that is calming. They are not afraid to admit mistakes and they can apologize when they have hurt or offended someone. Genuineness is so highly related to healthy human relationships that it is considered one of the primary qualities of good mental health.

How do you think the quality of genuineness in the religious educator might be nurtured? How might it impact one's ministry or catechesis?

**Affectively engaged:** The word "affect" means feeling. It refers to the ways we experience and express our emotions. The person who is "affectively engaged" is in touch with his or her feelings. Feelings are various subjective energy states designed by God to help orient us to our internal and external surroundings. They are meant to be guideposts for our behavior. For example, if I feel anger, that tells me that I have a need that is being thwarted. It is important that I allow the anger to help me identify the need, examine it, and choose a course of action that is helpful to me and respectful to those around me. Anger is sometimes called the "energy of protection."

If I feel joy in response to a particular behavior or relationship, I can be fairly confident that what I am involved in is good for me and for those around me. Joy is the "energy of sacred pleasure." Although different cultures place different emphasis on when, how, and with whom feelings can be expressed, the ability to do so appropriately is another primary indicator of good mental health. The inability to do so suggests a lack of full human development and in the extreme may indicate a serious mental disorder.

We can have a good indication that our level of affective engagement is healthy by looking at our relationships. Expressing feelings in a healthy manner promotes good relationships with others and deepens intimacy. It is usually harder to get along with people who hide their feelings, act them out inappropriately, or don't seem to be able to talk about them.

What messages did you receive in your family of origin about expressing your feelings? How have these messages helped or hindered your relationships? your ministry?

**Self-aware:** Self-awareness is not the same as genuineness, but is closely associated with it. Self-aware people have a realistic appraisal of their gifts and limitations. (Genuineness involves acting in accord with this awareness.) Persons who are self aware know themselves well. In addition, their perception of themselves is congruent with how most others see and experience them. Self-aware persons have a good ability to pick up cues in the environment, cues which help them know how their behavior is impacting others. This ability to perceive tells them when their words or actions are being received and when they are not.

This is a very important quality because it enables us to know when to make important adjustments in our behavior in order to enhance our interpersonal relationships. For example, if a highly self-aware person is talking to a group, and notices that people in the group are beginning to look out the window and yawn, he or she will be aware of this and make the necessary accommodations, such as taking a break or shortening the presentation. A less self-aware person might not notice or try to interpret the group's reaction and keep on talking.

Reflect on the difference that self-aware and less self-aware persons have on a religious education environment, on a parish, or school community.

**Truthful:**  We all know what it means to tell the truth. However, the quality of truthfulness in a person goes beyond simply avoiding lies. Truthful persons are in touch with the inner truth of wisdom and they try to live it. They have a depth of understanding and an ability to convey it that honors the deepest reality in a relationship or a situation. They can be counted upon to manifest integrity in their dealings with people. We are all familiar with the phrase from John's Gospel, "The truth shall set you free" (John 8:32). Truthful people know this reality from experience. They have the inner freedom that comes from living an uncomplicated and authentic life.

Truthful persons are honest in their use of language. They do not use words to manipulate or confuse others. Rather, they are verbally clear when they speak. The phrase, "what you see is what you get" is sometimes used to describe persons who have the inner quality of truthfulness.

How might using gender inclusive language be an example of truthfulness?  of compassion?

**Centered:**  The centered person is steady and not easily shaken. Regardless of the level of turmoil around them, centered people seem able to maintain their inner balance. They keep things in perspective and are inclined neither to catastrophize situations nor minimize them. Centered people tend to get things done because they are not distracted by unimportant events around them. They have a sense of purpose and balance that guides them from the inside.

This inner directedness makes them less bothered by external pressures, changes, and unexpected events. They do not depend on external affirmation to guide their decisions and actions. At the same time, they are flexible enough to change when change is needed. The quality of centeredness that facilitates catechetical leadership is rooted in prayer, in relationship with the God who is always present.

When and how frequently do you experience this kind of centeredness in your life?

**Conscious of personal and interpersonal boundaries:** One aspect of ministry we are hearing more about today is that of boundaries. Maintaining appropriate boundaries, and making sure the vulnerable are safe when in our care, should be a "given" for those who serve in ministry. Yet, reports of sexual abuse and malpractice by clergy and other ministers have made it abundantly clear that maintaining appropriate boundaries cannot be assumed, even among those who have committed themselves to serve the Gospel. Some ministers appear to have been unaware that all ministries in the Church confer some degree of power on the minister. Power involves the capacity to influence others. Depending on the psychological and emotional health of the individual minister, that power can be used to enable great growth and creativity, or it can cause immense pain.

Whenever I use my power to make myself more comfortable at the expense of those I am to serve, I am abusing my ministry power. Leaders can help people or abuse people by the way they exercise the power inherent in their role. Being given power as a minister involves a sacred trust, one that must be handled with great care and awareness. While it might seem obvious, it needs to be emphasized that it is always a violation of power if a person in a position of catechetical leadership becomes sexually or romantically involved with someone he or she is serving in the capacity of minister. Mary Angela Shaugnessy's article on the Practicalities of Catechesis summarizes the legal issues involved in this matter.

There are other types of power violations that are not sexually abusive, but may be very hurtful to others. Interrupting people who are speaking, taking over or re-doing things that others have done without consideration of their feelings, monopolizing conversations, being passive-aggressive, controlling behaviors, and having a "bossy" manner are all examples of power abuse.

How conscious are you of the ways you use power? Can you give some examples of ways that a catechetical leader might abuse his or her power?

**Committed to justice:** The Prophetic books of the Hebrew Scriptures give central emphasis that the people of God must live justly and promote justice for all. Many of the Gospel stories are about Jesus reaching out to the poor, the disenfranchised, the outcast. Theologians and scripture scholars often speak of this as the "preferential option for the poor." In other words, God's justice was slanted toward those who had the least opportunity to have their voices heard in the religious and political society of their day. In our effort to teach the Catholic faith to children and adults in the faith community, this emphasis on justice and inclusivity should be given the same prominence in our catechetical classes as it is given throughout the Scriptures. The catechist whose own life bears witness to justice will be the catechist who is best able to do this in a way that is believable. Sharing one's resources, being generous with one's gifts, speaking up for the rights of the oppressed, displaying a welcoming attitude toward those who live at the fringes and margins of the community, offering compassion, all such actions should mark the life of anyone who is a leader or pastoral minister in the Catholic Church.

In biblical times, there were whole categories of people who were automatically considered outcast, or unable to participate fully in the religious and social life of the times—the poor, the lame, the deaf, the blind, lepers, prostitutes, strangers, foreigners, women.

Who are the groups or categories of persons today who are marginalized in our religious communities? What particular responsibility does the catechetical leader have toward these people? What actions on behalf of justice could be transformative for your parish or school community?

## Questions for Reflection
- Make a list of your specific catechetical responsibilities and ask yourself if you feel sufficiently competent to perform them.
- Do you have the resources you need? the educational background? the teaching skills or experiences? the self-confidence?
- Can you identify your limitations or concerns? Can you ask for help if you need it?

## Come and See:  Competencies of the Catechetical Leader

When we have met someone who truly moves and inspires us, there is a natural desire to want to introduce that person to those we love. We instinctively want the people closest to us to share the transformative experience. This is what happened with the Samaritan woman. As John reports it, the woman left her water jar, went back to the city, and began to tell the people about her experience with Jesus: "Come and see a man who told me everything I have ever done! He cannot be the Messiah, can he?" (John 4:28-29)  The woman knew enough religious history to make a connection between Jesus and the expected Messiah. At the same time, her faith did not provide her with certainty. She still had questions: "He cannot be the Messiah, can he?" We know very little else about the Samaritan woman's faith experience or its impact on the people. But her ability to communicate it was enough to get the attention of those she told. They wanted to meet him too. "They left the city and were on their way to him" (John 4:30).

Perhaps this is the essence of good catechetical leadership—being open to meeting God in the everyday places of life. Experience personal transformation, not a transformation that answers all questions or removes all doubts, but the kind that creates an energy inside of you that compels sharing the faith. Tell the people. Perhaps some of them will then make their way to the God who has spoken to your heart.

Clearly, "telling the people" in such a way as to compel their attention and evoke their response requires that certain people skills accompany one's faith convictions. The Samaritan woman had to be believable as she told of meeting Jesus or the people would never have gone themselves to find him. She had to be able to make her message heard. What are some of the skills that assist us in getting a message across? What personal competencies help the catechist enable people to move from information about the faith, to formation in the faith, to transformative faith experience?

When considering competencies of catechetical leadership, it might be helpful to think in terms of the particular job description or responsibilities that you must carry out. Obviously, if your ministry involves teaching religious education to young children, in addition to having access to the content that needs to be taught, it would be important to know something about effective teaching methods with this age group, appropriate disciplinary techniques, a general ability to communicate with children, and a true enjoyment in working with them. It would not be necessary to have an advanced degree in religious education, ten years of experience, or expertise in canon law.

Aside from the specific competencies related to particular areas of responsibility, having a broad range of "people skills" will enhance any catechetical leader's effectiveness. Some of these include:

- The ability to listen
- The ability to use words clearly
- The ability to notice non-verbal emotional "cues" in an individual or group
- The ability to manage conflicts in a healthy way
- The ability to include others, especially those who are shy or feel left out

- The ability to work well on a team or with groups of other people
- The ability to promote others, to want them to "shine"
- The ability to work with differences without being threatened
- The ability to motivate others, to focus group energy toward a common goal

There are many good and readable books available on identifying and improving one's skills with people. The bibliography includes some of them. Reading these books, however, will be most helpful if your life history and personal relationships already reflect a reasonable level of emotional health. Communications skills work best if they are coming from someone whose heart is already people oriented. Qualities and competencies support and enhance each other.

## They Were Astonished That He Was Speaking to a Woman: Partnership Among Women and Men in Catechetical Ministry

The astonishment reflected by the disciples of Jesus when they found him speaking with the Samaritan woman was understandable given the highly patriarchal practice of the times. Both in the Jewish religious structures, and in most of the Greco-Roman world, women held inferior positions. They were regarded as the property of their fathers and husbands, and often counted, along with the animals, among the spoils of war. Women were considered ritual unclean during menstruation and after childbirth. They were excluded from any central involvement in Jewish religious rituals. Jewish men did not speak to women in public, not even their wives. The fact that Jesus did so has been interpreted by many Scripture scholars as one of the major examples of his ethic of inclusive love, an ethic that affirms the fundamental equality of women and men.

The early Christian community seemed to take this ethic of inclusive love seriously in its practice and teaching, as evidenced by writings such as the letter to the Galatians. Later in Church history, however, the question of gender became more strongly influenced by the Greco-Roman philosophies which placed women below men on the hierarchical "ladder of being."

Today, the Catholic Church recognizes that sexism can no longer be tolerated. Though the Church now speaks of the equality of women and men hundreds of years of patriarchal practice do not easily give way to newly re-claimed visions of inclusive love and mutuality. Much work remains to be done to fully realize the vision of male-female equality that the Church now articulates in its official teachings.

While theologians, Scripture scholars, and Church leaders continue to struggle with issues related to male-female equality, catechetical leaders will no doubt encounter some tensions around this issue in their own efforts to be educators for justice. While some areas of disagreement remain, some very strong statements on the part of the Church give an encouraging mandate to those who would be educators in the Catholic faith. Among them are many made by Pope John Paul II, including the following statement in his Apostolic Letter, *On the Dignity and Vocation of Women:* "The biblical text provides sufficient bases for recognizing the essential equality of man and woman from the point of view of their humanity." (#6)

For their part, catechetical leaders can best promote this teaching by their own witness in their relationships with women and men. Some of the following suggestions might be discussed:

- Become as informed as you can with regard to the issue of gender equality, especially as it relates to justice making and compassion. Know what the Church teaches clearly and unambiguously for social justice and the dignity of all persons.
- Identify any angers you might hold regarding this issue.
- Try always to use inclusive language, both in personal speaking and in preparing educational materials, songs, prayers, and announcements.
- Evaluate your own style of behavior with women (if you are a man) and with men (if you are a woman). What do you notice?
- When possible and appropriate, make sure that both genders are represented on committees, in group presentations, and in leadership efforts in the parish or school community.
- Be sensitive to the ways you treat boys and girls, or women and men. Do you call on one gender group more than the other? Do you give preferential treatment to one group over the other?
- Use gender inclusive examples when teaching or speaking.
- Reflect on your own personal history with regard to the issue of gender equality. What attitudes do you hold? What has influenced the formation of these attitudes?
- Do you identify any unresolved discomfort or anger towards one gender group?
- In what ways do you need to grow personally regarding this issue?

One metaphor Jesus uses to describe the reign of God is the festive table. It offers us the image of a banquet prepared for all God's daughters and sons. In this image, all people are invited and welcomed as equal partners. This image of the reign of God breaks down the usual barriers and divisions between people. There are no separate tables in the kingdom. It is no longer political or religious status that counts. It is no longer gender or economic class or racial background that is the determining factor. Only one thing matters; the willingness to see the world and its people with new eyes and an open heart, and to work for the peace and justice that God intends for all.

## They Left the City and Were on Their Way to Him:  When Catechetical Leadership Works

What gives religious education its "sticking power" for the future? What is it in catechesis that lingers on in people's lives long after definitions have faded from memory and the exact content of religious education classes may have receded into the background places of the mind? In the early days, it was simply the experience of Jesus; the face to face, eye to eye contact, the conversations held at wells that could neither be forgotten or dimmed by the passage of years. That has not changed. Jesus provided the sort of religious education/faith formation experience that went beyond people's minds and into their very being. He listened. He felt. He cared. He heard their questions. He respected their limitations.

Jesus expressed his convictions about the reign of God in ways that were understandable to those who were open to hear. He faced conflict and tension. He became involved in people's lives. He was not a remote savior dispensing hillside lectures from a safe distance. He was particularly tender toward those others shunned or found unacceptable according to cultural mores. He asked his friends to stay with him when he felt troubled. He did not cling to being divine when being human got hard.

Today's religious educator will be effective in providing transformational experiences for people to the extent that he or she can enable these same kinds of deep heart connections to occur, connections which build people's self-esteem and confidence in the possibility of their own goodness and holiness. It is this kind of education that lasts over time. The *General Directory for Catechesis* stresses that "catechesis must have a catechumenal style, as of integral formation rather than mere information; it must act in reality as a means of arousing true conversion" (#29).

Consider again the Samaritan woman at the well. She was not an expert in matters of religion. Her personal life reflected mistakes. She had not lived in perfect obedience to the law. Even so, her heart held an excitement about the coming Messiah. And she was honest, honest enough to speak the truth about her own life, and honest enough to challenge Jesus: "How is it that you, a Jew, ask a drink of me, a woman of Samaria?" (John 4:9) Then, she found out that they shared a common thirst. Perhaps it was this deep thirst that allowed her to linger there, and, eventually, to become the premier catechist of the Christian Scriptures.

## Questions for Reflection:

- Which scripture stories speak to you about what might be considered Jesus' "catechetical style"? What were his primary concerns as a teacher? What are yours?
- As you read the various qualities and competencies described in this essay, with which do you find yourself in greatest agreement? Are there any you disagree with? What do you find most challenging?
- What has been your own personal story regarding the gender issue? What life experiences have shaped your story? How has your awareness grown? Do you know women and men whose experience of oppression or liberation has been different from your own? What convictions do you hold about male-female equality? What commitments?

## Bibliography

Bolton, Robert, Ph.D. *People Skills: How To Assert Yourself, Listen to Others, and Resolve Conflicts*. Englewood Cliffs, NJ: Prentice-Hall, 1996.

Ferder, Fran & Heagle, John. *Partnership: Women and Men In Ministry*. Notre Dame, IN: Ave Maria Press,1989.

Ferder, Fran. *Words Made Flesh: Scripture, Psychology & Human Communication*. Notre Dame, IN: Ave Maria Press, 1986.

Ferder, Fran & Heagle, John. *Your Sexual Self: Pathway to Authentic Intimacy*. Notre Dame, IN: Ave Maria Press, 1992.

John Paul II. *On the Dignity and Vocation of Woman*. Boston, MA: St. Paul Books & Media, 1988.

Josselson, Ruthellen. *The Space Between Us: Exploring the Dimensions of Human Relationships*. San Francisco, CA: Jossey-Bass Pub., 1992.

# 8
# Planning and Improving
# Parish Catechesis
### Diana Dudoit Raiche

## Need for Planning

An executive friend of mine once shared an inspirational vision that gave him a sense of direction in his business practices: He who fails to plan, plans to fail. Planning is an activity shared by people in all walks of life at various levels from managers of major corporations to teachers in classrooms and parents in homes. Wherever and whenever planning occurs, planners have three things in common that will be the subject of this essay: they operate out of a specific vision; they plan specific tasks based on that vision; and they evaluate in order to name and improve the status quo. Creating a plan is more than just an unavoidable exercise; it is as much an art as it is a skill.

Planning, unfortunately, is neither universally praised nor practiced. When the serendipity of life presents a difficult situation that no one could have anticipated, some people question the value of even the best laid plans. People do not just question the wisdom of a plan in hindsight; they often simply never get around to planning. Especially busy people often find that a demanding, frenetic schedule generally does not leave enough time for planning unless they call "time out."

Another deterrent to planning is not having an end in sight. A Director of Catechetical Ministry once invited a talented parishioner to become involved in a specific project. In doing so, the Director shared the rationale behind the particular activity that was the subject of the invitation. The parishioner interrupted the director mid sentence to share a startling personal discovery: "For years I have poured myself into church related activities. In listening to you describe why I am being asked to do this project, I just realized that in all the times before, I did not really know where the work was headed!" The moral of this true story is: A plan has to be directed toward a particular purpose that is grounded in a vision.

Planning for improvement offers many more advantages than disadvantages. From a purely secular perspective, planning may fall on a continuum anywhere from drifting like a ship without a rudder to micro-managing every detail. From a faith perspective, planning is thoroughly compatible with relying on the grace of God while exercising God-given talents to accomplish a specific task. A constant affirmation of the Catholic theological tradition is that "God's grace works through nature"—our efforts. In the hands of a skilled leader, a plan can be just what is needed to chart a course of action for implicit and explicit desired outcomes. A plan can also be the impetus for mobilizing people to make a difference through coordinated efforts.

## Questions for Reflection

- In your own life experience, do you find that you have time to plan, take time to plan, or plan a time for planning?
- Recall a time when the final product of intended outcome of an activity influenced your planning process? Contrast that planning experience with a time when the end was not readily apparent.
- What empowers you to 'see' the final, intended outcome of a project? How do you know when you have captured and appropriated the 'vision' of a particular project? In your experience, does owning a foundational vision for a project or initiative make a significant difference in the outcome?

## Elements of Catechetical Planning

Planning is considered vitally important to the catechetical endeavor as evidenced by the treatment the topic gets in *Sharing the Light of Faith* (1977). This *National Catechetical Directory* (*NCD*) for the United States directs leaders to plan for catechesis at parish, diocesan and national levels according to the overall mission of the Church. In outlining eight elements considered common to all planning systems, the *NCD* suggests that these elements be applied when organizing for catechesis. When engaged in planning of any kind, it is important (a) to clearly understand the essential mission and overall objectives of the project at hand; (b) to assess the needs of the project and the resources required to meet those needs; (c) to determine both long- and short-term goals; (d) to translate initiatives intended to accomplish stated goals into concrete activities which are prioritized; (e) to develop a budget that shows what resources are available to support the initiatives; (f) to create conditions that are favorable to the performance of concrete activities; (g) to commit to on-going review and evaluation of all parts of the planning and implementation process; (h) to restate, when necessary, goals and concrete activities (*NCD* #22).

Planning and improving catechesis may affirm or challenge current catechetical practices to a lesser or greater degree. In one instance, these two correlative operations may not call for any change in the current catechetical plan. On the other hand, if an evaluation of the status quo suggests that there has been insufficient planning for the catechetical enterprise, or if the current plan for catechesis is inconsistent or incompatible with the Church's foundational vision for catechesis, then a major overhaul of the entire catechetical agenda may be in order. Whether a change is interpreted as radical or slight, every responsible leader understands that one must plan for change. Effective leaders usually plan to bring about improvement or enhancement of the status quo. If that improvement means change, so be it.

## Leadership Vision Sets the Standard

Within the context of the eight essential elements necessary to any planning process, it is necessary to acknowledge two significant influences on planning and improving catechesis. First, those involved in catechesis must be aware of the foundational vision for catechesis articulated by the Church over time. Second, it is critically important that catechetical leaders have an ability to appropriate the stated foundational vision, and from it, develop a specific plan for the catechetical enterprise in a particular parish or school. Whatever the vision may be, once recognized and appropriated, a vision will not only influence the planning process, but it will also be detectable in whatever plan has been developed and employed in the past to improve catechesis.

Although some people assume that leaders are successful because they "see" more than the average person, possess an unlimited supply of inspiration or have a magnetic personality, anyone who has observed effective leaders in action can recognize that big dreams, inspiration, charisma and vision are typically accompanied by equal amounts of planning and hard work. Thomas Edison defined genius as 99% perspiration and 1% inspiration. Recognized leaders readily admit that they work at being good leaders. They not only seem to possess a clear sense of direction based on a personally held vision, but competent leaders are also capable of devising a plan to actualize such a vision. A plan helps a leader improve upon past successes and incorporate important lessons learned from personal past mistakes as well as the errors of others. Planning is always a continuous process that helps leaders become proactive rather than reactive.

## Vision for Leaders

Leaders have the kind of vision that allows them to see the world from a different perspective. They are equally gifted at seeing through obstacles that camouflage a clear direction and navigating through obstacles more gracefully. Such leadership qualities attract the trust and loyalty of other participants. Leaders with vision see possibilities where others may see problems. Sometimes, leaders can turn real problems into opportunities. For example, while still a student, a young man with dyslexia thought that what every struggling college student needed was a 24 hour copy center that could offer a wide variety of print related support services. His idea launched a unique way to put technology at the service of students. From a modest beginning as a storefront operation, his vision spawned a multi-million dollar enterprise that he named Kinko's.

Entrepreneurs are not the only type of farsighted leaders. Martin Luther King, Jr.'s now famous "I Have a Dream" speech left no doubt that his inspirational dream for justice was firmly rooted in biblical images of the Exodus and the Promised Land. The vision he advanced through a non-violent plan of action influenced the course of history and the civil rights movement in the United States.

Likewise, the announcement of an ecumenical council by Pope John XXIII on January 25, 1959, surprised not only the world, but many within the Roman Catholic Church. Pope John saw a Church in need of updating (*aggiornamento*) in its internal structure (vitality *ad intra*) and its stance towards the needs and demands of the peoples of the world (vitality *ad extra*). He recognized that the modern world seemed to be drifting farther and farther away from Gospel values. The Pope hoped that such an updating would enhance the ability of the Church to read the signs of the times and help Christians everywhere actively engage the modern world in order to exercise greater Christian influence on it. The sixteen documents of Vatican Council II (four constitutions, nine decrees and three declarations) provided a plan to realize Pope John XXIII's vision for updating the Church.

## Vision for Catechetical Leaders

Catechetical leaders are called to manifest some of the same qualities and characteristics all good leaders exhibit. In addition, those who lead catechetical efforts are also required to demonstrate a Gospel vision. Theirs is a unique perspective of the world that originates in Sacred Scripture and the tradition of the Church.

Catechetical leaders may possess exceptional spiritual qualities and obvious competencies in scripture, doctrines of the faith, and liturgy. Along with these gifts and skills, they may also have a secure grasp of the purpose, principles and processes of catechesis. Catechetical leaders may even be especially gifted at facilitating a well-balanced interrelationship among the faith community, participants and catechists in furthering the catechetical agenda of the Church in a particular diocese and local parish. However, like other successful leaders who are motivated by an inspirational vision that is clear to them, catechetical leaders concretize the overarching mission of the Church by devising a specific plan of action for a particular people in a particular location. Planning not only advances the communication of a shared vision, but as a process, it advances accomplishments that, in turn, can be interpreted as improvement. With a plan to guide activities, everyone involved in catechesis is better able to stay focused on the big picture.

## Questions for Reflection

- Do you recognize the eight essential elements to planning named in *Sharing the Light of Faith* as truly essential? When have you experienced planning that included all of these elements? Have you been involved with planning that did not incorporate these elements?
- How do you feel when you are involved in a project that is well (or poorly) planned? What has been you best/worst experience in a planning process? Reflect on "why?"
- When you are engaged in planning, how do you plan? Is it a solo operation for you? Do you work in a consensus group? Do you experience planning as an on-going process? Do you set aside time for planning? Why or why not?
- Describe the vision for catechesis that motivates your experience of the catechetical endeavor in a short phrase.

## Vision in Documents for Catechesis

In each age, a new generation is called to read the signs of the times that are ever changing. The age old Gospel message and long-standing Church teachings need to be articulated to a new audience in a language that can be understood. Catechetical leaders who have inherited the legacy of Vatican II have learned to rely on key catechetical documents for a well-grounded catechetical vision. A vision for the catechetical mission of the Church inherent in these documents guides catechetical leaders as they steer toward new horizons.

In 1971, the *General Catechetical Directory* (*GCD*) laid out the basic principles that govern the components and organization of the catechetical enterprise, such as the nature, purpose and goals of catechesis, and the content, context, and means. It clearly placed the entire catechetical enterprise under the umbrella of ministry of the Word. The *Directory* acknowledged developments that came out of the catechetical renewal and honored the contribution that the social sciences (psychology and sociology) had made and applied those developments to catechesis. *Sharing the Light of Faith*—the *National Catechetical Directory*— adapted the principles articulated in the *General Catechetical Directory* for the catechetical endeavor in the United States.

In 1997, the Congregation for the Clergy presented a new *General Directory for Catechesis* for the universal Catholic community. Clarifying the nature of catechesis even further, the new Directory intends to prompt study and deepen research in catechesis to better respond to the needs of catechesis and the norms and directives of the Magisterium. The *GDC* articulates a balance between the contextualization of catechesis within evangelization found in the apostolic exhortations *Evangelii Nuntiandi* (*EN*, 1975) and *Catechesi Tradendae* (*CT*, 1979), and the appropriation of the content of the faith found in the *Catechism of the Catholic Church* (*CCC*, 1992). While acknowledging that evangelization depends on the Word incarnate and catechesis is rooted in the Word of God in Scripture and tradition, the *GDC* highlights the place of the *CCC* as a "reference point for the transmission of the faith in catechesis" (*GDC* #8).

The *GDC* builds upon the trajectory set in the original sixteen documents of Vatican II and further nuances a vision for catechesis that had been developing in recent documents, such as *Evangelii Nuntiandi* (*EN*, 1975) and *Catechesi Tradendae* (*CT*, 1979). In promoting evangelization as foundational to a catechetical vision, the *GDC* places catechesis as one of three moments in the total process of evangelization: missionary activity, catechetical activity and pastoral activity. Catechetical activity, a gradual, Christocentric activity—always done in stages—is more clearly designated in the *GDC* as a two fold process: as initial catechesis according to the norm of the *Rite of Christian Initiation of Adults* (1972), and as formation in faith within the context of evangelization. As in the 1971 *Directory*, the 1997 *Directory* maintains that adult catechesis guides all other forms of catechesis. In addition, it declares that

> Post-baptismal catechesis, without slavishly imitating the structure of the baptismal catechumenate and recognizing in those to be catechized the reality of their Baptism, does well, however to draw inspiration from 'this preparatory school of life' and to allow itself to be enriched by those principal elements which characterize the catechumenate (*GDC* #91).

When planning for the improvement of catechesis, catechetical leaders at all levels are required to heed the vision for catechesis articulated in an on-going fashion. More recent documents need to be read within the context of previous catechetical documents.  Sometimes the seed of an older idea may be contained within a seemingly new concept.  Catechetical documents continue to nuance the vision for catechesis making a vision that is ancient, ever new.

Responsible planning for catechesis will necessarily take its cue from the more recent *General Directory for Catechesis* and *Catechism of the Catholic Church*; however, catechetical leaders will also need to consult a body of previous documents on approaches to catechesis that have emerged since the close of Vatican Council II.  The direction as well as the important distinctions for the catechetical enterprise sketched in these documents appropriately inspire planning for catechesis.  Such planning is ordered toward improving catechesis.

Identifying a vision for catechesis within these documents is foundational to the catechetical endeavor.  A true vision is inherently a farsighted view of a new reality or a new paradigm.  It is not merely a personal idea based on a personal agenda.  A vision contains within it foundational principles that stand the test of time and bear good fruit. If a vision is not embraced and personally held by catechetical leaders, even the most pristine and perfectly articulated vision will be ineffective.

## Planning for a Catechumenal Style of Catechesis

There once was a young man who wanted to learn from a Zen master. Before the master would accept him as a student, the young docent was invited to share a cup of tea.  The Zen master began to fill the cup until it was overfull and the tea spilled over in waves on the student's hand.  The student protested, "Master, the cup is overflowing!"  The wise master retorted that the student, too, like the cup, was overflowing with his own ideas and concerns.  The master kindly instructed the student to become empty of personal pet ideas and opinions and to return when there was space inside to receive and accept new knowledge and ideas.  Only then would the master agree to accept the student as a true disciple.

The disciples of Jesus were also students. Like the would-be students of the Zen Master in the previous story, some of Jesus' disciples were overfull with their own ideas about what a Messiah should be and how a Messiah should usher in the Kingdom of God.  Others sat at Jesus' feet, listened and learned. Catechetical leaders need to become students who are open to learning, eager to identify their personally held vision for catechesis, and then willing to hold that vision in the light of the Church's stated vision. Such a comparative exercise is necessary because plans for catechesis emerge out of an appropriated vision.

Eager to plan for improved catechesis, a catechetical leader looks for principles in which to ground the planning process. The *General Directory for Catechesis* links catechesis with a catechumenal style and thus with catechumenal principles. A catechumenal style of catechesis incorporates formation rather than mere information since catechesis is about arousing a true conversion within another human being (*GDC* #29). Such a style intends, by God's grace, to bring about a maturity of faith, not merely the memorization of a body of knowledge. It is certainly compatible with ongoing catechesis without slavishly mimicking the four periods of the *Rite of Christian Initiation of Adults* (pre-catechumenate, catechumenate, purification and enlightenment, mystagogy).

Acquisition of knowledge does not necessarily move a person to conversion of heart nor integrity of life style. A good example of this reality is sometimes seen on a Catholic university campus where students, regardless of faith affiliation, take a survey course in Christianity. One student who professed to be an atheist learned the appropriate data, gave "correct" answers based on the data, wrote stellar exams, and passed the course with an "A." However, at the end of the course the student willingly admitted that although it was a fine course, the student had not embraced a personal belief in God or in Jesus Christ or in Christianity. Knowledge of Christian data is not the same as appropriation of Christian faith, a Christian vision of life, or a Christian life-style. A plan for catechesis that embodies a catechumenal style incorporates knowledge of Christian faith but also goes beyond the accumulation of knowledge to effect conversion of heart—to become a disciple of Jesus.

A catechumenal style is essentially about conversion. When infant christening was the single most formative image of baptism that landscaped the imagination of Roman Catholics, conversion was, and sometimes still is, assumed. At the level of intuition, Catholics may readily agree with Horace Bushnell (1802-1876) "that a child is to grow up a Christian, and never know himself as being otherwise." However, in a society where Christian nurturing is more difficult because popular culture does not affirm or support Gospel values, conversion can no longer be taken for granted. More and more, adults are not bringing their infants to the waters of baptism as readily as in the past. That reality is evidenced by the growing number of children of catechetical age who are unbaptized, or who are baptized but uncatechized and properly belong in the catechumenate process adapted for children. And even if a child's conversion has already begun, we should remember the broader Catholic tradition that conversion is a lifelong process more than a particular experience.

In a society where conversion and Christian nurture can not be presupposed, and in a Church where parents at times are as much in need of catechesis as their children, many more catechetical leaders are asking questions beyond what data need to be taught at what time of life. A much more fundamental question emerges:  What is it that we do when we cooperate with the movement of the Holy Spirit to facilitate Christian conversion in people of all ages?  This is a question that goes beyond what book to choose, what facts or doctrines to teach, or how many contact hours in formal religious instruction are required.  When catechetical leaders begin to ask what it takes to facilitate conversion for adults, adolescents, and young children, then the search for what makes up a "total curriculum" emerges.

When a catechumenal style drives a "total curriculum," intentional catechesis lasts for an extended time, that is, long enough for conversion of faith to become strong and visible in an evangelical way of life.  The length of time a person is involved with catechesis plays a critical role in the conversion process.  In initial catechesis, an appropriate amount of time may vary according to the age, background and personality of an individual.  Adults, adolescents, and young children all need appropriate amounts of time in the beginning stages of conversion.  It is noteworthy that they do not all necessarily require the same amount of time for conversion to begin.

Once conversion takes hold, however, it must take root and mature.  That is why catechesis must always be ongoing.  If it is ongoing, it perdures throughout the seasons and cycles of life and helps a person understand that life is a truly spiritual journey.  Every plan for catechesis must account for a catechesis that is not completed at the end of the eighth grade, high school, confirmation, or any specific course of study at a college or elsewhere.  A plan for catechesis necessarily embraces a variety of ways to continue to nurture everyone in the faith community in every age and stage of life.  The *GDC* often reiterates that lifelong catechesis—mentoring constant growth in holiness of life—is the vision for every Christian community.  Such a plan also accommodates marginalized segments of society; mentally and physically challenged people of all ages; rural, urban, academic and artistic environments as well as senior citizens.

Paragraph #75 of the *RCIA*, which is rooted in the document *Ad Gentes* of Vatican II, gives a succinct outline of four essential elements of the catechumenal style intended to facilitate conversion.  Within a context of an extended period of time and with an intention to bring about conversion and maturity of faith, these four elements supply the content of a "total curriculum" approach to catechesis: 1) catechesis grounded in the Word of God, 2) catechesis nurtured in a community of faith, 3) catechesis supported by appropriate liturgical celebrations, 4) catechesis directed towards personal apostolic witness and mission to the world. Each of these four elements must be supported by sound catechetical materials that translate the faith story, found in Scripture and Tradition, prayed in the liturgy, experienced in the community and manifested in apostolic activity into age appropriate language.

## The Word of God in Catechesis

The Word of God incarnate in the person of Jesus and mediated now through Scripture and Tradition guides every catechetical leader. St. Jerome asserts that "ignorance of the Scriptures is ignorance of Christ" (*CCC* #133). Therefore, a plan for catechesis necessarily attends to sharing, proclaiming, celebrating, teaching, learning and living the Word of God that comes through Scripture and Tradition.

Through tradition, (Latin, *traditio*; Greek, *paradosis*), we come to understand that beliefs, doctrines, rituals, and even Sacred Scripture are transmitted in the context of a faithful, believing, and ordered community of faith. In contrast to the Tradition-Scripture tug-of-war evident in the history of theological debates, Vatican II's *Dogmatic Constitution on Divine Revelation (Dei Verbum)* presented a non-dualistic view of Tradition and Scripture. "Sacred Tradition and Sacred Scripture, then, are bound closely together, and communicate one with the other. Flowing from the same divine well-spring, both of them merge, in a sense, and move towards the same goal" (*DV* #9).

Tradition has a content, an active or passive process, an apostolic or post-apostolic source, and a written or unwritten form. Functionally, tradition preserves the Church's collective memory, but it also anticipates the future. In relation to society, it can be public or private; universal, regional, or local. The binding nature of tradition can be normative or non-normative. Tradition can refer to Scripture as an embodiment of the first transmission of the Gospel, but it can also refer to the transmission of Christian doctrine after the canon of Scripture was finalized. Catechetical leaders must be the first to understand that "the task of giving an authentic interpretation of the Word of God, whether in its written form or in the form of tradition has been entrusted to the living teaching office of the Church alone" (*DV* #10). According to *Dei Verbum*, this authority, exercised in the name of Jesus Christ, does not render the Magisterium superior to God's Word. Rather, the Magisterium submits to the Word of God as its servant; it teaches only what has been handed on to it. The Church acknowledges that developments in its teaching can correctly be accepted as a progression or a deepening of insight into divine truth. Catechetical leaders are challenged to more fully understand their role in transmitting the Word of God and are called to stand within tradition when planning and improving catechesis.

Through Sacred Scripture, we come to understand that God's Revelation is complete and definitive in Jesus Christ. For that reason, catechesis is always Christocentric. Jesus Christ is the complete and fullest expression of divine revelation. A plan for improving catechesis can never take the centrality of Jesus for granted. We live in a culture that is counter-Christian yet commercializes the Christmas holidays into a hype that obscures the real reason for a Christmas season. Within such a culture, Christians are challenged to communicate the person and message of Jesus Christ in everyday life.

This point was made very clear to a Catholic who taught fifth grade in a public school. One of the students in the class had a bracelet that boldly displayed the name of Jesus. The fifth grade student had won the bracelet as an award for a job well done in a catechetical session in a parish-based religious education program and wore the prize with a sense of pride. While at lunch one day, another student in the class was intrigued by the Jesus bracelet and tried to get a better look at it. The teacher found it hard to imagine that this child had never heard or seen the name of Jesus before, and thought perhaps that the student was attempting to call undue attention to himself. Nonetheless, in a loud voice across the lunch table this young boy stood up and shouted: "Hey! Who is that Jesus dude?" A Jesus bracelet may not appear to be a very significant way to evangelize a group of children; however, in this case, it prompted an eleven-year-old to respond to the boy's question. In simple language that could be understood by the other students at the lunch table, this fifth grader was able to share why the bracelet was meaningful to her and give witness to Jesus Christ and to the Catholic faith tradition in a public school setting.

Unfortunately, sometimes the centrality of Jesus to the catechetical endeavor also becomes lost in a sea of well meaning faith-related activities. To give the Word primacy in any faith formation process is not as easy as it may appear. The fact that scripture passages are included in catechetical lessons may not be adequate. Familiarity with and use of sacred scripture must be accompanied by love of the Word of God as well as basic knowledge of Catholic interpretation of scripture. How scripture is handled by a catechist or parent is as important if not more critical than the fact that scripture is incorporated in catechetical materials. For example, is scripture an add-on feature to a catechetical session based on a pre-selected theme? Is scripture used as a proof text taken out of the context in which a passage was written? Does the scripture have any relationship to the prayer of the Church according to the cycles of the liturgical year?

In a catechumenal style of catechesis, scripture is a starting point for catechesis. Not only does scripture find a suitable ally in a shared Christian praxis methodology, but scripture also provides a springboard for exploring doctrinal teachings and traditions particular to the Roman Catholic faith. In a catechumenal style of catechesis a human story meets the Faith Story. Both unfold gradually together according to the organization of scripture throughout the liturgical year. Introducing those being formed in the faith to a rhythm of scripture based on the liturgical year while also introducing them to shared Christian praxis equips Catholics at an early age to understand both a Catholic approach to scripture and a process of critical reflection on scripture in the context of personal experience and personal application.

## The Role of the Community in Catechesis

Advertising images together with an upward mobility mentality exert tremendous influence on young people to accept the myth of a homogeneous American overculture. Yet, ethnic, cultural and regional characteristics thrive in spite of these influences. Children absorb regional and familial peculiarities as thought and speech patterns, accents, or mannerisms quite unselfconsciously in their early formative years. Within a few years of life, attitudes, perceptions, beliefs and behaviors learned at home or from those with whom we have bonded condition us to be eager for or cautious of new experiences.

A person's first encounter with a "world" different from a family of origin, home town, or cultural milieu can have an unsettling impact. Such an event may evoke a range of emotions from delight in unexpected diversity to fear of dangerous differences. The early formative patterns may be modified over a life time, but in times of anger, stress, or excitement the telltale signs of our origins generally appear rather spontaneously in a particular colloquialism, accent, belief or even prejudice. That is the power the formation community has on all of us. The conditioning we appropriate from the group of people with whom we have been reared or have a strong bond, for good or ill, leaves an indelible mark we either try to live up to or live down. Some people are able to reinvent themselves along life's way with greater or lesser success. Acts of human expression are essentially acts of self-revelation.

The experience of formation in the Christian community is very similar. Tertullian, writing in the third century, was the first to acknowledge that "Christians are made, not born." The making of Christians in the early Church depended on the active presence of a community of Christians. The Christian way of life became distinguished by its fraternal love, high moral stance and gatherings for prayer. Christians became known for the support they offered each other and to all who were in need—especially "the poor." The good example of fellow Christians helped to form catechumens, those in training to become Followers of the Way of Jesus, and the newly initiated into a particular kind of Christian lifestyle. A common denominator for Christians was belief in Jesus as the Messiah, as the one who brought salvation. However, a careful reading of Paul's letters to the various Christian communities shows just how diverse those early communities were. His epistles reveal how much these communities retained geographic and ethnic distinguishing characteristics even as they embraced the same Christian faith.

From the earliest time, to be a Christian meant to be in a faith community, for God is a community of Persons: Father, Son and Spirit. Even the solitude of imprisonment did not diminish a Christian's connectedness to the Christian community. Oftentimes, members of the community supplied fellow Christians with physical as well as spiritual support in times of need. Because of their baptism in the name of Jesus Christ, Christians experienced themselves as connected to the visible community of believers and to the community of the faithful departed, the communion of saints.

Gathering with a formative believing community is characteristic of a catechumenal style of catechesis. A catechumenal style of catechesis acknowledges that people learn from one another, are uplifted by good example, and are challenged by the Gospel message that manifests itself in the lives of fellow believers. In a catechumenal style of catechesis the process of initial as well as ongoing conversion is aided by Christians who are seasoned in the spiritual journey and know how to point the way for others who are less experienced or lacking in knowledge. A Christian experience of community is of prime importance for the process of conversion, and needs special attention as a key component in a catechumenal style of catechesis.

Who then makes up the Christian community? This is a question that deserves thoughtful attention. No one can deny the value or necessity of a family or a small ecclesial community or even a sixth grade class in a Catholic school or a confirmation class at the parish for helping people form an identity with the Christian community. These smaller groups of Christians offer an important yet more limited and somewhat insular experience of Christians being in communion with each other. There will always be special segments of a whole community with whom we have a special affinity and consistent contact. However, if we are to take a catechumenal style of catechesis seriously when planning for catechesis, the formation community must extend beyond insular small groups. The Christian community is more than "my" class or group. The Christian community embraces people I know well and some I know less well; people who are like me and people who are very different.

The best example of a smaller segment of the whole Christian commu-

nity is a liturgical assembly of gathered believers from which more special-
ized segments of the community originate. In the act of worship, a Christian
community manifests self-definition and creates its identity. For Roman
Catholics who embrace the idea of a universal Church, inculcating the
community with a proper sense of itself beyond congregationalism is critically important.

When gathered in the name of Jesus for prayer, for sacraments, and
especially when gathered for eucharistic liturgy as a Sunday assembly, the
total community is called to continual conversion beyond comfort zones.
One of the scenes from the movie *Romero* captured this idea of who makes
up the Christian community most appropriately. Archbishop Romero baptized infants at his parish after Mass each Sunday. A very wealthy and
influential friend of his asked the Archbishop if he would baptize her baby.
Of course Romero was delighted and told her she could bring her baby to
the Church on Sunday when he baptized all the children in the parish. The
wealthy friend wanted a private baptism in her own home with just her
family present. Accustomed to a privileged life and more private practice
of her religion, she became visibly distressed when the Archbishop refused
to baptize her child in a private ceremony. As the scene unfolded, it became
obvious that her concept of a Christian community was very different from
the Archbishop's. Offended at the Archbishop's suggestion, she shouted a
scathing protest: "You don't expect me to have my baby baptized with a
bunch of Indians, do you?" That is exactly what Archbishop *Romero*
expected. Romero saw each person as a child of God. In his eyes, baptism
makes us all members of the same family—the Christian community. This
scenario highlighted two irreconcilable perceptions of who makes up the
Christian community.

Accepting a limited segment of the community as a substitute for the
whole Christian community, especially the community that gathers as a
Sunday assembly, has far-reaching debilitating effects. Smaller groups can
become too insular and too intolerant of those who are outside the group.
Planning that is based on a catechumenal style of catechesis should prompt
catechetical leaders to break down barriers that exist within a Christian
community. For example, if an uneasy relationship exists between Catholic
schools and parish-based catechetical programs over use of facilities, times
for celebrating First Communion, or funds allocated for religious instruction, catechetical leaders must strive to create a sense of community so that
different groups experience unity of purpose. Human differences should not
become occasions for human divisiveness for a community of Christians.
When a parish community accepts each person and every small group as
part of one family in faith, then getting the best for "my" group will have

no place in a planning process for catechesis.

Catholics in the United States who are accustomed to a private, personally oriented life, tend also to be private in matters of faith. The practice of keeping faith private is sometimes seriously challenged by catechetical leaders who embrace a more comprehensive, universal concept of community. For example, planning based on a catechumenal style of catechesis may promote a parish-wide celebration for First Communion within the context of the Sunday assembly. At such a celebration, concern for Johnny's or Suzy's special day would not take precedence over the joy of joining the Christian family at the Eucharistic table on Sunday, the primary day for remembering the paschal mystery. When a broader understanding of community replaces a more restrictive one, young people who prepare for sacramental celebrations may be paired with prayer partners from the whole community. A more comprehensive understanding of Christian community could encourage catechetical leaders to facilitate mentoring relationships between youth and aging populations within a faith community.

The way catechetical leaders plan community events and work with smaller segments of the larger community to knit them together as a cohesive unity will have a formative impact on how people of all ages are catechized about who makes up a community. Catechetical leaders who embrace a catechumenal style of catechesis strive to incorporate the whole community as partners in the catechetical enterprise. Such action can expand a community's imagination not only about who makes up a community of faith, but also about how a community can embrace an expanded role in evangelizing and catechizing for conversion.

## Questions for Reflection

- What distinction and development do you think is implied in expanding the notion of catechesis from an aspect of the ministry of the Word (*GCD*-1971) to catechesis as a work of evangelization in the context of the mission of the Church (*GDC*-1997)?
- In your opinion, what are the implications of the baptismal catechumenate as an inspiration for catechesis? How might this vision for catechesis be consistent with or different from the current vision of ongoing post-baptismal catechesis with which you are familiar?
- How does a catechumenal style of catechesis contribute to a "total curriculum" in catechesis? What distinguishes an information-based catechetical program from a formation process? How does the latter include the former?

## The Place of Liturgy in Catechesis

A catechumenal style of catechesis takes liturgy very seriously. Catechetical leaders who take a catechumenal style of catechesis seriously will need to become as educated about liturgy as they are about religious education. Knowledge of liturgical documents and liturgical principles are as important to catechetical leaders as they are to liturgical specialists. Catechetical leaders do not have to be experts on the structure of liturgical rites, prayer texts, symbols, and ritual actions, but they should know something about each of these. Such knowledge does not put catechetical leaders in competition with presiders and pastoral ministers who are directly responsible for liturgical celebrations. Rather, being properly informed about liturgy prepares catechetical leaders to catechize people of all ages appropriately about liturgical prayer and sacramental spirituality. Catechetical leaders must know how to prepare people of all ages to celebrate liturgy well.

Formation in faith and personal conversion are central to a catechumenal style of catechesis. They are not only prerequisites for participation in liturgy, but each is also a dimension of the faith journey that is nurtured by liturgy. Liturgy is not just something we do; liturgy also acts upon us. Each person has the potential to become transformed as a result of having undergone a liturgical experience that connects liturgy to life.

Liturgy involves action; it engages the whole person, or at least it should engage all the senses along with the intellect. Liturgical action is shared between the presider and the gathered believers for the assembly has a critical role to play in gestured prayers, postures, and sung or spoken responses. People remember more of what they do than what they read or hear. This relationship of action to learning is contained in a key liturgical principle: *lex orandi, lex credendi*—as the Church prays, the Church believes. It is imperative that catechetical leaders know that good liturgy builds faith, and poor liturgy can diminish faith.

Catechetical leaders have an obligation to plan for catechesis in such a way that liturgy is seen as essential, not optional. Planning for catechesis should acknowledge that participation in liturgical celebrations is of primary importance and should become a sacred habit. Catechesis for liturgy assumes that people willingly and faithfully participate in the sacramental life of the Church with regularity.

Catechetical leaders are often called upon to plan for liturgical celebrations. Mindful of the formative and nurturing power liturgy has on people of all ages, they are obliged to know where to find the principles that guide liturgical planning. In the interest of promoting liturgical instruction and active participation of the assembly at liturgy, catechetical leaders should be familiar with *Sacrosanctum Concilium (SC)*, the *Constitution on the Sacred Liturgy (CSL)*, the first of the documents to come out of Vatican Council II. The Constitution sets forth a vision for liturgy that is still a challenge for many within the Roman Catholic Church. Paragraph 14 of the Constitution states that "the Church earnestly desires that all the faithful be led to that full, conscious, and active participation in liturgical celebrations called for by the very nature of the liturgy" (*SC* #14).

To participate in liturgy fully, actively, and with mindfulness, people need to know what liturgy celebrates and why. In addition to knowing that bread and wine become more than symbolic in the course of the eucharistic liturgy assemblies and leaders alike need to know that bread, wine, scripture, fire, water, oil, cross, presider and assembly are primary liturgical symbols. When these symbols are used in liturgical action, they create another language, an analogical language. Catechetical leaders must not just know the vocabulary of liturgy, but must also know how these symbols function in a liturgical celebration. The primary liturgical symbols should not be supplanted by unnecessary "props" that a particular catechist may think are clever embellishments for a particular liturgical celebration.

Full and active participation goes beyond specific "spoken parts" assigned to certain individuals because they read well, i.e., lectors, readers of introductions before Mass, or readers for the general intercessions. Music is integral to liturgy. It not only accompanies liturgical action with a primary symbol but also highlights the dialogue that exists between a presider and the assembly. Even if catechetical leaders are not professional musicians, they are called to know and follow the norms for liturgical music found in *Music in Catholic Worship* (1972, 1983).

Likewise, worship space needs informed attention. Working within the architectural perimeters of available worship space is a challenge for some catechetical leaders. Too often, they are unaware how the "decoration" and arrangement of worship space contributes to or detracts from a proper celebration of liturgical prayer.

Catechetical leaders can more effectively lead others to full conscious and active participation in liturgy by knowing something about the use of the human body at prayer, the full use of ritual symbols, and the influence that furnishings, vesture, vessels, and images have when planning for liturgy (*Environment and Art in Catholic Worship*, 1978). It is incumbent on catechetical leaders to understand how, why, and when these liturgical elements and symbols are used in liturgical prayer. Both before and after liturgy, catechetical leaders are charged with planning ways to make the analogical liturgical language accessible to everyone, not just presiders and liturgy planners.

Paying attention to the place of liturgy in catechesis is critical to planning and improving catechesis. For each time a catechist "plans" a school, class, or special interest group liturgical celebration that violates key liturgical principles, the formative and nourishing power of liturgy to build faith and strengthen conversion is diminished. When the time comes for sacramental celebrations, catechetical leaders are in a privileged position. They can help people of all ages prepare for specific sacramental celebrations, and then beyond initial preparation, help them learn how to reflect on liturgical experiences.

Catechetical planners are also called upon to communicate that, within the Roman Catholic tradition, experience of liturgical celebrations and formal religious education programs are not either/or interchangeable components. To insure that catechesis is comprehensive, formative, and incorporates a "total curriculum" approach, liturgy and religious education are both required and must work "hand-in- hand." It is just as essential to reflect on an experience of liturgy after the fact as it is to prepare for a liturgical experience before the celebration. It is virtually impossible to reflect on an experience one has not had. Although a limited experience with liturgical celebrations is better than no experience, holding up a consistent connection to the liturgical life of the Church is more than an ideal. Catechesis that adverts to a catechumenal style presumes that liturgy is experienced, that people of all ages consistently attend liturgical celebrations, and that the liturgical experience is made engaging for people's lives by liturgy planners and presiders.

## Apostolic Service in Catechesis

When catechetical leaders embrace a catechumenal style for catechesis, a link between liturgy and social justice concerns becomes more apparent. In a catechumenal style for catechesis, commitment to apostolic service goes beyond civic laws, social activism, or service projects. Apostolic service is a commitment to being in mission for the gospel—it is integral to Christian identity. It is appropriate that this commitment flows naturally and spontaneously from prayer, especially liturgical prayer. The *Constitution on the Sacred Liturgy* clearly points out that liturgy is the "summit toward which the activity of the Church is directed; and at the same time it is the fount from which all the Church's power flows" (*SC* #10).

Personal faith and conversion are meant to be strengthened through liturgical experiences in which the gospel of Jesus Christ is experienced as good news. A truly converted person wants to share the good news they have experienced and seeks to reach out to other members of the human family who are marginalized, disenfranchised or downtrodden. In such a case, social justice concerns often well up from within a person of faith so strongly that the urge to reach out to others in need simply cannot be ignored.

It is axiomatic that prayer shapes belief; however, a necessary corollary to that rule is that belief also shapes action. The believer who commits to a life of prayer based on the Word of God prayed in the midst of a gathered, believing community of faith does not shy away from giving apostolic witness. Reaching out to others becomes a moral imperative. If one is in a powerless position to effect a change for the good, then merely raising the justice question is itself an act of social justice.

Catechetical leaders at national, diocesan, or parish levels who are conscious of a catechumenal style of catechesis recognize the inseparable connection between liturgy and apostolic service. Yet, if the average church-goer were to be asked what liturgy has to do with social justice, many would say "Nothing." A pastor in a large, affluent parish in southern California discovered that was precisely the opinion of many of his parishioners. When a politically charged proposition directed at eliminating some of the state's immigration prohibitions came up for a vote, he preached a homily one Sunday that connected the Gospel of the day to the plight of illegal immigrants. This particular parish had a long history of outreach ministry to immigrants in the surrounding area as well as to poor communities in Tijuana, Mexico. The proposition in question would have denied immigrants who had not yet obtained citizenship or green cards access to any medical or educational benefits from the state. These were the same immigrants who were hired illegally for lower wages by U.S. citizens. On the one hand, some segments of the population were eager to hire immigrants and eager to receive the benefits of their labor. On the other hand, some were convinced that offering medical and education benefits only served to lure more illegal immigrants than the state could accommodate.

In his homily, the pastor avoided the arguments of both political camps and talked about the dignity of personhood and the gospel imperative to help a brother or sister in need. By challenging the mentality that "there was no more room at the inn" the homily divided the community. The objection of the offended: Father had no business bringing politics into Church. The objection of the socially concerned: Where else if not in Church can one directly link real life situations to the Gospel message? The proposition passed; but the unease that this single homily released in the faith community did not soon pass. It was a situation no catechetical leader could avoid addressing in the context of religious education gatherings without appearing totally disengaged from reality and community concerns.

Catechetical leaders are called to intentionally build upon what an assembly hears and experiences at liturgy. It is one thing to teach about the intersection of liturgy and life. It is quite another to make such a connection in the context of real life situations. Reaching out to those in need cannot be seen merely as an add-on activity used to teach a lesson. Rather when catechetical leaders are planning and improving catechesis, they are obliged to find ways to integrate concern for social justice issues germane to the locale within the "total curriculum" for catechesis. When outreach to others in need is a conscious concern, a faith community is able to see the needs of those who are closest to them. Sending money and gathering food at times of natural disaster or special holidays are noble and needed activities. However, training a faith community to see local, regional, and universal needs while facilitating ways to show people how to help others as an integral part of a catechetical agenda has great value and far-reaching effects. The bumper sticker message "think globally, act locally" is an appropriate slogan for all faith-filled people.

## Materials and Environments to Support Catechesis

Each of the four content areas in a catechumenal style of catechesis (word, community, liturgy and apostolic service) need appropriate support materials and methodologies to insure a "total curriculum" approach to catechesis. Appropriate catechetical materials will necessarily attend to the doctrinal themes outlined in the four pillars of the *Catechism of the Catholic Church* (Creed, Liturgy and Sacraments, Moral life and the Ten Commandments, Christian Prayer and the Our Father) within a context of a catechumenal style of catechesis.

In a spiral curriculum that introduces the key doctrinal themes at an introductory level and then expands and deepens the presentation of the key concepts, students have an opportunity to expand and deepen their understanding of their Christian faith. When this approach is joined to a catechumenal style that specifically attends to the Word of God, the community of faith, liturgical experience, and apostolic service, students are introduced to aspects of Christian formation that bring about conversion to the person of Jesus Christ and foster identity within the Church community that gathers in his name. Catechetical materials need to present an integration of information and formation elements. Such an integration properly supports the goal of catechesis to link catechesis with baptism by way of a living, explicit, and fruitful profession of faith (see *GDC* #66).

It is important for catechetical leaders to remember that a lived faith is transmitted in a variety of ways: the family or the domestic church, parish catechetical programs, Catholic schools, basic ecclesial communities, intergenerational gatherings all working in conjunction with a myriad of catechetical print and media resources. Unfortunately, because of past or potential aberrations, there remains an inherent distrust of nonprofessional approaches to training children and adults in matters of faith. A recent revival of "home schooling" for religious education of children strikes a note of terror in some professional religious educators. In some circles, catechesis has been viewed as a special domain for specially trained people. The history of Catholics in the United States of America at the turn of the last century supported such a notion. Immigrant Catholics were generally poor and illiterate. In such a climate, the Catholic school played a tremendous role in advancing the Catholic faith through an educational mission. In this new millennium, a new wave of immigrants still face formidable challenges in striving to pass on their Catholic faith to their children.

If catechetical leaders intend to accept adult catechesis as the norm for all catechesis, then planning for improving catechesis will have to take the role of all kinds of families into consideration more intentionally. Families are defined as the domestic church and as such have a special responsibility and obligation to preside over the spiritual as well as the physical welfare of the family unit. It saddens many catechetical leaders to interact with adults who feel inadequate and unqualified to share their personal, sometimes privatized faith with their children and other adults. To be called upon to teach others about the faith or, more particularly, to share scripture with them is beyond the imagination of far too many Catholics, especially Catholic parents. Whether practicing or inactive Catholics, many parents lack the means or the confidence to hand on their Catholic faith tradition. Any plan for improving catechesis must attend to the spiritual needs of all kinds of adults in every situation and for parents who are single, married, or divorced with or without joint custody of their children. One special challenge of parishes is to sponsor programs for parents and see to it that they have the resources for handing on their faith.

Families are not alone in introducing a new generation into the practice of Catholic faith. Intergenerational gatherings give members of the community at every age and stage an opportunity to learn from each other. It is said that faith is caught, not taught. Who are the chronologically and spiritually young observing? From whom do they absorb their perceptions, beliefs, attitudes and behaviors? Intergenerational groupings for catechesis offer a community natural avenues for mentoring relationships. An intergenerational form of catechesis mimics other natural groupings for all kinds of important human activity. Human beings are socialized according to particular patterns. Not only young people, but inexperienced people learn first by observation. When wisdom figures of a faith community are not in close contact with the young and neophyte members of the community, traditions are diluted and the community suffers. Spiritual maturity needs as much attention as every other kind of maturation: physical, emotional, psychological, and intellectual.

*Lord of the Flies* by William Golding tells the story of a group of boys who are stranded on an island. As they begin to develop savage ways, the boys realize that if they are to survive, it will be necessary for them to plan and to form some kind of civilization. They organize themselves into hunters (doers) and firekeepers (thinkers). Before long they are at war with each other. Although Golding is writing about the conflict that exists between the mind and instincts and implies that human beings cannot survive without the restraint that conscience supplies, the absence of adult wisdom figures for nurture and guidance is a striking void.

In many ways, modern civilization isolates young people in much the same way as the stranded boys in Golding's story. When faith-filled adults are absent in the lives of the chronologically and spiritually young, a kind of wilding ensues. Intergenerational catechesis offers many more diverse examples of how faith-filled people live. One catechist devised a very effective assignment for young people who were preparing for sacraments. While at Sunday liturgy, these students were asked to observe members of the faith community as they received Holy Communion. One fifteen-year-old boy astounded the catechist when he reported that it was easy to tell who had real faith when they received Eucharist and who appeared to take the host out of habit. In his opinion, people with real faith visibly displayed their belief in the real presence of Jesus in the Eucharist. The quality of faith the young man observed in other members of the community made him think about the kind of faith he would like to have.

## Questions for Reflection
- What elements in a liturgical experience contribute to helping a gathered assembly engage in  full, active and conscious participation of  the liturgy
- If doing good works nets the same effect for people and situations in need of improvement, what difference does it make if those good works are motivated by Gospel values that are learned through liturgical experiences?
- How do catechetical materials with which you are familiar incorporate and promote information and formation aspects of the catechetical agenda?
- What benefits and challenges are inherent in incorporating an intergenerational approach to catechesis?

## Ongoing Evaluation and Planning

Having an ongoing evaluation process for people, programs, pedagogical methods and processes is an essential component for planning and improving catechesis. Since catechesis should be an on-going process that continues throughout the stages of the life cycle, then on-going evaluation makes immanently good sense. Engaging in an evaluation process gives catechetical leaders an opportunity to recall the essential catechetical mission and the agreed upon stated objectives for that mission. Evaluation also encourages catechetical leaders to reassess the catechetical needs of a particular environment and the resources that are available to meet those needs. Sometimes the result of an evaluation process allows catechetical leaders to focus more clearly on the long- and short-term goals that support the catechetical enterprise. An effective evaluation process can help leaders identify whether the current strategies used to accomplish the defined catechetical goals have produced the desired outcomes. If they have not, then catechetical leaders know that the time is right to develop new initiatives in the form of concrete activities and priorities and then to find the resources to support these initiatives.

Conditions favorable to new initiatives are essential. If conditions are unfavorable or even hostile to new initiatives, then catechetical leaders are faced with the task of creating conditions that are favorable. That may mean additional training for collaborators in catechetical ministry. It may require a shift in emphasis or style of catechesis. When evaluating catechetical efforts, catechetical leaders need to engage in an evaluation process that is multi-faceted. As important as catechetical materials are, to evaluate only catechetical texts is to miss the panoply of components that make up a "total curriculum" for catechesis.

The oldest and most experienced organization to begin assessment for religious education in the United States is the National Catholic Educational Association. The NCEA initiated religious education surveys in the early 1970's. Today this professional organization for all Catholic educators provides two religious education assessment instruments that help catechetical leaders evaluate the catechetical agenda for a particular identifiable group.

*Assessment for Catholic Religious Education (ACRE)* surveys students at several age levels: elementary, junior high and senior high school. This religious education tool surveys religious knowledge as well as beliefs, perceptions, attitudes, and behaviors of young people. Unlike achievement tests, this evaluation tool does not focus primarily or exclusively on individual student performance. Rather, individual student responses are compiled into a group report. Such a report provides catechetical leaders with a profile of the level of religious literacy and faith expression of a particular group.  When catechetical leaders compare the compilation of data based on student responses with the desired outcomes based on previously agreed upon catechetical goals, objectives, strategies and activities, they have a "snap shot" of the status quo.  Such information provides catechetical leaders with a real basis for making sound judgments about the direction a catechetical program has been taking in a given environment.  The population profile generated by these composite reports may be construed as an affirmation, or a cause for concern by catechetical leaders.  In either case, both catechetical leaders and faith communities benefit greatly by having reliable data upon which to base a decision to stay with a particular set of initiatives or adopt "in-flight" corrections to the present catechetical course of action.

To facilitate assessment for adults, NCEA provides a second survey, *Information for Growth (IFG)*.  This instrument also provides confidentiality for adults who participate in the survey, and gives an adult sufficient information to determine areas of strength and where there is a need for further spiritual growth.  The *IFG* is ideal for catechists in parish-based religious education programs or teachers and staff members in Catholic schools; newly initiated adults who have entered the Catholic church through the catechumenate process; women and men who are preparing for religious life; or any identifiable group of adults such as parents' groups or small base communities.

## Planning and Improving Catechesis

The reality of who Jesus is does not change; however, our understanding of who Jesus is in the course of our lives does change if we are growing intellectually, emotionally, psychologically, and spiritually.  The challenges that life poses impacts all forms of human growth including spiritual growth.  Likewise, spiritual growth effects the way we face life's challenges.  It is fitting, then, that efforts for catechesis should be ongoing, patterned after an adult approach, and grounded in authentic practices for formation as well as accurate and appropriately developed information.

Planning and improving catechesis requires a sound vision and able leadership from catechetical leaders at all levels of Church responsibility.  Every leader has an obligation and responsibility to plan ways to implement a vision for catechesis that promotes the good news that Jesus Christ incarnates.  To consciously focus every human resource in all kinds of environments on efforts to improve catechesis requires human intelligence, will, talent and skill. Catechesis happens when people who have experienced conversion in Jesus Christ are compelled to share the fruit of their faith with others.  To that end they plan.  They focus energy on nurturing and communicating the Word that is entrusted to a believing community who regularly gathers in the name of the One who gives life.

To avoid self-deception, secure catechetical leaders willingly engage in ongoing evaluation to inform the on-going process of planning and improving catechesis. The spiraling image is an important one for catechesis. It reminds catechetical leaders that faith grows in depth and breadth. Information and formation must work in tandem to insure that the spiral is centered in the source of Christian life—Jesus Christ—and stays balanced. To that end, planning and improving catechesis requires a well-articulated vision for catechesis, a well-devised plan to implement that vision, and catechetical leaders eager to evaluate and discern the communication of the Spirit of God in every new age.

## Questions for Reflection

- Does a vision of catechesis as an aspect of the total process of evangelization affirm or challenge your understanding of catechesis?
- What are the implications of planning for improving catechesis in your parish or school?
- Name three specific things you can do to plan and improve catechesis in your area of influence?
- What methods and tools of evaluation do you use to assess the health and vitality of your program?

## Bibliography

Duggan, Robert D. and Maureen Kelly. *The Christian Initiation of Children: Hope for the Future.* New York: Paulist Press, 1991.

Greinacher, Norbert and Virgil Elizondo. *The Transmission of Faith to the Next Generation.* Edinburgh: T&T Clark LTD, 1984.

Hater, Robert. *The Relationship Between Evangelization and Catechesis.* Washington, DC: USCC, National Conference of Diocesan Directors of Religious Education, 1981.

*The Liturgy Documents: A Parish Resource.* Third Edition. Chicago: Liturgy Training Publications, 1991.

Marthaler, Berard L. *The Catechism Yesterday & Today: The Evolution of a Genre.* Collegeville, MN: The Liturgical Press, 1995.

Morris, Thomas. *The RCIA: Transforming the Church—A Resource for Pastoral Implementation.* New York: Paulist Press, 1989.

National Conference of Catechetical Leadership. *National Certification Standards for Professional Parish Directors of Religious Education.* Washington, D.C.: NCCL, 1996.

Parent, Neil, ed. *Educating for Christian Maturity*. Washington, DC: USCC, Department of Education, 1990.

*Rite of Christian Initiation of Adults*. Chicago: Liturgy Training Publications, 1988.

*Sharing the Light of Faith: National Catechetical Directory For Catholics of the United States*. United States Catholic Conference, 1979.

Warren, Michael, ed. *Source Book for Modern Catechetics*. Winona, MN: St. Mary's Press, 1983.

# 9
# Practicalities of Catechesis
## Mary Angela Shaughnessy

On a typical afternoon, the hardworking catechetical leader pauses in the midst of checking class lists, calling substitutes for two of the regular catechists, verifying signatures on permission slips for a Confirmation service trip to a nursing home, reading the latest minutes of the parish council and religious education board, and completing a diocesan questionnaire regarding insurance benefits for employees. In the midst of all this, she looks for the third time at a phone message from the mother of a second grader who is threatening a lawsuit because an older child pushed hers onto the pavement and he sustained bruises, and according to her, is in incredible pain. The catechetical leader thinks quietly, "All I ever wanted to do was bring the Gospel of Jesus Christ and the truth of the Catholic faith to young people. What happened? It seems I have become a personnel director, police officer, counselor, baby sitter, lawyer, and paper pusher. Sometimes I wonder if religious education is really about rules, regulations, lawsuits, and paper work. How do my job status and benefits protect me as DRE or catechetical leader?"

This essay offers a beginning response to these questions. The practicalities of catechesis can seem to overshadow the mission of catechesis. Knowledge of these practicalities, and understanding their legal implications, can help busy catechetical leaders keep a sense of balance and perspective that can only enhance ministry. Before we look at the practical issues pertinent to catechetical leadership, we invite you to reflect on the following questions.

## Questions for Reflection
- Which parts of your ministry are the most satisfying? The least satisfying? The most time consuming? Do you see ways you could more effectively manage administrative details and thus have more time for the work of evangelization?
- When the topic of civil law and religious ministry is mentioned, what are your feelings? If someone asked you to state some legal principles that you know apply to religious education programs, what would you say?

## Catechetics and the Law

Canon law or church law establishes certain norms for religious education. It is somewhat rare, though not unheard of, for a catechetical leader to run afoul of canon law. Diocesan catechetical leaders and pastors generally recognize and require correction of questionable practices. At all times, catechetical leaders are expected to uphold the teachings of the Magisterium of the church.

Standard 538.012 of the *National Practicalities Standards for Educators* requires the following abilities of educators with regard to civil legal concerns:

Develop policies and programs that reflect the appropriate implementation of legal responsibilities relating to the screening and supervision of volunteers, negligence, corporal punishment, fire laws and procedures, health procedures, permission slips, search and seizure, defamation, child abuse, sexual abuse, and other related issues.

Constitutional law is the main source of civil law affecting public education programs in the United States today. In the majority of public education cases, persons allege deprivation of constitutional rights. Persons in private institutions cannot sustain such allegations because contract law, not Constitutional law, governs private institutions—such as those operated by the Catholic Church.

Catechetical leaders will recognize the existence of certain constitutional rights. The First Amendment guarantees freedom of speech, press, assembly, and religion; the Fourth Amendment protects against unlawful searches and seizures; the Fifth and Fourteenth Amendments guarantee due process.

The U.S. Constitution and state constitutions protect persons from arbitrary governmental deprivation of their freedoms. Persons in religious programs, however, cannot claim these protections because they are in private programs, not public ones.

These restrictions may seem unfair, yet a similar price is paid by anyone who works in a private institution. If a person works for an automobile manufacturer, the person may be required to wear a uniform, and the person may not be permitted to exercise freedom of speech if the contents of one's actual words or symbolic expression are unacceptable to the employer. For example, the auto worker is not permitted to appear in a commercial for a competitor. Similarly, a religious education program can prohibit statements that contradict the teachings of the Catholic Church.

The bottom line is that when one enters a private institution such as a parish, one voluntarily surrenders the protection of the U.S. Constitution.

The catechetical leader, catechists, volunteers, and students are free to end employment or participation, but so long as the person remains in the institution, constitutional protections are not available. Thus, a catechetical leader does not have to accept behaviors about which the public sector has no choice and is even required to protect.

## Fairness and Due Process

Public entities must be concerned with constitutional issues. While administrators of religious education programs are not bound to recognize Constitutional rights, they are required to act in a manner that is fair. Some legal experts talk about a "smell" test. If an action "smells" wrong when a person examines it, it may be suspect. For example, if the pastor were to tell an individual, "You are dismissed from employment or participation in programs, and I am not giving you a reason," an objective observer would probably find that the action "smells" wrong. Although such an action may be perfectly legal in employment situations due to the "at will" employment doctrine—a private sector employer can fire without reason or with a good reason—being legal does not always equate with being right. A wise person once said, "What's legal and what's right could get married tomorrow because they're not related." Unfortunately, there is at least as much fact as fiction in that statement.

Most attorneys would agree that the best law is, like medicine, preventive. The best defense is having tried to follow the right course in the first place. Catechetical leaders must realize that despite their best efforts in any and all areas of religious education they may face lawsuits. Nonetheless, all catechetical leaders should be fair in dealings with others. For this they have the mandate of the gospel. In addition, a basic tenet of contract law, the main source of the law governing religious education, is the covenant of good faith and fair dealing, a pledge to treat other people the way one would like be treated.

## Questions for Reflection
- What policies and procedures does my program/parish have for dealing with discipline of young people? Are they fair?
- How could our policies and procedures be improved? How could they be implemented more effectively?

## Federal and State Statutes

Federal and state statutes and regulations, many of which have constitutional bases, comprise a second source of the law affecting Catholic catechetical leaders and other pastoral personnel. If a statute requires that all who operate educational programs within a given state follow certain directives, then all educational programs are so bound. So long as what is required does not unfairly impinge upon the rights of the Catholic Church as a religious institution and can be shown to have some legitimate purpose, catechetical and other educational programs can be required to comply.

Federal antidiscrimination law does permit religious institutions to give preference to members of that religion in hiring and acceptance into programs, so a catechetical leader can refuse to consider non-Catholics for paid or volunteer positions and to admit non-Catholic young people to a religious education program. Other antidiscrimination laws do provide protection for persons who face discrimination because of their membership in certain protected classes:  race, color, national origin, age (persons over 40 are protected), and handicapping condition/disability. Catechetical leaders must ensure that no discrimination on the basis of such protected class status occurs.

One particular type of discrimination posing special challenges is disability discrimination. Although there appears to have been no definitive court ruling on the applicability of the *Americans with Disabilities Act* to churches and church programs, other federal and state anti-discrimination laws may apply. Thus, prudent catechetical leader will strive to make reasonable accommodations for people with disabilities. There is no law requiring that any accommodation sought by persons with disabilities must be provided. Financial exigency can prevent even reasonable access being provided, as existing laws allow an institution which would face severe financial hardship in providing such accommodations to decline to do so. Care must be taken to ensure that financial exigency is not used as an excuse. If a parish were to hold that an elevator cannot be provided in the religious education program, and then spent $500,000 on other parish improvements, the existence of true financial exigency could be questioned if the *ADA* is found to apply.

A question often asked regarding disabilities is, "Does each parish have to provide religious education services for the deaf, blind, mentally or physically challenged?" The answer is that services do not necessarily have to be offered at a specific site, but they must be available somewhere within a reasonable distance. For example, a diocese might designate one parish to be the service provider for deaf people. If, however, a parent of a special needs child insists on the child's inclusion in the parish program, every reasonable effort should be made to accommodate the request. The key term to keep in mind always is reasonableness.

## Sexual Harassment:    A Form of Discrimination

Today's catechetical leaders have surely read and heard much about sexual harassment. No longer is sexual harassment something that is found only between two adults or between an adult and a child. School children claim that they have been sexually harassed by peers, and courts are granting money damages to the victims. What can catechetical leaders do to ensure the sexual safety of people in their programs? First, they must understand what sexual harassment is. Every comment that is made concerning gender is not sexual harassment. For example, a male student who states, "Everyone knows boys are better at football than girls," or a catechist who declares, "I'd rather teach girls than boys because boys are rowdier than girls," is likely not guilty of sexual harassment. Title VII of the *U.S. Civil Rights Act* of 1964 mandated that the workplace be free of harassment based on sex. Title IX requires that educational programs receiving federal funding be free of sexual harassment. Some states are also enacting laws governing gender harassment; the above referenced comments could be considered as gender, but not necessarily sexual, harassment.

The Equal Employment Opportunities Commission issued guidelines which define sexual harassment, forbidden by Title VII as:

Unwelcomed sexual advances, requests for sexual favors, and other verbal or physical conduct of a sexual nature when:

- Submission to such conduct by an individual is made explicitly or implicitly a term of employment;

- Submission to, or rejection of such conduct by an individual is used as the basis for an employment decision;

- And any such conduct has the purpose or effect to interfere with an individual's work performance, or creates a hostile or intimidating environment.

The above definition concerns employment conditions; however, "education" can be substituted for "employment" in the definition, and the basis for Title IX violations would be evident. Specifically, Title IX states:

No person in the United States shall, on the basis of sex, be excluded from participation in, be denied the benefits of, or be subjected to discrimination under any education program or activity receiving Federal financial assistance.

While the amount of financial assistance necessary to trigger protection has not been established, most Catholic parishes or parish-sponsored programs, particularly those associated with schools, have taken some government funds or services at some time and, thus, would be well-advised to comply with Title IX as far as possible. Courts, including the Supreme Court, are vigorously supporting persons' rights to be free from sexual harassment. Most legal experts agree that Title IX can apply to Catholic schools. Since religious education programs are sponsored by parishes in much the same manner as are schools, it seems that religious education program participants should also be protected from sexual harassment.

One of the most important actions a catechetical leader can take with regard to sexual harassment is to implement clear policies defining sexual harassment and detailing procedures for dealing with such claims. Most dioceses currently have sexual harassment policies that should be implemented in all parishes. Catechetical leaders, catechists, and staff should sign a statement, "I have received and read the sexual harassment policy for the diocese/parish, and recognize the parish/diocese's right and obligation to enforce it." If nothing else, this will heighten peoples' consciousness to be alert to such infringements and claims.

It is far easier to prevent claims of sexual harassment than it is to defend them. Employees, catechists, and volunteers should participate in some kind of in-service training that raises awareness of sexual harassment and gender issues. All must understand what types of behaviors can be considered sexual or gender harassment. Finally, of course, sexual harassment and other forms of demeaning behavior have no place in any religious education program. Guarding the dignity of all members of the parish community should be a priority for all catechetical leaders—as it is a mandate of Christian faith.

## Questions for Reflection
- What areas of discrimination law cause you the most concern as a catechetical leader? Why?
- How will you address issues of discrimination in your catechetical ministry? What policies does your program need? How will you monitor compliance?

## Search and Seizure and Other Issues of Privacy
One of the privileges of living in the United States is the right to be free of unreasonable intrusion into one's private affairs. One main concern is the issue of search and seizure. The Fourth Amendment to the U.S. Con-

stitution protects the right of persons to be secure in their persons and property. If a governmental agency searches persons and property without a warrant, the results of the search are considered poisoned and cannot be used against the person searched or the owner of property. The right of students in public schools to be free from searches has been severely limited by the case of *New Jersey v. T.L.O.*, 105 S. Ct. 733 (1985) which held that students in public schools cannot be granted the same privacy that adults have. The court ruled that school officials need have only reasonable cause to conduct a search and do not have to obtain a search warrant before proceeding with the search.

Because the prohibitions against searches are based on the Fourth Amendment to the Constitution, they apply only to government agencies, not to private agencies such as religious education programs. Nonetheless, catechetical leaders should have some kind of stated policy for searching young persons and/or seizing their possessions. Searching a student's person should require "more" cause than searching a desk or locker.

Lockers and desks are parish property. The catechetical leader and catechists have every right to examine them and their contents. A religious education program strengthens its position with students and parents by including in handbooks a statement such as, "The parish is co-tenant of lockers and desks and reserves the right to search them at any time without notice."

## When and How to Conduct a Search

If a catechist or catechetical leader believes that a young person is carrying a dangerous item on his or her person, he or she should ask the student for the item. If the student refuses, the student can be asked to empty pockets, book bags, purses, back packs, etc. If the student still refuses, the adult must make a choice. Obviously, if the adult believes that others are in danger, he or she will have to take whatever action appears necessary to gain possession of the item. There is no requirement that adults expose themselves to grave harm, but adults are expected to act reasonably. If all else fails, the police should be contacted. If it is possible to contact the catechetical leader or other administrator, the catechist should do so before beginning a search.

If the situation permits, the best course of action would appear to be to contact the parent and have the parent come to the site and conduct a search of the student. Such a procedure is a serious one and should be undertaken only in grave circumstances. When possible, catechetical leaders should contact the appropriate diocesan personnel or attorneys for advice. The pastor should always be notified as well.

While constitutional protections do not apply, religious education programs and their personnel can be subject to tort suits (private civil wrongs) of assault and battery and/or invasion of privacy if a student is harmed as a result of an unreasonable search. Carefully developed policies and procedures should guide any search and seizure; a common sense "balancing test" should be applied in each case. Is this search and its possible effects worth finding whatever it is the catechetical leader or staff member is seeking?

For example, an exhaustive search for a student's lost dollar does not seem worth the effort. After asking if anyone has seen the dollar, the adult would be well advised to lend the student a dollar, if necessary, rather than to disrupt the educational environment by a search. If the young person has lost an expensive piece of jewelry, the catechist might conduct a more expansive search. Approach is most important. Saying to a group of young persons, "Let's all help Johnny look for his watch. Let's all look in our book bags to see if it could have fallen into one by mistake," while the adult examines his or her own bag, avoids the trauma of young persons being singled out for accusation. Our Church teaching affirming the dignity of each person and a commitment to treat everyone the way Jesus would should be the guiding principles in any search and seizure situation.

## Records and Privacy

An issue related to invasion of privacy is confidentiality of records. The contents of student files should be released only to authorized persons. Even program personnel should be given access to files only for appropriate program-related reasons. Parental signatures should be required before records are sent to anyone. Of particular concern today in matters of privacy is the issue of non-custodial parents; many young persons are not in the physical custody of both biological parents or are in a shared custody situation where living is divided between two homes. Catechetical leaders may often find themselves facing a non-custodial parent who wants a copy of student records or other information. The *Buckley Amendment* grants non-custodial parents the right of access to student records. There is a difference of opinion among legal experts concerning the applicability of this Amendment to private institutions. Some scholars interpret the law as not affecting religious institutions. Others believe that religious institutions can be held to its requirements.

There has been no definitive case concerning the *Buckley Amendment* and a Catholic institution. It is this writer's opinion that religious education programs, like Catholic schools, should voluntarily comply with the law. If one chooses not to comply, one runs the risk of becoming a test case in the courts. There are common sense reasons, also, for allowing non-custodial parents involvement in the lives of their children. Unless there is a court order to the contrary, a non-custodial parent should be allowed to discuss a child's progress and should be given unofficial copies of reports, if requested. Of course, a non-custodial parent has no right of physical access to the child unless granted that right by a court.

Catechetical leaders would be well advised to include a provision such as the following in parent/student handbooks: "This program voluntarily complies with the provisions of the *Buckley Amendment*. Non-custodial parents will be given access to unofficial copies of student records, and catechists will be available to discuss the student's progress unless a court order providing otherwise is filed with the catechetical leader."

An alternate inclusion would be the requirement that divorced parents file a court certified copy of the custody section of the divorce decree with the program office; such a procedure would help to protect the rights of everyone in the family.

While religious education programs are not held to the same Constitutional privacy safeguards as are public institutions, all catechetical leaders should be concerned with protecting the rights of young people entrusted to their care. Prayerful and thoughtful reflection and planning will help ensure that programs have the necessary information, and that the privacy rights of persons are respected.

## Questions for Reflection
- How do I ensure that the privacy rights of students and their parents are respected?
- Does my program have policies governing non-custodial parents and access to information, records, and physical access to children? If yes, are they consistently implemented? If no, what policies and procedures do we need?

## Keeping Confidences: What Can You Tell? What Must You Tell?

One complex situation facing catechetical leaders today is that of students sharing confidential information. Today's young persons may well face more pressures and problems than the young persons of any other generation. Broken homes, alcoholism and drug addiction, sexual and physical abuse, depression and violence were certainly found in earlier eras but they seem to be more prevalent, or at least more openly acknowledged, today than they were when the majority of today's catechetical leaders were children and adolescents.

The responsibility for receiving student confidences and advising students in both day-to-day situations and crises can be overwhelming. Busy catechetical leaders may well say, "What am I supposed to do? I know I'm not a professional counselor, psychiatrist, or a social worker but I'm the one the student trusts, the one the student has consulted. Are there certain legal issues involved in receiving student confidences? Is there matter that must be made known to others, even when the student has asked for and received my promise of confidentiality?"

These are good questions. No one can afford to think that he or she can help all students all of the time. If a student were to come to a catechist or catechetical leader and state that he or she is experiencing shortness of breath and chest pain, the adult would quickly summon medical assistance and the student's parents. Yet, psychological problems are no less serious than physical ones, and the lay person who attempts to deal with such problems unaided may well be courting tragedy for both self and student.

Confidentiality is generally held to mean that one individual will keep private information private, and will not reveal it. Thus, the penitent in the Sacrament of Reconciliation rightfully expects that the subject matter of confession will be held sacred by the confessor and will not be revealed to anyone. Indeed, there are accounts of priests who have died rather than break the seal of confession.

Friends share confidences with each other. One individual may say to another, "This is confidential. You cannot repeat it." The person speaking in confidence has a right to expect that the confidant to whom the information is given will keep the matter confidential. But there are recognized limits to what friends will keep confidential if the health or safety of the person giving the confidence is at risk.

It is not as unusual as one might think for an adult, however, to believe that a student who is talking about suicide is not serious, can be talked out of the planned action, or is not capable of carrying out a suicide threat. As child and adolescent psychiatrists report, young people do not generally comprehend the finality of death and do not consider the long-term ramifications of suicide. If a student tells a catechist or catechetical leader that he or she is going to harm self or others, the catechist or catechetical leader must reveal that information even if a promise of confidentiality has been given. Teachers who fail to act on the information can be sued for failure to warn when tragedy occurs.

It is a widely held myth that counselors, physicians, psychologists, and social workers have legal immunity from responsibility for any injuries that may arise from their not acting on confidential information. Such a belief is not grounded in law or fact. The only two privileges protecting confidential conversations which seem to remain in the law are that of priest/ penitent and attorney/client. Even the husband/wife privilege which allowed a spouse to refuse to testify against a spouse has been largely abandoned. Clearly, there is no privilege for a catechetical leader or catechist, unless the person is a priest hearing confession or an attorney who can claim attorney/ client privilege.

In light of the above information, a catechetical leader must presume that no legal protection exists for those who receive student confidences. What should the adult do who wants to be a role model for young persons, who wants to be approachable and helpful? The answer is simple: lay down the ground rules for confidentiality before you receive any confidences. Tell students that their confidences will be respected except in cases of danger to health, life, and safety. If a student asks to talk to the catechetical leader or catechist in confidence, the ground rules should be reiterated before the student begins to share.

Another confidentiality situation is presented by the practice of journal writing. Religious educators, like all teachers, have long recognized the value of student journal writing. This practice does, however, carry a real risk of student disclosure of information that the educator is compelled to reveal. Catechists must set the same rules for journal confidentiality as discussed above. Catechists must understand that they are expected to read what students write. If the catechist cannot read the assignment, then the assignment should not be made. Journal writing has a place in today's religious education curriculum, but adults must be sure that students understand the parameters of the assignment and the adult's responsibility of reporting threatened danger.

In one very relevant school case involving confidentiality, *Brooks v. Logan and Joint District No. 2, 903 P.2d 73 (1995)*, parents of a student who had committed suicide filed an action for wrongful death and a claim for negligent infliction of emotional distress against a teacher who had assigned the keeping of journals to her class. She stated that she had not read the entries in question, as she had told students that they could simply indicate pages they did not want read and she would not read them. The lower court granted summary judgment (a ruling that there is no case) in favor of the teacher and the school district. However, the appellate court reversed the finding, and held that there were issues of fact in existence which could only be determined at a trial; thus, the teacher will have to defend herself in a trial.

The above information indicates that allowing students the option of not having journals read poses real legal problems. A general rule is, if the teacher assigns it, the teacher reads it. If the teacher doesn't have time to read the entries, the teacher doesn't assign journal writing. Catechists and catechetical leaders often ask about the keeping of a prayer journal which the supervising adults never collects or reads. So long as the prayer journal is never read, a teacher may be able to avoid liability for failing to read. If the keeper of such a journal wants to share an entry or entries with a teacher, the teacher should require that the student read the entries to him or her.

A final confidentiality concern is posed by the retreat and other faith sharing settings. The retreat experience is extremely important for today's Catholic young people. However, students are often very vulnerable in such situations. They may share stories of child abuse, sexual harassment, family dysfunction, even possible criminal activity. While encouraging students to share, the group leader must once again set the ground rules before the sharing begins. To repeat, this means making clear that any behavior which endangers oneself or others must be reported to the appropriate authorities. The use of peer leaders does not lessen the responsibility of the supervising adults. Student leaders must receive instructions regarding confidentiality and reporting rules, and must communicate them to group members.

To meet the ever-changing legal challenges posed by confidentiality issues, the wise catechetical leader will establish and enforce ground rules for dealing with student confidences, and will seek assistance from diocesan officials and/or parents when appropriate.

## Questions for Reflection

- What has been your experience regarding issues of confidentiality?
- What conversations have you had with the catechetical team at your school or parish about privacy issues and confidentiality?

## Gangs and Religious Education

A number of issues, including confidentiality, are presented by gang membership. In the last decade or so, the word "gang" has taken on a very different meaning than it had twenty, thirty, or fifty years ago. Many readers remember their parents or grandparents referring to the good times they had while they "ran around with a gang of friends." Today, the word "gang" has taken on a sinister meaning connoting fear, violence, and domination. Suddenly, it seems everyone is clamoring for educational programs to do something about the presence and activities of gangs. Many dioceses are writing and implementing policies concerning gangs.

The first step in developing policy is to define exactly what a gang is. A 1991 California case, *The People v. Ralph Gamez*, 235 Cal.App.3d 957, 286 Cal. Rptr. 894 was significant in its definition of gangs. The court stated that the proper term to use when discussing problematic gangs is "criminal gang-like behavior." Unless one's state law has a different term or definition, diocesan and/or local leaders would be well-advised to adopt such a designation.

An analysis of *Gamez* and similar cases leads to a clearer definition of criminal gang-like activity. One archdiocese (Louisville, Kentucky) offers this definition:

> Criminal gang-like activity involving membership in a criminal gang is defined as an ongoing organization, association, or group of three or more persons, whether formal or informal, having as one of its primary activities the commission of one or more criminal acts.

Pastoral and catechetical leaders should understand that the intent to commit criminal acts is what distinguishes criminal gang-like activity from other types of group activities. Moreover, it is not membership in a gang in and of itself that is a problem; it is the criminal activity.

Some may be tempted to think that enumerating all possible criminal offenses is useful in policy writing. In actuality, the issue of gangs is one that is better dealt with in general, rather than specific, terms. The term, "criminal gang-like activity," includes all possible offenses; attempts to enumerate all offenses can result in omission of some, or an argument by an aggrieved student that what he or she did was not terroristic threatening or property damage, for example.

## Gang Attire, Symbols and Behaviors

The wearing of colors has long indicated membership in a gang. Any catechetical leader has the right to forbid such displays. However, it is not always easy to identify what exactly constitutes the display of gang colors. In one state, for example, two university athletic teams have different school colors. So gang members wear university sweatshirts, jackets, and other emblems to denote their membership in a particular gang. Certainly, there is nothing wrong with wearing a college sweatshirt and it is very difficult, if not impossible, to determine who is supporting a team and who is displaying gang colors.

If a catechetical leader suspects or notices criminal gang-like activity at any time during educational and related activities, the pastor should be notified immediately. Second, the catechetical leader will seek appropriate advice concerning investigation of the suspicion or allegation, and will proceed to gather data.

Third, if the catechetical leader determines or strongly suspects that any young person is involved in criminal gang-like activity, the student's parents or guardians should be notified and disciplinary action taken when appropriate. In the case of suspicion without any convincing evidence, a warning concerning the consequences for any one who engages in criminal gang-like activity may be given. Written documentation of any meetings should be kept.

Fourth, if a criminal act has occurred, the catechetical leader has a legal responsibility to notify local law enforcement officials and to assist the officials as far as possible in their investigation(s). A catechetical leader should focus on what was actually done that is/was wrong, rather than on membership in a gang. If a parish rule has been broken, the breaking of the rule should be discussed and appropriate sanctions given. If a crime has been committed, the focus should be on the crime and its consequences.

Sometimes, a student needs help to avoid or terminate membership in a gang. Catechetical leaders should have some training or know where to contact trained persons so that students can be helped in avoiding or disengaging from gangs.

The days of simply announcing that some activity or association is wrong and expecting immediate student compliance are gone. It is every catechetical leader's responsibility to help in the creation of a community in which persons have no desire to engage in criminal gang-like activity.

## Catechist/Student Relationships

Catechists, as well as catechetical leaders, often find themselves counseling students in personal matters. It is not unusual for a catechist to find him or herself in the position of "surrogate parent" for a young person. Students often entrust catechists with confidential information, as discussed elsewhere in this chapter. Catechists, many of whom have little training in professional counseling, often have questions about what is appropriate in interacting with students outside the classroom or parish setting. There are few guidelines available; catechists and others may find themselves dealing with situations that pose personal and legal risks for the adults as well as the students. There is a growing number of lawsuits in which parents threaten and/or pursue legal action against an educator whose actions they view as unwise, inappropriate, sexually motivated, or interfering with the parent/child relationship.

## Sexual Misconduct

One end of the student/catechist relationship spectrum is represented by sexual misconduct. Sexual misconduct can be alleged in apparently innocent situations. Students can misinterpret touching, and catechetical leaders and catechists may easily find themselves facing child abuse charges. Prudence is in order whenever a catechist touches a student.

Another kind of problem is posed by a student who believes that a catechist has not responded to efforts to achieve a closer relationship. Such a student may accuse a catechist of inappropriate conduct as a retaliatory measure. Catechetical leaders and catechists must be aware that serious consequences can result from an allegation of child abuse, even if the allegation is proven to be false. At the very least, such a false allegation can be extremely embarrassing for the catechist.

If a child abuse report is made, authorities will question the alleged perpetrator and make a record of the allegation. In some states, lists of suspected or reported child abusers are kept. Thus, it is imperative that catechists protect themselves and the students they teach by practicing appropriate behavior with young people. To avoid even the slightest hint of impropriety, a catechist should avoid being alone with a single student behind closed doors unless a window or other opening permits outsiders to see into the area. A good question to ask one's self might be, "If this were my child, grandchild, niece, nephew, would I have any objection to a catechist relating with him or her in this manner?"

## Other Problematic Behaviors

Catechetical leaders and catechists must remember that they are professionals rendering a service. Just as a counselor or psychiatrist is professionally bound to avoid emotional involvement with a client, a catechist should avoid becoming so emotionally involved with a student that objectivity and fairness are compromised. Catechists must remember that they have many young persons for whom they share responsibility and who need and may desire the catechist's attention. If a relationship with a student keeps a catechist from responding to other student needs on a regular basis, the catechist and the catechetical leader should seriously examine the appropriateness of the relationship.

In seeking to assess the appropriateness of an adult/child relationship, some mental health professionals recommend asking one's self questions such as: Whose needs are being met? Is there a boundary between student and adult? Where and what is it?

The following adult behaviors could be considered inappropriate, depending on the totality of the circumstances:

- dropping by a young person's home, particularly if no parent or other adult is present
- frequent telephoning of the student
- social trips with a student
- sharing of catechist's personal problems.

Serving as a catechist in these times is both a privilege and a challenge. It is indeed tragic when a catechist or catechetical leader is forced to relinquish that gift because of inappropriate choices.

## Questions for Reflection

- Do all catechists, staff and volunteers have a working understanding of privacy and confidentiality?
- If yes, how can we strengthen the understanding? If no, how can we establish appropriate policies and procedures, and provide training?

## Negligence and Religious Education

Negligence is the most common of all lawsuits filed against educators. Negligence is the "fault" against which catechetical leaders and other parish administrators must guard; however, what may be considered negligence in one court may not be considered negligence in another. It is much better, obviously, to avoid being accused of negligence in the first place than to take one's chances on the outcome of a lawsuit.

Since negligence is an unintentional act or omission which results in injury, a person charged with negligence is generally not going to face criminal charges. Persons who bring successful negligence suits are usually awarded money damages in amounts calculated to compensate for the actual injuries suffered. It is possible, though rare, for a court to award punitive or exemplary damages if the court is shocked by the negligent behavior. In assessing whether a person's behavior is negligent, a court will use the "reasonable person" test: Would a reasonable person [catechist] in this situation have acted in this manner? "Reasonable" is whatever the jury or other fact-finder decides it is.

Courts also rely on the principle: "The younger the child chronologically or mentally, the greater the standard of care." Ninth grade participants in religious education programs, for example, would not ordinarily require the same level of supervision that kindergarten students need. Some people believe that children and older students can never be left unattended. Such a belief is mistaken. Courts recognize that emergencies can arise and that students might be left alone while the supervisor is taking care of the emergency. Judges expect, however, that supervisors will have told students at other points, such as the beginning of the term and periodically thereafter, what they are supposed to do if the supervisor has to leave. At minimum, rules might require that students remain in their seats when no adult is present. Catechetical leaders should consider developing a staff rule that students are not to be left unattended unless absolutely necessary, and that proper procedures are followed in an emergency. Ordinarily, a catechist should be able to tell some other adult that he or she has to leave the students.

There are real risks associated with religious education programs. In some programs in which volunteers are used as substitutes in the absence of the regular catechist, the supervising volunteer may not even know the student's names. He or she may not be skilled in teaching and classroom management techniques. Catechetical leaders should insist that all persons who supervise students, even the individuals who are on the substitute list, participate in an orientation in which appropriate skills can be addressed and cultivated.

There are **four elements** which must be present before legal negligence can be found: **duty**, **violation of duty**, **proximate cause**, and **injury**. If any one of these elements is missing, legal negligence cannot be present. Let us explain each element.

The person charged with negligence must have had a **duty** in the situation. Educators are not responsible for injuries occurring at a place where or a time when they had no responsibility. A catechetical leader, catechist, or program volunteer walking through a mall on a weekend, does not have a legal duty to students who are also walking through the mall. Within the religious education setting, students have a right to safety and catechetical leaders and catechists have a duty to protect the safety of all those entrusted to their care. Catechetical leaders have a duty to develop and implement rules and regulations guiding catechists in providing for student safety.

One situation that presents problems from a negligence standpoint is that of the student who arrives early and/or is not picked up at dismissal time. All staff must understand that students must be supervised from the time they arrive at the religious education site until the time they depart. If parents are late picking up their children, an adult staff member must remain with the students until the parents arrive. Catechetical leaders may want to consider some sort of penalty for repeated violations of these rules. Perhaps a fine could be imposed, or a student could be denied participation in some social activity.

Whatever procedure a catechetical leader chooses, at no time may a participant be left unattended or placed in front of a locked door to await the arrival of parents. Courts have indicated that administrators and staff members can be held responsible for participant behavior occurring on parish premises before or after programs and for the consequences of the behavior.

The 1967 New Jersey school case of *Titus v. Lindberg*, 228 A.2d 65 illustrates the extent to which educational officials can be held liable. In

*Titus* the principal was found negligent and responsible for student injury occurring on school grounds before school because: he knew that students arrived on the grounds before the doors were opened; he was present on campus when they were; he had established no rules for student conduct outside the building; nor had he provided for student supervision. The court ruled that the principal had a reasonable duty to provide such supervision when he knew students were on the property before school.

It should be easy to see how a situation similar to that in *Titus* could arise in a religious education program. Who will supervise the early arrivals and the late pick-ups? This dilemma might well be taken to the supervising board for the development of a policy statement. Courts expect some policy as to when students may arrive at a program site, what rules they are to follow, what kind of supervision will be provided, and the penalties for noncompliance.

In any situation, common sense has to prevail. Textbook solutions are rarely available for persons working with young people. For example, a catechist who realizes on her way home that she has left an article at the religious education site and returns to retrieve it could discover that a student is outside waiting for a ride and no other adult is present on the premises. The reasonable catechist would wait with the child until parents arrive or until some other transportation arrangement can be developed.

The catechist might think that it is not her duty because she normally wouldn't even be on the premises; however, a court could well decide that the point is that she was there and should behave in a professional manner. In the situation just described, a catechist may be tempted to put the child in her car and take him or her home. However, should a catechist elect to take such an action and an accident occurs, the catechist would be liable.

Negligence cannot exist if the second element, **violation of duty**, is not present. Courts understand that accidents and spontaneous actions can occur. If a catechist is properly supervising students during a break and one student picks up an object, throws it, and thus injures another student, the catechist is not responsible. However, if the supervising adult were to allow object throwing to continue without attempting to stop it and a student were injured, the catechist would probably be found to have violated a duty.

Similarly, a catechist who leaves a classroom unattended to make a personal, non-emergency telephone call will usually be found to have violated a duty if a student is injured and it can be shown that the catechist's presence could have prevented the injury. If it can be shown that catechists often left students unattended while the catechetical leader, through inaction or inattention, did nothing about the situation, the catechetical leader has violated a duty as well.

Under the legal doctrine of *respondeat superior* (let the superior answer), administrators are often held responsible for the actions of subordinates. In determining whether the superior is liable, courts pose questions such as these: Has the superior developed a clear policy for staff conduct in dealing with situations such as the one which resulted in injury? Has the supervisor implemented the policy? Are staff members supervised in this regard?

The violation of duty must be the proximate cause of the injury. The court or jury has to decide whether proper supervision could have prevented the injury and, in so deciding, the court has to look at the facts of each individual case. Proximate cause is not necessarily synonymous with direct cause. For example, in the object-throwing example cited above, the student throwing an object would be the direct cause of the injury; however, the catechist's failure to intervene in the situation would be the proximate cause of the injury.

A well-known case which illustrates the concept of proximate cause is *Smith v. Archbishop of St. Louis*, 632 S.W.2d 516 (Mo. Ct. App. 1982). A second grade teacher kept a lighted candle on her desk every morning during the month of May. She gave no special instructions to the students regarding the dangers of lighted candles. One day a child, wearing a crepe paper costume for a play, moved too close to the candle and the costume caught fire. The teacher had difficulty putting out the flames and the child sustained serious physical and resultant psychological injuries.

The trial court ruled that the teacher's act of keeping the lighted candle on her desk was the proximate cause of the child's injury. The court discussed the concept of foreseeability; it was not necessary that the teacher have foreseen the particular injury but only that a reasonable person should have foreseen that some injury was possible. The concept of foreseeability is important. Would a reasonable person foresee that there is a potential for injury? Religious education programs contain the potential for injuries like the one in *Smith*.

**Proximate cause** is a complex legal concept. Religious education programs pose special dangers because participants are not in the traditional school setting. Their energy can stimulate their taking risks that could expose them to dangers. Catechetical leaders would be well-advised to hold regular staff meetings to discuss the program, catechists' expectations, and foreseeable problems. These matters can then be analyzed in the light of health and safety requirements.

The fourth element necessary for a finding of negligence is **injury**. No matter how irresponsible the behavior of an educator, there is no legal negligence if there is no injury. If a catechist leaves twenty first-graders unattended for thirty minutes and no one is injured, there is no negligence in a legal sense. In order to bring suit in a court of law, a person has to have sustained an injury for which the court can award a remedy.

In developing and implementing policies for supervision, the catechetical leader must ask, "Is this what a reasonable person in a similar situation would be expected to do?" The best defense for any administrator in a negligence suit is a reasonable attempt to provide for the safety of all through appropriate rules and regulations. The best defense for a catechist is a reasonable effort to implement rules and regulations.

Because of the seriousness of the dangers posed by religious education programs, a greater standard of care will be expected of catechists than would probably be required of teachers in the traditional school setting. Catechetical leaders and catechists are expected to keep all equipment in working order and to render areas used by young people as hazard-free as possible.

Thus, catechetical leaders must take a proactive approach with regard to the elimination of hazards. All activities should be carefully monitored. All staff, paid and volunteer, should receive thorough and ongoing orientation and instruction. The reasonable catechetical leader supervises staff. The catechetical leader who practices prevention by constantly striving to eliminate foreseeable risks will avoid costly lawsuits and injuries.

## Religious Education Handbooks:    Are They Necessary?

After the first weeks of the religious education program, a catechetical leader may give a sigh of relief that the opening went well, and the business of Catholic religious education is moving forward. It is never too early or too late, however, to evaluate policies, procedures, and documents. No documents are more important than the faculty and parent/student handbooks.

Catechetical leaders, catechists, and parents may ask why a certain item isn't covered by a handbook policy or procedure or may state that what is written in a handbook does not seem sufficient for situations that arise. These are important observations and they need to be captured and recorded when made, not later when it is time to revise the handbook(s) for the coming year. The catechetical leader might consider utilizing a simple index card method for suggested revisions. Anyone who has a suggestion for inclusion or deletion in handbook(s) should note that suggestion on an index card. Only one suggestion per card is allowed. In the spring when handbooks are usually revised or updated, the catechetical leader can sort cards by topic. Then, the catechetical leader or handbook committee can consider each idea. Such an approach makes revision much easier, and does not result in frantic efforts to recall what people said at previous meetings. Such a process also fosters greater participation, and therefore ownership, among staff members.

## Minimum Components of Catechist Handbooks

There are six minimum topic areas that should be included in any catechist handbook:

1) the philosophy and mission of the parish and program
2) a list and explanation of teaching duties, including a working definition of what constitutes good catechesis,
3) a list and explanation of non-teaching duties,
4) the policy and procedures for administrative supervision and evaluation of catechists,
5) a list and explanation of personnel policies, and
6) sample forms.

These six areas are by no means exhaustive, but they provide a broad, legally sound framework. Almost everything that a catechetical leader would want to include in a handbook can "fit" into one of these categories. For example, a policy on the law relating to child abuse reporting, is a non-teaching duty. A policy that reflects an awareness of students with special needs in classrooms can be placed under the category of teaching duties.

## Parent/Student Handbooks

Parent/student handbooks are, in the opinion of this author, preferable to having simply a student handbook or two separate handbooks. The parents are the parties that can be said to have contracted for the religious education of their children. In enrolling their child(ren) in the program, they are agreeing that both they and their child(ren) will abide by program rules and regulations.

The parent/student handbook should include policies and procedures in the following areas:

1) Philosophy and Mission,
2) Admission Policies,
3) Academic Expectations concerning catechesis,
4) Communication—how does the parent communicate with catechists or the catechetical leader?
5) Discipline Code, including rules, regulations, penalties, and exceptions,
6) Extra-curricular Activities, including policies on participation and exclusion from activities,
7) Parent/Student's Signed Agreement to be bound by the handbook.

Such an agreement, which should be on a detachable card or a separate sheet, can state the following or similar words: "We, the parent(s) of _____, agree to be governed by this program handbook for the religious education year _____. We recognize the right and responsibility of the parish to make rules and enforce them."

Since situations can arise that were not foreseen at the time of writing a handbook, the catechetical leader should always reserve the right to amend the handbook. Parents and students should be promptly notified of amendments.

### How Binding Are Handbooks?

A sizable number of court cases hold that handbooks can be legally binding, in the same way as other contracting documents are. Some administrators have inserted disclaimers into handbooks stating that they are not legally binding contracts. There are ethical issues that should be considered before a catechetical leader publishes a handbook to which catechists or parents or students are bound, but which the catechetical leader does not consider as binding the parish. Since courts generally resolve any ambiguity in favor of the person who did not construct the document, it is easy to see how problems can arise. The wise leader will always attempt to balance ethical and legal issues in decision-making.

### Questions for Reflection
- Does my parish have handbooks? If yes, are they adequate? Do they need revisions? If no, how can we develop them?
- What items would I want to include in handbooks?

### Boards of Education:  Roles and Responsibilities

Religious education year beginnings offer many activities and challenges for all who work in the ministry of religious education. One important activity is the opening board meeting. New board members may be attending their first meeting. Questions and concerns surface. Good orientation helps board members understand their roles and those of the catechetical leader, principal (where appropriate, as in boards of total Catholic education), and pastor. Board members who have a clear understanding of the rules for board operation have a greater chance of functioning efficiently and effectively than do those who have no such understanding.

The relationships between and among pastors, catechetical leaders, and board members should be mutually beneficial; thus, it is important that the legal role of the board be carefully outlined and the scope of its authority delineated. Board members have a right to the information and documents they need in order to perform their job effectively.

## Canon Law

Canon law governs the function of boards, just as civil law does. There is no such creature as a board with absolute jurisdiction. Any institution or program that calls itself Catholic is subject to the bishop in what is traditionally called "matters of faith and morals."

## Powers

The school or religious education board has power to recommend and/ or adopt certain courses of action, always subject to the ratification of the pastor or canonical vicar. Board members must understand that power is vested in the board as a body, not in individual members. The role of the board is development of policy, even if policy has to be approved at a higher level.

Policy is usually defined as a guide for discretionary action. Thus, policy will dictate what the board wishes to be done. Policy is not concerned with administration or implementation; the board should not become involved in how its directives will be implemented or with the specific persons who will implement them. For example, a board might state as a policy that confirmation would be received by eighth-graders. The board would not be concerned with how the policy is implemented. Administrative decisions are the day-to-day management choices of the catechetical leader. It is important for everyone to understand these distinctions.

Generally, boards will recommend and/or set policies in the major areas of program, finance, personnel, and plant. A board might approve the budget, approve programs and handbooks, determine hiring and dismissal policies, and possibly oversee facility planning. Other areas of board action might include grievance procedures, extra and co-curricular activities, building safety and usage, and disciplinary code approval.

When tensions arise, board members must keep their responsibilities to the diocese and to the Church in view. If a board member cannot support a policy (and support does not necessarily mean agreement; it does mean a willingness to live with and support the decision), then change must be sought through appropriate channels. If change cannot be achieved and a board member still cannot support the policy in question, then the person's only real choice is to resign from the board. The board of a parish or religious education program is not free to adopt a policy at variance with those of the diocese.

Board members, then, have two basic responsibilities: 1) to recommend and/or approve policies and 2) to support the persons who implement those policies. Becoming involved in internal program conflicts only weakens the authority of both the board and the catechetical leader who, nonetheless, should keep board members informed about problematic or potentially problematic situations so that board members will be able to respond in an intelligent manner if questioned.

## Board Handbooks

Board members will find a thorough handbook to be an invaluable aid in learning about the parish/program and about board membership. Orientation can be structured around the contents of the handbook. The handbook should begin with the parish or program mission/philosophy.

The handbook should also include the constitution and by-laws of the board. Parishes and/or programs may have set by-laws and constitutions from the bishop or his delegate. These documents, written by persons with authority, should give detailed information about the scope of authority, the role of the board, board accountability, and practical aspects of membership, procedures, and meetings.

All policies, including diocesan policies and ones adopted by the board, should be included in the handbook. Policies should be dated and any revisions should be clearly noted.

Formal minutes of all meetings should be kept. Board members should be responsible for filing these minutes in their handbooks and keeping them in good order so that they can be passed on to their successors.

Appropriate financial information, such as budgets and audits, should be readily available in the handbook. Official parish or program handbooks should be included in appendices or as separate documents in a board binder.

## Other Issues of Board Membership

Board members have a sacred responsibility to keep the confidences they receive in their capacities as board members. This responsibility should be noted in the handbook and stressed in orientation so that no board member loses sight of this trust.

Every board should have a mechanism by which it evaluates its functioning. Boards may also be responsible for ensuring that a formal evaluation of the catechetical leader is done. However, board members should not conduct such evaluations alone. One or two board members may serve on an evaluation committee, but non-board members with special expertise should also be included on the committee. Board members can and should address the catechetical leader's work with the board, but all other aspects should be left to the evaluation committee. The pastor or person who makes employment decisions about the catechetical leader should receive evaluation data and board recommendations, and make a final decision.

A board of total Catholic education or a board of religious education should be a support and a resource for the catechetical leader who should experience them as such. Sometimes, seemingly insurmountable differences can arise; in the final analysis, the pastor or canonical vicar must make binding decisions.

## Questions for Reflection

- What do you see as some of the advantages of working with a Board or Commission of Education? What would be some of the challenges?
- What would be the ideal membership of a Board of Education in your particular setting? How would you go about recruiting for such a Board?

## Conclusion

The work of a catechetical leader may appear to be overwhelming. Practical matters of day-to-day leadership could be all-consuming. All catechetical leaders must reflect on their true mission and call, as stated in the Congregation for the Clergy's *General Directory for Catechesis*, Part III, #138:

> In the school of Jesus the Teacher, the catechist closely joins his action as a responsible person with the mysterious action of the grace of God. Catechesis is thus an exercise in "the original pedagogy of the faith." The transmission of the Gospel through the Church remains before all else and forever the work of the Holy Spirit and has in Revelation a fundamental witness and norm.

> It is God's work that catechetical leaders are doing. If the catechetical leader is faithful to prayer and to the tasks of administration, the practicalities of day-to-day leadership will remain within the boundaries of civil law in the same way that Jesus required his followers to render unto Caesar what was Caesar's and unto God what is God's.

## Bibliography

Shaughnessy, M.A.  *Civil Law and Ministry.*  Mahwah, N.J.:  Paulist Press, 1998.

_____.  *A Legal Primer for DREs and Youth Ministers.*  Washington, D.C.:  NCEA, 1992.

_____.  *A Primer on School Law:  A Guide for Board Members in Catholic Schools.*  Washington, D.C.:  NCEA, 1988.

_____.  *Religious Education and the Law.*  (2 vols.), Washington, D.C.:  NCEA, 1996.

Shaughnessy, M.A., et al.  *Ethics and the Law:  A Teacher's Guide to Decision Making.*  NCEA, 1993.

_____.  *Volunteers in Catholic Schools:  Legal Considerations for the Administrator.*  Washington, D.C.:  NCEA, 1993.

# 10
# Claiming and Breaking Ground: The General Directory for Catechesis
### Thomas H. Groome

On August 15, 1997, the Congregation for the Clergy—the Vatican agency entrusted with oversight of the Church's catechetical ministry— issued a new *General Directory for Catechesis* (*GDC*). The *GDC* replaces even as it builds upon and amplifies the *General Catechetical Directory* of 1971. Like its predecessor, it is likely to set the tone and tenor of catechesis throughout the universal Church for at least another quarter century. For all concerned about the Church's catechetical ministry—which the *Directory* says should be every Christian—but especially for catechetical leaders, this is a major document.

The essays in this collection, *Empowering Catechetical Leaders*, were already being written when the *GDC* was issued. Relying at first on an unofficial translation, our authors knew that it was imperative to subsume the wisdom and sentiments of this document into our essays. In fact, the new directory proved to be a great boon to our writing. Our authors have drawn upon its insights as relevant to their topics, but it also seems fitting to end this collection with a brief essay that introduces the document as a whole.

If you have not had the opportunity to read it, we urge you to do so. In addition to reading it out of loyalty to the Church—this is a normative statement from the Church's teaching office for the universal Catholic community—it is an inspiring statement about catechesis. It will be a helpful and worthy companion to catechetical leaders for the foreseeable future.

## Questions for Reflection
- Imagine you were writing a directory to guide the catechetical ministry of the universal Church (not just in the United States). What themes would you be likely to discuss?
- What guidelines and directives would you be sure to suggest?
- If you have had an opportunity to read the new directory, what are some of your sentiments in response to it?

## A "Fantastic" Directory

With both of us in a hurry and moving in opposite directions, a colleague queried, "how's the new *Directory*?" I simply said, "fantastic!" With more time, of course, I would add nuance—as academics do for a living—and locate the document and my response in their historical context. But at the end of the day, I would stand by my "fantastic" assessment.

One contextual clue to my initial response is that "rumor had it" this could be a regressive document, reversing the ground gained for catechesis with the documents of the Second Vatican Council and official statements since then, like *Evangelii Nuntiandi* (1975) of Pope Paul VI, and *Catechesi Tradendae* (1979) of Pope John Paul II. And though all Vatican directives concerning the *Catechism of the Catholic Church* (1992) have insisted that it be appropriated into the catechetical renewal anointed by Vatican II, there have been notable attempts to use the *Catechism* to "turn back the clock" for catechists.

The *GDC* gives no solace to restorationist sentiments. At the outset, it quotes Pope Paul VI's reference to the documents of Vatican II as "the great catechism of modern times" (#3), notes that "the catechetical renewal developed in the Church over the past decades continues to bear very welcome fruit," and lists its significant achievements (#24). The remainder of the document does what one would hope for; it gathers up wisdom from the Church's long-term and most recent experience as catechist—claiming the ground gained—and then breaks ground toward new horizons for this pilgrim people of God. I say again, "fantastic!"

## A Bird's-Eye View

The document has five sequential parts that focus on the nature and purposes of catechesis, its content, how to go about it, who are its participants, and its location in the particular Church and culture.

The very title of Part I—Catechesis in the Church's Mission of Evangelization—summarizes the understanding of the nature of catechesis reflected throughout. Evangelization is "the process by which the Church, moved by the Holy Spirit, proclaims and spreads the Gospel throughout the entire world" (#48). Then, catechesis is one function—the more formative one—within that overarching umbrella. "Catechesis, distinct from the primary proclamation of the Gospel, promotes and matures initial conversion, educates the convert in the faith, and incorporates him [or her] into the Christian community" (#61). As such, catechesis is to be "a school of faith, an initiation and apprenticeship in the entire Christian life" (#30).

The purposes of catechesis—already hinted in its nature—are stated variously but all are shaped by the core conviction that the "heart" of

Christian catechesis is the person of Jesus Christ. Thus, the defining intent is "to put people . . . in communion and intimacy with Jesus Christ (#80), to "apprentice" them to Jesus (an oft-repeated term), promoting "full and sincere adherence to his person and the decision to walk in his footsteps" (#53).

This "maturing of initial conversion" (#82) entails forming people in Christian identity by incorporating them into Christian community (#68). However, beyond nurturing "a deep ecclesial spirituality" (#28), catechesis promotes "the integral development of the human person and of all peoples" (#18).

In fact, the ultimate catechetical intent is to build up the reign of God (#34)—"a Kingdom of justice, love and peace" that was "so central to the preaching of Jesus" (#102). As "catechist of the Kingdom of God" (#163)— what a lovely title—Jesus preached and lived a "message of liberation" and effected a "radical liberation" in human history (#104). By the power of the Holy Spirit, Christian catechesis should help Jesus' apprentices to continue what he began (#103).

Part II, entitled "The Gospel Message," offers "norms and criteria" for what should be taught—the "content of the Gospel message" (#s 92, 93). Note first—lest one presume the stereotypical cognitivist meaning—that for the *GDC* "content" has "cognitive, experiential, [and] behavioral" aspects (#35). Later, it summarizes this holistic sense of "content" in more traditional ecclesial language as *lex credendi*, *lex orandi*, and *lex vivendi*—what Christians are to believe, how they are to pray and worship, how to live one's faith in the world (#122). Then, its guidelines can be summarized as threefold.

As to be expected, the first guideline for what to teach is "the word of God contained in Sacred Tradition and in Sacred Scripture" as they are understood within the Christian community and "given an authentic interpretation" by the Church's Magisterium (#95, 96). Earlier, the *GDC* expressed a concern that in the aftermath of Vatican II, Catholic catechesis had become too scriptural, neglecting "the Church's long experience and reflection" congealed in its tradition and taught by the Magisterium (#30). Now, while reiterating that "Sacred Scripture should have a pre-eminent position" (#127), the *GDC* calls for a rebalancing that attends carefully to both Scripture and Tradition, and within the guidance of the community of faith.

The second guideline for content is the *Catechism of the Catholic Church*, which the *GDC* refers to repeatedly as "the doctrinal point of reference for all catechesis" (#93, 121). The Catechism, "structured around the four pillars which sustain the transmission of the faith (the Creed, the Sacraments, the Decalogue, the Our Father)" (#122), provides "a sure and authentic reference text for teaching Catholic doctrine" (#121).

The third guideline draws together the previous two, and proposes that people can be given access to the comprehensive nature of Christian faith—all Christians are so entitled—by constantly attending to "the seven basic elements" or "seven foundation stones" of catechesis, namely "the three phases in the narration of the history of salvation"—the Old Testament, New Testament, and life of the Church, and then to the "four pillars" of Creed, Sacraments, Morality, and Prayer (#130).

Part III, entitled "The Pedagogy of the Faith" has a fascinating undergirding thesis, namely that all approaches to catechesis should reflect "the divine pedagogy"—how God reveals Godself to humankind. In gist, God's methodology is "according to the mode of the receiver." This means shifting focus from the teacher to the learners, to the "fundamental experiences" of those being taught and presenting the faith in ways most likely to touch into the hearts and lives of people (e.g., #133).

This student-centered pedagogy was also used by Jesus in the Gospels. And while catechesis is "forever the work of the Holy Spirit" (#138), its human agents—through whom the Spirit works—should employ approaches consonant with "the school of Jesus the Teacher" (#138) and appropriate to the people being taught (more on approach below).

Part IV, entitled "Those to be Catechized" reiterates the constant imperative "for adaptation to those to be catechized"—echoing its recommended pedagogy. Then it reviews the "permanent catechesis" (an oft-repeated phrase) that is to take place in the life of every Christian and Christian community. Beginning with a normative emphasis on adults, it outlines catechesis from infancy to old age, and raises consciousness about catechesis for people with special needs (e.g., the disabled, handicapped, marginalized).

Part V, "Catechesis in the Particular Church" highlights the seriousness with which the local Church must take its task as catechist, emphasizes the careful and thorough training of catechists and catechetical leaders, and gives some guidelines for organizing catechetical ministry.

## Some Demurrings

Before my very positive assessment of the *GDC*, let me note some demurrings—nuances to my "fantastic" evaluation when in a hurry. Others, I'm sure, will add more nuances, and I could too, but here I list three and describe them—in ascending order of demurring—as a wonder, a reservation, and a downright criticism.

My wonder is about the wisdom of placing catechesis totally and exclusively within the context of evangelization. Now it is true that the *GDC* expands evangelization to something the whole Church must do and is itself ever in need of—"in order to evangelize the world with credibility." Though it retains "an accent on missionary character" (#33), this is not the hege monic proselytizing of previous eras which presumed that all must become Christian in order to be saved. And catechesis "is always called to assume an ecumenical dimension everywhere" (#197), must help to overcome all forms of religious prejudice and ignorance of other religious traditions (#198); and help "in particular . . . to overcome every form of anti-Semitism" (#199).

And who knows?  Maybe the sense of being evangelizers and mission- aries again will give those of us in old inculturated faith traditions that "fire in the belly" we need to catechize effectively—with enthusiasm and excite- ment (what Augustine called *hilaritas*).  This is surely what Pope John Paul II intends by calling for "a new evangelization."  But I cannot help won- dering if evangelizing zeal is not more likely to be effective in explicitly mission contexts—where the Gospel is still "new."  Undoubtedly, all Chris- tians are called by baptism "to hand on the faith," but is missionary evan- gelization the most empowering way to think about this ministry for all catechists and in every context?  We will see!

My reservation is about the oft-repeated insistence that "the model for all catechesis is the baptismal catechumenate" (#59). The *GDC* looks only through this lens, never recognizing that though a rich angle of vision, it is only one perspective.  Consequently it tries to fit—nay squeeze—every aspect and kind of catechesis within the paradigm of the catechumenate— and specifically the *Rite of Christian Initiation of Adults*.

Now, it is true that for adult converts to Christian faith one can "map" their emergence into Christian identity as a catechumenal dynamic—ever gradual and Christocentric—from first interest in the Gospel, to conversion, to profession of faith, to life-long journey into holiness of life (#56); or, stated in *RCIA* terms, from the pre-catechumenate, to the catechumenate, to purification and illumination, to mystagogy (see #88). But, for example, is this the most illuminating and helpful way for parents to understand their catechetical function?

Indeed, I remember my mother addressing her brood of nine children on occasion as "a bunch of pagans" (as when no one remembered to say "grace"), but we presumed—or hoped—that this was not her defining estimation of us. Might it not be even more helpful for parents to think of "sharing faith" with their children, of nurturing them in Christian identity, of setting them afoot on their journey home to God?  There was much wisdom in Horace Bushnell's oft-quoted phrase of 1860—in criticizing the undue emphasis on conversion by the revivalists of his day—that "children should grow up as Christian, not remembering a time when they were otherwise."

I am thoroughly convinced of the pastoral effectiveness of the *RCIA*. Likewise, with appropriate adaptation, the catechumenal model can be very effective for initiating older children who have not been nurtured in the faith. The *GDC* itself hits the mark when it says that "the catechumenate truly and properly belongs" to "not-baptized adults" (#172). Beyond that, to imagine all catechesis being done in a catechumenal mode may be too much of a stretch. I doubt if it will be helpful for committed parents who share their faith with their children from the very beginning of life, nor for catechists who work with "cradle Catholics" in well established Christian communities.

Further, my colleague Jane Regan makes the point that the catechumenate, by its nature, is a process of socialization. As such, it may not encourage people to raise critical questions about the Church itself, and in the interest of formation can set aside the prophetic voice.

My criticism is the language pattern of the document. First, there is way too much of it because of pervasive repetition. The *GDC* could say well what it says in half its present length (over 250 pages) and be more likely to be read.

But beyond the length, it is not nit picking to lament that the language pattern is egregiously exclusive. Now one could not hope for a "purist" document on this issue at this time; even a token of sensitivity would be welcome. There is none—a foolish choice, at least for the English translation. I can only imagine the response when American women catechists read that they can become "sons in the Son" (#99), or are "to grow . . . towards the maturity of a free son" (#139), or are "to become the perfect Man" (#142). I hope they won't simply give up on the *GDC* and put it aside. This fine document deserves a better rendering.

## Questions for Reflection
- What are your own responses to the *GDC*'s emphasis on evangelization? On a catechumenal paradigm for catechesis?
- What positions will you take on these issues as a catechetical leader?

## The Gift of New Horizons
Here I will confine myself to noting three great expansive horizons that the text lays out to inspire the work of catechesis; they are: a holistic understanding of Christian faith, inclusivity regarding the participants in catechesis, and a comprehensive pedagogy.

**1) Holistic Christian faith.** By this I mean a broadening of Christian faith to engage the whole person—head, heart, and hands—and inviting a wholesome and holy life after the way of Jesus.

Karl Rahner once wrote that in the aftermath of the Council of Trent (1545-63), the Church tended to define faith as intellectual assent to its stated doctrines; in consequence, catechesis could settle for a question/answer catechism—laying out clearly the beliefs to be believed and memorized. However, suggested Rahner, the current catechetical renewal was catalyzed by Vatican II's return to a more holistic notion of faith—thus requiring a more holistic catechesis.

Be Rahner correct or not, that the Church understands faith in a holistic way is solidified and amplified in the *GDC*. Faith is a way of believing, a way of worshipping, and a way of living (*credendi, orandi, vivendi* #122); it is cognitive, affective, and behavioral (#35); it engages people's minds, emotions, and wills; it is to permeate how we make meaning out of life, the quality of all our relationships, and the ethic by which we live (#16).   In consequence, catechesis is to promote a lived, living, and life-giving faith; it is to inform, form, and ever transform people as faithful apprentices "in communion and intimacy with Jesus" (#80).

It is simply not possible to be a disciple of Jesus within one's head alone; one must be formed to "walk the walk" as well as to "talk the talk." Though the *GDC* states often that knowledge of the faith is important (e.g., #85), Christian faith requires "integral formation rather than mere information" (#29), "an apprenticeship of the entire Christian life" so that "the entire person, at his [her] deepest levels, feels enriched by the word of God" (#67). As such, "formation for the Christian life . . . comprises but surpasses mere instruction" (#68).

In sum, "as the vitality of the human body depends on the proper function of all of its organs, so also the maturation of the Christian life requires that it be cultivated in all its dimensions:  knowledge of the faith, liturgical life, moral formation, prayer, belonging to community, missionary spirit. When catechesis omits one of these elements, the Christian faith does not attain full development" (#87).

**2) Inclusivity of participants in catechesis.** By this I mean that every Christian and Christian community is to be both catechized and catechist. All are to be continually nurtured in Christian faith, enjoying "permanent catechesis" from infancy to old age. "Adhering to Jesus Christ sets in motion a process of continuing conversion, which lasts for the whole of life" (#56). What a contrast to our stereotype that catechesis is only for children.

The document emphasizes repeatedly that baptism calls all to be catechists, and especially through the socializing power of Christian communities. The *GDC* repeatedly reflects that "the Christian community is the origin, locus, and goal of catechesis" (#254). Community includes "the family, parish, Catholic schools, Christian associations and movements, basic ecclesial communities" (#253). This makes catechesis "the particular responsibility of every member of the community" (#220). Following on, everything about the life of each community should be a source of catechesis for its individual members and for the community as a whole; for while the community catechizes it is ever in need of being catechized (#221).

Even for Catholic schools, the *GDC* emphasizes the shift that must take place "from school as institution to school as community." Here the crucial issue is school environment; it should be "an atmosphere animated by a spirit of liberty and charity" that by its very ethos helps "to orientate the whole of human culture to the message of salvation" (#259).

On the family as communal catechist the *GDC* is most insightful. Previous rhetoric about family catechesis seemed to put a didactic role upon parents but the *GDC* is more nuanced, placing emphasis on the ethos of the home. Understanding the family as "the primary agent of an incarnate transmission of faith" (#207), its function is to provide a "positive and receptive environment" and the "explicit experience and practice of the faith" (#178). And so, rather than formal didaction, family catechesis is "a Christian education more witnessed to than taught, more occasional than systematic, more on-going than structured into periods" (#255).

The *GDC* elaborates around the image of family as "domestic church"— revived by Vatican II. This highlights that the family is to participate in the various Christian ministries, reflecting within its life "the different aspects and functions of the life of the entire Church." (#225). In its own way, each family is to share its faith around the word of God, join in prayer and worship within the home, give witness to Christian faith and service to those in need.

Yet, the *GDC*'s attitude of "we're all in this together"— with everyone of every age and station being both catechist and catechized—does not at all diminish the need for designated catechists and catechetical leaders who are thoroughly prepared, spiritually, theologically, and pedagogically. The Church, local and universal, should encourage the "vocation of catechist," and give those so called both "basic training and continuing formation"; catechesis "is placed at risk if it does not rely on truly competent and trained personnel" (#233-234). For catechetical leaders there is need for "catechetical institutes" where "standards . . . will be more demanding" and which provide education for other functions of ministry as well (#250).

**3) A comprehensive pedagogy.** By this I mean broadening the dynamics of catechesis to actively engage people around their life experiences while giving access to the whole tradition of Christian faith.

It may help to put this broadened horizon in historical context. First, a distinguishing feature of contemporary catechesis has been a shift from a passive mode of being instructed to people actively participating in the teaching/learning dynamic, from silent reception to conversation and *Sharing Faith* together. The *GDC* canonizes this paradigm shift in pedagogy.

For example, catechesis should "promote active participation among those to be catechized" (#145), encourage "a sense of dialogue and sharing" (#159) in the immediate teaching/learning community; "in the catechetical process" every participant "must be an active subject, conscious and co-responsible, and not merely a silent and passive recipient" (#167). And the rationale for this is both anthropological and theological: "the active participation of all the catechized in their formative process is completely in harmony, not only with genuine human communication, but specifically with the economy of Revelation and salvation" (#157). Clearly, what Paulo Freire called "banking education"—depositing information in passive receptacles—is unworthy of the Church's catechesis.

Focusing specifically, then, on teaching method, the *GDC* favors a general approach that gets people to learn from their own lived experiences as they learn the faith tradition, bringing together these two sources of God's word. Here again, the historical context helps to appreciate the point being made.

For the past 50 years or so, there has been a debate between an experiential approach or a *kerygma*tic approach to catechesis—whether to emphasize people's experiences or the content of the faith tradition as reflected in Scripture. The *GDC* favors both—a comprehensive pedagogy—urging catechists to engage people's lived experiences as a locus of God's self disclosure and to faithfully teach the word of God as mediated through both—again—Scripture and Tradition.

That God reveals Godself in a normative and definitive way through both Bible and Christian tradition has long been a foundational conviction of Catholicism. And yet the balance of the two has not been well achieved in catechetical curriculum. The Reformers, with their cry of *scriptura sola*—scripture alone—triggered a Catholic overreaction of undue emphasis on tradition, to the neglect of Scripture. Then, as the *GDC* notes, with the post Vatican II enthusiasm to reclaim the centrality of Scripture, Catholic catechesis may have neglected tradition. The document calls now for the appropriate balance that duly honors both Scripture and Tradition. To coin a phrase, catechetical curriculum should reflect "the whole story" of Christian faith.

Why then should catechesis attend to people's lived experiences, making their lives an integral aspect of the curriculum? First, so that Christians may incarnate their faith, that they may reach beyond "information" about it to taking on Christian identity and living as disciples. The *GDC* summarizes with a bold statement: "this formation must be closely related to praxis; one must start with praxis to be able to arrive at praxis" (#245).

Then, the *GDC* affirms throughout that divine revelation continues in the existential lives of people, with God using "human events and words to communicate" (#38). Pedagogically, then, "every dimension of the faith, like the faith itself as a whole, must be rooted in human experience and not remain a mere adjunct of the human person" (#87). For the truth is that "experience promotes the intelligibility of the Christian message"; "experience is a necessary medium for exploring and assimilating the truths which constitute the objective content of Revelation" (#152). Catechesis is most effective as it presents every aspect of the faith tradition "to refer clearly to the fundamental experiences of people's lives" (#133).

So, claiming to reflect divine pedagogy, the document throughout recommends a method of correlating life and faith. For example: "on the one hand, [catechesis] assists the person to open . . . to the religious dimension of life, while on the other, it proposes the Gospel" (#147); "interpreting and illuminating experience with the data of faith is a constant task of catechetical pedagogy," the key task is to mediate "a correct . . . correlation and interaction between profound human experiences and the revealed message" (#153).

Further, "the relationship between the Christian message and human experience is not a simple methodological question. It springs from the very end of catechesis which seeks to put the human person in communion with God (#116). It is by "correlating faith and life" (#207) that "catechesis... bridges the gap between belief and life, between the Christian message and the cultural context" (#205).

On a related methodological note, the *GDC* highlights the role of critical reason in the affairs of faith—needed both for reflection on human experience and for understanding the faith tradition. Instead of blind faith, the *GDC* urges a "right understanding of the faith" so that "the truths to be believed are in conformity with the demands of reason." It notes that such critical understanding is needed "to overcome certain forms of fundamentalism as well as subjective and arbitrary interpretations" (#175).

It sees a place for memorization in catechesis—especially "of the major formulae and texts of the Bible, of dogma, of the liturgy, as well as the commonly known prayers of Christian tradition" but "such formulae should be proposed as syntheses after a process of explanation" (#154). In other words, memorization should be subsequent to understanding and appropriation.

And there are other aspects of this document that are significant contributions; it reminds Catholic Christians that there is a hierarchy of truths to our faith—that not all is of equal centrality; it repeatedly calls for inculturation—for the Gospel to become truly indigenized into every context; it urges appreciation of God's revelation as reflected in other traditions, and so on. But I have said enough! This document sets an irreversible milestone to mark the ground gained by contemporary catechesis, and invites the Church's catechetical ministry to reach into new horizons. In any day and age, "that's fantastic."

## Questions for Reflection

- What insights do you find in the *General Directory for Catechesis* for your own work as a catechetical leader?
- Are there specific decisions emerging for your ministry in your context? How do you imagine implementing your insights and decisions?

---

Note: This article appeared in a slightly different format in the summer 1998 issue of *The Living Light*, vol. 34, no. 4. It is used here with permission of the U.S. Catholic Conference.

# Contributors

### Wilkie Au
Wilkie Au, Ph.D., is Director of Spiritual Development Services in the Archdiocese of Los Angeles and Adjunct Professor of Theological Studies at Loyola Marymount University, Los Angeles.

### Michael Corso
Michael J. Corso, Ph.D., holds the doctorate in Theology and Education and a Master's Degree in Systematic Theology from Boston College. He is currently the Coordinator of Continuing Education and Supervised Ministry at the Institute of Religious Education and Pastoral Ministry at Boston College, and the Director of Religious Education at St. Ignatius Church in Chestnut Hill, MA.

### Fran Ferder
Fran Ferder, FSPA, Ph.D., D.Min., is Co-Director of Therapy and Renewal Associates, a counseling and consultation service located in the Archdiocese of Seattle; a part-time faculty member in the Graduate School of Theology and Ministry at Seattle University; an author of several books and articles; and a national and international speaker. Dr. Ferder has been a resource for catechetical leaders for over twenty years both through her writing and speaking.

### Thomas H. Groome
Thomas Groome is a professor of theology and education at Boston College. He completed his doctorate in education and theology (Ed.D.) at Columbia University Teacher's College and Union Theological Seminary, New York.

### Michael Horan
Michael Horan holds the Ph.D. from The Catholic University of America. He is an Associate Professor of Theological Studies at Loyola Marymount University, Los Angeles. He has taught youth ministers and religious educators in graduate programs at St. John's University, Jamaica, New York, St. Mary's University of Minnesota, Winona, Minnesota, the University of St. Thomas in Houston, Texas, and Boston College.

## Carl J. Pfeifer and Janaan Manternach

Dr. Carl Pfeifer and Dr. Janaan Manternach both hold the Doctor of Ministry (D.Min.) degree from St. Mary's Seminary, Baltimore, MD. They have been influential religious educators for over three decades. In 1993 they received, as a husband and wife team, the National Conference of Catechetical Leadership award for outstanding contributions to catechetical ministry. As assistant directors of the former National Center for Religious Education/CCD, they were involved in work on *To Teach As Jesus Did*, the *General Catechetical Directory*, and the *National Catechetical Directory*.

## Diana Dudoit Raiche

Diana Dudoit Raiche is pursuing the Ph.D. in religious education/catechetics at The Catholic University of America and is the manager of religious education surveys at the National Catholic Educational Association. She is a frequent workshop presenter at catechetical and liturgical conferences and serves as a team member for institutes on the catechumenate for adults and children for the North American Forum on the Catechumenate.

## Jane Regan

Jane Regan holds the Ph.D. from The Catholic University of America. She is on the faculty of the Institute for Religious Education and Pastoral Ministry at Boston College. Her primary focus for research and teaching are in the areas of adult education and leadership formation. In addition to her academic work, Dr. Regan gives presentations and workshops throughout the United States.

## Mary Angela Shaughnessy

Mary Angela Shaughnessy is a Sister of Charity of Nazareth who has taught at all levels of Catholic education from elementary through graduate school. She holds the JD degree in law from the University of Louisville, and the Ph.D. in educational administration and supervision from Boston College. Sister Mary Angela is Professor of Education and University Counsel at Spalding University, Louisville, KY.